# HELPING MALTREATED CHILDREN

## School and community involvement

# HELPING MALTREATED CHILDREN

## School and community involvement

**Michael Halperin, Ph.D.**

Director of Child Abuse Services,
Associated Marriage and Family Counselors,
Auburn, Alabama; Director of Development Research,
Tuskegee Institute, Tuskegee, Alabama; formerly,
Director of Child Abuse Prevention Service, Inc.;
Elementary School Principal; Graduate Faculty,
University of North Florida,
Jacksonville, Florida

*with assistance from*
**Pamela Shuman**

**The C. V. Mosby Company**

ST. LOUIS · TORONTO · LONDON    1979

To my parents
**Marvin and Leah**
who gave me their love
and my wife
**Sandra**
who nurtured it.

The C. V. Mosby Company
11830 Westline Industrial Drive, St. Louis, Missouri 63141

**Library of Congress Cataloging in Publication Data**

Halperin, Michael, 1941-
    Helping maltreated children.

    Bibliography: p.
    1.  Child abuse—Prevention.    I.  Shuman, Pamela,
joint author.    II.  Title.
HV713.H14        362.7′1        78-31527
ISBN 0-8016-2020-1


C/VH/VH   9  8  7  6  5  4  3  2  1  02/A/283

# Preface

For no apparent reason, Tim started another fight at recess this morning. Susan continued to stare out the window during the reading lesson. Kim's cold lingered into its third week and threatened to develop into bronchitis. Sammy came to class with belt marks on his arms and neck again. For the third time this month, Jennifer stole another child's lunch and ate it herself. Guiltily, Anna confided to her teacher that her father came to her room last night to fondle her. Steve got both the teacher's and students' attention this afternoon when he launched into a 10-minute temper tantrum. Sally came to school very early this morning and finally left for home when the last teacher left the building. What is the common element that binds these youngsters together? All of them are maltreated children who may be enrolled in the neighborhood school.

Because child abuse and neglect take many forms, the term *child maltreatment* is inadequate to describe the range of behaviors it encompasses. Qualification is required to differentiate between limited and extensive abuse and between injurious and destructive neglect. Therefore, a distinction must be made between "marginal" maltreatment, defined as abuse or neglect that hinders a child's growth, and "severe" maltreatment, which threatens the health, welfare, or very existence of a youngster. In cases of severe maltreatment, citizens must involve the governmental agencies specifically empowered to protect children from serious harm. Informed, caring individuals, including educators, parents, and community members, can help families to replace marginal maltreatment with healthy nurturance. It is with these children and their parents that this book is primarily concerned.

The central proposition of this volume is that educational institutions can and must assume responsibility for identifying the marginally maltreated child and for aiding both youngsters and their families. What do day-care workers, school teachers, or principals know about child abuse? They know that maltreatment adversely affects both the social and intellectual growth of children. They understand that harshly punished children frequently use violent methods to express their feelings. They recognize that children who need glasses or medication are unable to devote themselves fully to schoolwork. They realize that children who are ignored or belittled at home see themselves as unworthy of affection and may use any technique to gain attention. These things educators know intuitively about children.

It is with the day-care center, preschool facility, or elementary school that each family with a child must eventually come in contact. Thus, educational institutions function as the one common denominator in the lives of all maltreating families. Though we know that infants and small children too young for school are maltreated, as many as 75 percent of all maltreated children are in attendance at a care or school facility while they are mistreated at home. As adults concerned with the welfare of youngsters in their charge, educators can no longer fail to recognize the responsibility they share with the community to aid maltreated children and their families.

This book is designed as a starting kit for people concerned with education's obligation to maltreated children. It speaks to the teacher, administrator, or school board member who is concerned about helping to improve the quality of life for children and their families. It addresses interested parent and neighborhood groups who view the school as an integral part of community life. It has application for professional social service workers who look to the school for assistance in helping their mutual clients. It serves as a useful introduction for inclusion in undergraduate and graduate teacher and administrator preparation programs at the university level. In short, the person who is concerned about children and about the role that education can play in their lives has a stake in understanding what schools can do to prevent and remedy child maltreatment.

This book is not meant to be an exhaustive study of all aspects of child maltreatment and family dynamics. Rather, it is a suggestive work aimed at defining child maltreatment and what is known about it, generating thought about the educator's role in dealing with maltreated children and their parents, and proposing plans that can be modified and implemented in individual schools, school districts, and communities. The reader who comes to this book seeking extensive theoretical evidence concerning child maltreatment will be disappointed. Other sources are currently available to fill that need, and a number of them are cited in the annotated bibliography included at the end of this volume. By design, only enough theory has been included to lay a foundation for understanding the basic dynamics of child maltreatment, while the emphasis is placed on action in the form of a proven model for identifying and treating abused children and their families. This model was forged by necessity and modified by practical application. As the principal of an elementary school, it became apparent to me that many of the youngsters who were having problems in school were also experiencing difficulties at home. Their families functioned in ways that did not allow them to meet the needs of the children. It became clear to me that the school had an obligation to attempt to help both the youngsters and their families, and at that point the model began to take shape. Elements that were successful were refined and sharpened; those that proved ineffective were eliminated. Thus, a sound process with which schools can help the victims of maltreatment, both children and their parents, has emerged. This model retains the flexibility necessary in any process involving human dynamics, for it incorporates within it alternatives that may be employed depending on the individual circumstances of the school and its staff, community, and clients.

This book had to be written now, for already it is too late. Daily, children with whom we work are being brutalized: beaten, physically neglected, and emotionally scarred. As people concerned with and believing in education, we must develop our knowledge of child maltreatment, sharpen our skills in dealing with maltreated children in our schools, and cultivate attitudes and programs that reach out to maltreating families within our communities. Only then can we warrant both the respect of the community and the self-esteem that should be ours.

This book would not have been written without the involvement of Pamela Shuman, a dear friend and colleague who assisted me in all aspects of the work. I am also grateful to Tom Healy and Ed Gray for their encouragement and to Karen Burns, Donna Britton, and Becky Aiken for typing the numerous drafts of the manuscript. Finally, to the students and teachers of North Shore Elementary School in Jacksonville, Florida, from whom I learned so much, I am deeply appreciative.

**Michael Halperin**

# Contents

# CHAPTER 1

# Why should schools become involved in fighting child maltreatment?

There is little argument that the major function of schools is to facilitate learning. Taken in the narrowest sense, schools are concerned with the academic development of children. Yet, as every person involved in education knows, social, emotional, and physical factors can interfere with intellectual growth. In recent years, schools have come to view learning as a matrix of classroom, home, and personal influences that work together either to help children achieve or conspire to block their progress.

Educators recognize that a child is more than a bundle of cognitive skills. For decades, elementary school report cards have included evaluations of adjustment factors, thus highlighting the importance of emotional and social characteristics in the development of a child. Cumulative records include comments on how successfully children deal with peer and adult relationships as well as their level of cognitive acquisition. Clearly, then, educators acknowledge that the intellectual development of each child is integrally linked to unique personal factors.

Schools not only concern themselves with the intellectual and social development of children, but also have begun to accept expanded responsibility for the general health and welfare of youngsters. Once believed to be the sole province of the home, schools started decades ago to offer annual vision and hearing screening tests, and many have expanded their roles to include general physical examinations and immunizations. With government assistance, free and reduced-price breakfast and lunch programs are being provided to youngsters who might not receive nutritional meals otherwise. Thus, ensuring the physical well-being of children has come to be recognized as another legitimate service schools should offer to their young clients.

In addition to benefits provided directly to children, schools have broadened their mission to become important community resources. The concept of the community school, which offers learning experiences to adults in the late afternoon and evening, is firmly established throughout our country. Even the smallest neighborhood frequently schedules courses designed to help its residents develop the knowledge and skills they desire. People can brush up on their writing technique or take brush in hand and learn to express themselves through painting. They can learn how to care for potted plants or how to make the pots in which to plant them. Courses on self-hypnosis help people block out the concerns of the day, while offerings in interpersonal relations teach them to show and respond to their feelings for others. Thus, schools are not only for children, and they deal not only with academic areas. Many have become responsive neighborhood centers that attempt to meet the comprehensive needs of their communities.

Because schools are designed to foster human development, anything that interferes with this goal is properly the concern of educators. Thus, we come to the central proposition of this book: schools have a responsibility to help maltreated children and their families. The child who is harshly punished at home, the youngster who is physically neglected, the child who is not given the love he or she needs, the child who is constantly belittled: all these children are being maltreated. The parent who is frustrated by life, the adult who looks to his or her child for emotional support and is disappointed when the youngster cannot supply it, the father who believes he must be physically tough with his child, the mother who sees her own bad qualities in her youngster and rejects the child: all these parents are maltreating their children.

Child abuse has gained a great deal of publicity recently through lurid newspaper headlines involving children who have been stabbed, burned, tortured, starved, and similarly victimized by their parents. Yet, in a broader sense, child maltreatment describes a phenomenon so commonplace that it almost escapes notice. It represents the failure of parents to meet the physical, psychological, social, and emotional needs of their children. It refers to a pattern of child-rearing practices that are satisfactory neither for the child nor the parent, but are not abandoned because the parent has no alternatives to substitute. While conservative estimates place the number of severely abused children at approximately one million a year, many times that number of youngsters are being harshly punished bodily and psychologically, uncared for physically and emotionally, and shunted aside literally and figuratively by their parents. It is these children who have difficulty settling down to work in a classroom; it is these youngsters who plead for the attention and affection of their peers and teachers; it is these children who have difficulty keeping up with the class academically, although there appears to be no reason why they are not learning. In short, it is these children who are maltreated by parents who generally love them but who, through lack of knowledge or simply because they are overwhelmed, have trouble fulfilling the role of parent.

The Education Commission of the States recently commented: "American education is potentially a major resource for helping abused children and their families. But this potential has rarely been tapped and, as yet, has never been fully utilized."[1] What factors give schools and educators the opportunity to play a positive role in the lives of maltreating families? Let us examine several generalizations about education in this regard.

If a family has children, sooner or later they must be enrolled in a day-care facility or elementary school. Thus, the school stands as a common contact point for all families with youngsters. Further, this contact is maintained on a daily basis over an extended period. The dual factors of frequency and longevity of teacher-student relationships facilitate positive attitudes toward the teacher and school on the part of the child and an empathic understanding of the problems of the child on the part of the educators. Both these factors are key elements in identifying and working with maltreated children and their families.

It is not known exactly how many children are of preschool and school age when maltreatment occurs in their homes. However, based on a study of nearly thirteen thousand confirmed cases of serious physical abuse, Dr. David Gil has estimated that at least 50 percent of the incidents involved school-age youngsters who were seen daily by teachers.[2] If we add to this figure the number of younger maltreated children who attend day-care facilities and the youngsters who are victims of other kinds of maltreatment, it becomes clear that educators routinely deal with the vast majority of maltreated children in America.

When youngsters enter school, they are generally eager to learn, for they find the classroom a place of challenge and adventure. Most recognize their teachers as loving adults who care deeply about them. Teachers play significant roles in children's lives; in some cases they are among the few adults youngsters meet. Children are predisposed to trust their teachers if the adults seem honest and interested, and this trusting relationship offers solace and reassurance to children in general and to the maltreated child in particular.

Just as children usually view schools and teachers in a favorable manner, so parents are predisposed to see them in a positive light. Many parents place a high premium on education. If schools demonstrate interest in parents and children, adults are likely to view educators as concerned professionals in the field of child development. When schools encourage parental participation in education, parents generally consider teachers natural allies both of their youngsters and themselves. A close relationship between school and home is based on the teacher's and parent's mutual desire that each child progress satisfactorily. Thus, parents perceive the well-functioning school as an institution concerned with the welfare of the child and, by extension, the well-being of the whole family.

In short, when schools establish good relations with children and their parents, they possess an important advantage that wise educators seek to maintain. Schools are generally viewed not as punitive institutions desirous of finding fault with children or parents, but as helping places dedicated to identifying and eliminating factors that block development. From this perspective, schools encourage problem solving rather than problem manufacturing, and it is in this vein that they can be useful in aiding maltreating families.

One of the functions of an educational institution is to evaluate pupil growth in academic, emotional, social, and physical areas. Periodic student appraisals are an important element in assessing individual's progress and in charting a specially designed future course of study in light of previous gains. Present evaluation methods allow the educator to identify the slow learner, the immature child, the withdrawn or hostile youngster, and the child who has an untreated medical problem. As basic an evaluative tool as daily attendance can indicate that a problem exists; it may be medical or it may have some other source. Some assessment may point to specific causal factors; the poor reader whose eye screening shows that glasses are needed is a case in point. Generally, however, it is easier to diagnose a condition than to identify its root.

It seems appropriate for schools to consider that a maltreating home may be responsible for the poor progress of a child. By reviewing the assessment results and talking briefly with the child about his or her family, a number of possible maltreatment situations may be revealed. In reality, schools have the information they need through existing sources to hypothesize that conditions within the home are related to a child's problems in school. What is being advocated here is that consideration be given to maltreatment as a possible underlying condition blocking satisfactory development.

It is hardly a revolutionary idea to suggest that many of the problems students have in school stem from their homes and families. Yet, all too often when educators suspect that a poorly functioning family is responsible for a child's behavior or lack of progress, they shrug their shoulders as if to admit defeat. Just as children have been turned around by a concerned teacher, so families can be helped to reshape themselves by schools and educators.

Parent-teacher conferences initiated by either party have a long and generally rewarding tradition. Parents frequently look to teachers both for evaluation of their children's progress and advice on how it might be improved. Through such conferences, teachers and parents share their perspectives on the child and, through the process of interchange, often gain useful insights about the youngster. This increased understanding acts as a bond not only between the child and the adults involved, but also between the teacher and the parents. When viewed as a concerned, nonjudgmental ally, the teacher is in a strong position to help parents solve what may seem to them to be the unending problems of parenthood.

As any experienced educator knows, some troubled parents actively seek help from teachers. "Since the divorce, I have had a lot of personal problems to work out," one parent offers. "I can't make that boy obey even though I spank him when he is bad," another says. "Sometimes I wish that kid would run away from home," yet a third parent reveals. Such openness on the part of parents can be viewed as a plea for aid. The sensitive educator can help parents understand both their own feelings and the needs of their children. Through such contact, parents can be assisted in establishing more satisfactory relationships with their children.

Though some parents want help, teachers also know of those who claim that the school is being overly critical of the child and, by extension, of the youngster's family. "There's nothing wrong with a little roughhousing. I want the kid to grow up to be a man," one parent claims. "You teachers try to run everybody's lives," another retorts. Such comments reflect the defensiveness many parents feel when they suspect that they are not doing a very good job of parenting. Teachers who can assure the parent that their ultimate concern is not to accuse but, rather, to safeguard the welfare of the child can begin to establish rapport with many parents. Eventually, teacher and parent working together can make the life of the family more satisfactory for all involved.

Yet, it is recognized that teachers are not totally altruistic, nor should they don the garb of full-time social workers. A teacher's primary job remains in the classroom helping students to learn. Even as educators work with parents, however, they advance the cause of learning. When a family functions better, educators can expect that children will achieve more satisfactorily. Their behavior will improve as they realize they do not have to be disruptive to be noticed. Their ability for self-control will increase as they learn that actions have natural consequences, either for better or worse. Their ability to deal with other people will improve as they gain self-confidence through positive reinforcement. Their erratic mood changes may subside as they understand that life has continuous elements of predictability on which they can rely.

Thus, not only do the lives of maltreating parents and their children become more enjoyable as both learn positive ways to deal with each other, but also the teacher's lot is improved. As the amount of maltreatment a child experiences at home decreases, teachers find improved learning and fewer factors that distract from the basic business of education. As there are fewer problems in the classroom and as those that occur become manageable, the rewards of teaching become less diluted and more numerous. If this seems to say that helping maltreated children and their families serves the self-interests of educators, then the message is clear.

By this point the reader may be asking, "Isn't child maltreatment too serious an issue for an educator to tackle alone?" In incidents of severe maltreatment, the answer is yes. When the abuse or neglect a child suffers is so extreme as to endanger health or life, then it is time to call in professionals in the field of child welfare. Yet, schools and educators already share responsibility for identifying maltreated children, though many are unaware of their legal obligations in this area. Legislation in all fifty states either specifically requires schools or more generally demands that all citizens make reports to protective services agencies when they believe the safety and welfare of children are jeopardized by their homes. In these serious cases, educators have both a legal and a personal duty to involve designated governmental agencies; failure to report may result in prosecution of the educator or, more important, serious harm to the child. This subject will be discussed in detail in Chapter 2, What is Child Maltreatment? Yet, it is important to emphasize at this point that the vast majority of maltreatment cases do not involve life-threatening circumstances. For children who are in serious danger at home, the weight of the law and of social service agencies can be brought to bear to safeguard them. Marginally maltreated children, however, have no advocates to protect them. They remain virtually unnoticed and too frequently unaided. Though these youngsters are ill-fed or clothed, often absent from school, or emotionally and socially impaired because they lack a loving, supportive home, their cases do not fit legal definitions of maltreatment; therefore, governmental agencies are both disinterested in and powerless to help these children. It is the school that is in a position to know of their situations. It is the educator who cares enough about these children to expend the energy necessary to help them and their families. Perhaps the original question should be rephrased, "Isn't child maltreatment too serious an issue for an educator *not* to tackle?"

In all but the most serious cases of child maltreatment, schools have natural advantages over the social agencies that are designed to assist families. Generally, governmental departments are crisis oriented, and it is not until serious problems exist that people needing help come to their attention. Further, overburdened social workers with large case loads and limited resources frequently are unable to provide sustained aid for troubled families. Neither of these shortcomings exists for schools. Because of their daily dealings with children, educators have the perspective to recognize unfavorable situations as they develop and often before they reach monumental proportions. Since children and families remain the clients of the school for extended periods, educators can continue to provide long-term assistance to families as they become more functional, less destructive units.

Yet another factor that mitigates in favor of schools and against social service agencies involves public attitudes. Viewed as punitive powers backed by legal authority, social service agencies often alienate those they would help. On the other hand, the school, acting out of concern for the child, generally is perceived as enlisting the voluntary cooperation of parents in solving problems that affect both the school and the family. This more positive attitude toward schools and educators often facilitates the establishment of a working relationship aimed at helping the family.

Another advantage schools possess that social services agencies lack affects the pocketbook of each taxpayer in America. Governmental departments are expensive to operate. Further, health and welfare agencies are frequently the victims of a lack of continuity in general funding and in specific programs. Today's pet project becomes tomorrow's victim of budgetary cutbacks. Though schools also feel the pressures of fiscal stringency, it costs them little or nothing to implement a maltreatment prevention program utilizing existing school facilities and community resources. It would be naive to believe that large sums of money will be allocated to either governmental agencies or schools to cope with the problems of child maltreatment; yet, unlike social service departments, schools do not need to make extensive outlays of funds to become integral parts of comprehensive community programs on maltreatment.

It should not be concluded that social service agencies perform no useful functions in aiding marginally maltreating families, for they do. Though the maltreatment may not be serious enough to warrant their investigation, other factors affecting the family may fall within the legitimate scope of social service responsibility. Many schools routinely work with governmental departments to meet the needs of families they serve. For example, families that have been evicted and have no place to live have the potential to maltreat their children. They may look to the school for help, which, in turn, contacts an agency with access to temporary or permanent housing accommodations. Children who are ill-fed may reflect the simple fact that their parents are too poor to supply their nutritional needs. When the school puts these families in touch with the appropriate social service department, food stamps or other supplemental income sources may remedy the marginal child maltreatment. Thus, it is important that schools, with knowledge of their clients' needs, be aware of the full range of governmental services available so that they can direct families to existing sources of assistance.

Just as schools can enlist the aid of social services when needed, so they are in a unique position to mobilize a wide variety of community resources to help families and combat child maltreatment. They can develop awareness of the problems of children and parents through such local organizations as the PTA, private community service groups, and concerned church associations. The important first step in a comprehensive maltreatment program involves alerting the public to the problem of child maltreatment. Since research and empirical evidence clearly indicate that maltreatment is not limited to any one social, economic, or cultural class, it is imperative that communities recognize that there may be and probably are maltreating families within their boundaries. Next, community members must realize that the parents in such families are not brutal monsters, but people who need help to fulfill the role of parent more satisfactorily. An understanding of the dynamics and forms of maltreatment makes acceptance far easier for community members, while it removes much of the emotional revulsion that is a conditioned response to maltreatment.

Once acknowledgment of the existence of maltreatment is accomplished, the school can set about the task of training both educators and concerned community members to identify maltreated children and to help their families. Counseling involving teachers and suspected maltreating parents can be initiated to learn the needs of the family and to plan appropriate action to fulfill them. Severe maltreatment cases can be reported to protective services authorities, with the request that the school be kept informed of the progress of the cases so that it can provide additional supportive assistance to children and their parents. Families requiring employment information, day-care facilities, health care, and similar services can be referred to the governmental agencies or community organizations that exist to assist with such problems. Community volunteers can act as friends to maltreating parents, assuring them that parenting is a difficult job for all adults and that their anxieties and frustrations are shared by others.

In the classroom, teachers must pay special attention to the emotional, developmental, and educational needs of maltreated youngsters. Individual counseling may be necessary, as may reordered teacher expectations for these children. Trained lay people can act as aides in classrooms to give extra assistance to maltreated youngsters. They can counsel these children about problems and solutions that can be employed to deal with them. They can be friends to young people whose daily experiences with adults have been less than positive.

The task is not completed, however, once educators and interested community members have begun dealing with child maltreatment. The entire community must be aware of maltreatment and must recognize its signs. Thus a campaign aimed at the general public may be necessary to enlist the help of the entire community in the fight against maltreatment. Further, attention can be focused on the problems of parenthood through adult education classes to help poor parents become good parents and good parents become even better at their roles. In light of the emphasis on prevention of maltreatment, child development and family life courses can be included in the regular school curricula at the elementary, secondary, and college levels to prepare future parents for the awesome responsibilities they will face. If an assessment of community resources reveals a lack of adequate care for preschoolers, efforts to establish such facilities can be undertaken, including the founding of preschools, crisis nurseries, and in-home baby-sitting services. Such facilities allow maltreating parents to get jobs to improve the family's lot or simply to get away from the children when the pressures of life in general and parenthood in particular become unbearable.

Its educational task is only partially completed once a school has trained its teachers and community volunteers to identify and deal with maltreating families. Others within the community may need both preservice and in-service preparation in this field since their jobs bring them in contact with maltreating families. In this regard, day-care center workers, police officers, social service workers, and mental health personnel come to mind. They may be brought into the family for reasons unrelated to maltreatment; yet, if they are familiar with the symptoms of marginal maltreatment and the resources available within the community to help the family, these workers can alert agencies and schools to family needs before maltreatment becomes severe.

In addition to what may be thought of as the educational functions of the school concerning child maltreatment, which have already been mentioned, the school can perform a dual task in regard to a community wide program to deal with child maltreatment. First, the school can assess community needs, suggest ways to supply them, and identify when a proposed service duplicates an existing one. Thus, the school can act as a coordinating vehicle for community programs. Second, it can promote the use and effectiveness of community resources by informing the neighborhood of the existence of these services. It matters little how good a maltreatment program is if people do not know of its existence. The coordination of services and dissemination of information about them are joint activities of the school.

## Critical questions

No doubt a number of important questions have occurred to the reader while thinking about the issue of child maltreatment and the role advocated for the school and community in combating it. In the following pages, issues of critical concern to educators and community members are raised. Not all the questions have universal answers; some can only be evaluated in light of the unique circumstances of a particular school, the neighborhood it serves, and the amount and kinds of community support available.

**If educators and citizens have a responsibility to aid maltreated children and their families, why have schools remained relatively detached from the problem of maltreatment in the past?**

A number of factors have contributed to the lack of involvement of many schools in recognizing and dealing with maltreatment. The news media have added to the public's confusion about child maltreatment by portraying its victims as very young children usually too small to be enrolled in educational institutions. The "battered child syndrome" affecting children under three years of age has received great attention and has become synonymous in many people's minds with child maltreatment. Certainly, such cases point out the gross physical brutality of some parents toward their innocent children. Because of the fragility of their tiny bodies, very young children are more susceptible to serious injury than are older children. Yet, focusing concern exclusively on preschool-age youngsters as the victims of maltreatment ignores the fact that most maltreated children attend care facilities or schools daily. Thus, it may be that educators have previously dismissed maltreatment as a problem that affects only pre-schoolers. They are only now becoming aware that children they see daily are maltreated.

Just as the news media have concentrated on small children as victims, so they have publicized physical abuse as if it were the only kind of mal-treatment to which children are subjected. More widespread forms, including medical, emotional, psychological, sexual, and educational maltreat-ment as well as harsh physical punishment not severe enough to constitute physical abuse are generally ignored. Though these kinds of maltreatment do not normally cause children's deaths, their long-range destructiveness to large numbers of young lives demands that attention be paid to them. In short, for too long the public has received incomplete information on child maltreatment. Now that the whole story is known about it, educators and the general public are beginning to seek ways to help marginally maltreat-ed children and their families.

Educators have always known that some parents are better at providing for the needs of their children than others. Many schools have worked with maltreating families in the past to bring about positive changes. Generally, however, such efforts have been sporadic. Few schools have developed sys-tematic procedures for screening children to determine possible cases of maltreatment. Few have trained their staffs and community volunteers to identify and aid maltreated children in the classroom. Few have taught their staffs human relations and counseling techniques to help maltreating parents. Few have spearheaded community efforts to increase public awareness of the problem of maltreatment and of the community resources available to alleviate it. What is being advocated here is a comprehensive approach to child maltreatment that focuses on the school as the agency with access to all children.

### Can every school establish a program to identify and assist maltreating families?

Not every school is currently in a position to begin a successful mal-treatment program. The school that lacks community support will be un-able to enlist the aid of neighborhood groups and individuals necessary to provide important services to maltreated children and their parents. The school whose principal is so overburdened with paperwork that he or she does not have time to assume the position of educational leader cannot hope to implement a comprehensive maltreatment program. The school whose teachers struggle from day to day to keep the lids on their classrooms hardly can expect them to enthusiastically embrace the added responsibilities of helping maltreating families. The school that relies heavily on ridicule and corporal punishment to control children cannot label these techniques as maltreatment when they are administered by parents. In short, a school must make sure its house is in order before it turns its concern to maltreating homes.

When is a school ready to launch a program to deal with child maltreatment? There is no hard and fast rule that can be applied in this regard. Many schools are ready now; many need to solve a few internal problems and can then begin; others have a long way to go before they will be in a position to devote their energies to fighting child maltreatment. Yet, maltreated children cannot wait forever; too soon they will leave the school, and too soon they may become maltreating parents themselves.

### Should every school establish a program to aid maltreated children and their parents?

After a careful assessment of its students, if a school finds that none of them are suffering marginal or serious maltreatment, then that school probably does not need a maltreatment program that year. However, in this imperfect world it seems highly unlikely that such a situation will come to light. Good parents maltreat their children when the pressures of their lives weigh too heavily on them. Loving parents sometimes rely too extensively on physical punishment to solve their disciplinary problems. Concerned parents sometimes forget that childhood can be at least as frustrating as adulthood; they may withhold their emotional support when a youngster needs it most. Thus, the potential for maltreatment always exists, and it is the wise school that has resources to deal with it when needed.

If a community already has an adequate program of prevention, detection, and treatment, the school need not be concerned with beginning a maltreatment program. Though many communities have some means to deal with maltreatment, few, if any, have a comprehensive system. Thus, it falls to each school to design and implement programs to meet the full range of needs of its maltreated children and their families.

### Is the establishment of a program to fight child maltreatment compatible with the "back to basics" philosophy current in educational circles?

The back to basics drive in American education is an attempt to focus on the acquisition of fundamental skills as a jumping-off point for further educational development. In one sense, concern with maltreated children can be seen not only as compatible with but also as a product of the emphasis on basics. A child's home environment is fundamental to his or her development as a competent human being. The youngster who lacks proper nutrition or who is constantly belittled at home has been denied the basics of success just as surely as the child who has not learned to read. Thus, it seems incumbent on educators to assess each child to learn if he or she is being supplied with the physical, emotional, psychological, and social basics through family life, for if these fundamental areas are neglected, it becomes infinitely more difficult for the child to acquire the educational basics that will enable him or her to succeed in school.

Simultaneously with the back to basics movement in education is expansion of the roles schools are being asked to perform. Schools are becoming centers of local action and leading forces in dealing with neighborhood concerns. As grassroots institutions, they are broadening their scope to encompass the entire community they serve. Education as an ongoing process extending from infancy to old age is becoming increasingly the function of schools. It is in light of this new comprehensiveness demanded by their clients that aiding maltreated children and their families is seen as a legitimate responsibility of schools.

**Do schools and educators have the right to delve into family affairs when they suspect that maltreatment is occurring?**

Traditionally, the family as the basic unit of society has enjoyed a great deal of autonomy. Parents have generally viewed child rearing as their prerogative, as witnessed by the often repeated justification, "I will raise my kids any way I want." Parents do have substantial rights in regard to family matters. However, too frequently forgotten is the fact that parenthood also involves great responsibilities, for children have rights as well.

Most parents love their children and want them to grow up to be the best people possible. Yet, parents do not always know how to go about that task. They need help, but in a society that assumes that all parents know how to fulfill their roles, whom can they ask for assistance? One of the most damning labels that can be applied to an adult is that of "unfit parent." To avoid such shame, maltreating adults try to hide their inadequacies, but frequently the parents' shortcomings show up clearly in their children.

Educators not only have the right to investigate their suspicions of maltreatment, but also have a responsibility to children to see that their homes foster growth. Certainly no family is perfect; no parents are ideal. Yet, within broad guidelines, educators know what helps children to develop normally and what hinders their progress. Prying into family relationships out of idle curiosity is an unjustifiable invasion of the privacy of the family; trying to assess if a family needs help to function as a productive unit is a legitimate responsibility of those concerned with the welfare of its members.

**Is it right to ask children to report maltreatment that they have suffered at the hands of their parents?**

Our society puts a great premium on loyalty. The tattletale and the stool pigeon are demeaned as less than honorable. Is the teacher who asks children about their parents' treatment of them encouraging these youngsters to snitch?

Certainly teachers have no right to "grill" or "pump" children for information about their homes. Yet, teachers need to understand why a child acts a certain way or seems unable to learn at a satisfactory rate. As professionals concerned with child development, teachers must be discreet in their inquiries. If their suspicions of maltreatment appear confirmed by the child, they must be careful not to pass judgment and must avoid communicating to youngsters any negative feelings they have about the parents. The teacher's role in identifying maltreating families involves understanding problems needing solutions and not alienating children from their imperfect parents. Thus, teachers should feel free to talk with children about their parents as long as the discussion remains nonaccusatory, with its ultimate goal helping maltreated children and their families.

### Should schools tell children what good parenting is?

Many maltreated children fail to realize that not all youngsters are treated by parents as they are. Research indicates that the bulk of parenting skills are learned by children watching the ways their parents deal with them. When the youngsters grow up, they employ the same techniques with their children that their parents used with them. Thus, good or poor parenting is an intergenerational phenomenon.

One reason why the cycle of parenting rarely is broken stems from attitudes toward parenthood. There is an assumption that a person needs no training to be a parent. It is the most widespread unskilled occupation in the world, with no experience required to get the job. Yet, parenting is hard work, as any parent knows. It involves responsibilities of monumental proportions, dedication unparalleled in any other field, and knowledge not obtainable from most educational institutions.

Parenting and child development classes for junior and senior high school students already exist in some communities. Family life units have been incorporated into many elementary school curricula. Such experiences help children learn positive approaches to parenthood and, when handled skillfully, do not alienate children from their parents. In fact, they can help children understand the difficult tasks their parents have, and development of such empathic relationships can actually improve family life.

Certainly, the best way to inculcate positive parenting skills in children is for parents to practice them with their youngsters. Schools can counsel adults to be better models for their children. Both through direct instruction to young people and indirect assistance to parents, schools can play a vital role in preparing children for the most pervasive vocation of all: parenthood.

### Should parents be told that they are performing their roles poorly?

Just as no one has the right to tell a child that his or her parent is unfit, so it would be wrong to express that idea to the parent. Good human relations are essential in working with maltreating parents and their children. People who wish to help others must avoid imposing their views and opinions on them. Further, family patterns established over many years cannot and should not be summarily abandoned, for such a total break might lead only to a worsened family situation. Often parents can identify problem areas in their family's life; sometimes they need help in analyzing sources of conflict within the family. In both situations, educators can be of invaluable assistance in aiding families to focus on their problems and in attempting to find solutions to the difficulties.

Of equal importance to pinpointing problem areas is recognizing the rate at which the family can be expected to implement solutions. Change must occur at a pace comfortable for the family or it may become overwhelmed. It is essential that those who work with maltreating families be sensitive to their needs and capabilities; without this important ingredient, good intentions will have little effect.

However, educators should not be frightened off by this warning, for good human relations and sensitivity to the needs of others are a teacher's stock in trade. Daily, teachers evaluate the capacities of students and the rates at which change can reasonably be expected to occur. Daily, teachers recognize that some students are upset, while others are very pleased with themselves. Teachers possess the flexibility to deal appropriately with each of these cases. Thus, using these same skills with parents is not demanding acquisition of a new sensitivity, but merely employment of an existing one in a slightly altered arena.

### Can schools force families to stop maltreating their children?

If parents violate child abuse laws and jeopardize the lives or health of their children, then educators have a legal obligation to report these facts to the proper authorities. However, in marginal cases of maltreatment that do not fit legal definitions, schools can only provide the vehicles for change and have no power to demand it. The family that believes it knows best how to raise its children cannot be made to alter its patterns unless it is violating the law. It is well to accept from the outset that some families will refuse all efforts at assistance. Further, other families that say they want help will find it difficult to implement much of the aid they are offered. Just as not all children are receptive to new learning, so not all parents can avail themselves of the services afforded them.

Forewarned is forearmed, however, and educators who accept from the start that they cannot stop all maltreatment will be less likely to hold unrealistic expectations as they begin to work with maltreating families. It is heartening to remember that the majority of marginally maltreating parents are anxious for assistance. They want and need to share their feelings with other adults who understand them. Generally, maltreating parents do not want to hurt their children, but they know no other ways to deal with them. Educators cannot allow the few uncooperative parents to dissuade them from offering assistance to the many more who desperately need and want it.

### What will become of today's maltreated children if the school and community do not help them?

Some children are strong enough to undergo maltreatment and emerge virtually unscathed. The scars inflicted by their families seem to fade as they grow to maturity. Perhaps they find ways to gratify their needs outside the family, such as excelling in sports or throwing themselves into their schoolwork. Perhaps a relative or a member of the clergy takes special interest in these children and helps them to develop normally despite their home situations.

Not all maltreated children are so fortunate, however. Some are placed in foster care or in institutions until they are old enough to fend for themselves. Often these facilities fail to provide any but the physical necessities of life. Other maltreated children run away from home to escape what they view as intolerable conditions. Some are never heard from again; others are picked up by the police and either returned unwillingly to their families or placed in juvenile reformatories or detention centers. Running away is a crime for juveniles, no matter how deplorable their family life. Some flee reality through drugs, which offer temporary relief from the harshness of their lives. Still other maltreated young people become involved in early marriages and unwanted pregnancies, either to escape from their homes or to receive the affection lacking in their families. When they become parents, they frequently maltreat their children because they know only the parenting techniques their parents employed with them.

Some maltreated youngsters turn their anger and hostility against society. Crimes committed by juveniles constitute one half of all serious crimes in America.[3] As Dr. Vincent DeFrancis, a tireless leader in the field of maltreatment, writes, "Most juvenile courts, and for that matter, most people working directly in the delinquency field, are convinced that child neglect is a first step in the development of a delinquent."[4] Whether the young criminal mugs a person to get money, to vent his anger toward adults, or to prove to his peers that he is a man, he may be reacting to the maltreatment he has experienced in his home. One writer who has done extensive work in the study of children says, "nearly every child I have interviewed in a jail or reform school has been abused to some degree."[5] Since it costs thousands of dollars a year to keep a person incarcerated, the price of maltreatment is high both for society and for the antisocial individual.

Are the long-term effects of child maltreatment being exaggerated? It seems likely that its consequences are more pervasive than most people realize. Maltreated children must receive the help they need while they are young enough for it to make a difference in their lives. Before they turn to drugs, the school can help them learn positive ways to deal with life. Before they run away from home, the community can provide services to make their families more functional units. Before they turn to crime, the school can instill in them feelings of personal dignity and worth. Before they perpetuate the cycle of maltreatment, the community can expose them to sound parenting skills. In short, unless the school and community work together to help maltreated children today, they may become the drug addicts, runaways, prostitutes, criminals, or child abusers of tomorrow.

## Conclusion

Educators must assume leadership in the fight against child maltreatment. Because their primary responsibility is to facilitate the development of each child, they can no longer remain aloof from the problems of the abused and neglected youngsters who are their clients. School personnel must accept the reality that children they work with daily may be mistreated by adults who do not perform their parenting roles adequately. Each day that passes adds to the injury the child suffers; each incident of maltreatment takes its toll on the youngster.

Maltreatment shatters young lives and destroys families. In a broader sense, it literally can change the course of history. Lee Harvey Oswald, who killed President Kennedy, was a maltreated child; Jack Ruby, who shot Oswald, was a maltreated child; Charles Whitman, who stationed himself in the University of Texas Tower with an arsenal of weapons, was a maltreated child; Charles Manson, who led a bizarre cult of killers, was a maltreated child. Once these men sat in classrooms before teachers who might have changed their lives.

Today, maltreated children wait for teachers to help them. Yet, if educators remain uninvolved, they may one day see their former students' names splashed infamously across the front pages of newspapers. Educators' potential to aid maltreated children and their families is tremendous; if assistance is not given by schools, the results can be tragic.

### References

1. Education Commission of the States, *Education Policies and Practices Regarding Child Abuse and Neglect and Recommendations for Policy Development*, report no. 85, DHEW grant no. 90-C-407 (Washington, D.C.: U.S. Government Printing Office, 1976), p. 3.
2. David Gil, "What Schools Can Do About Child Abuse," *American Education*, April 1969, pp. 2-4.
3. Naomi Feigelson Chase, *A Child Is Being Beaten: Violence Against Children, An American Tragedy* (New York: Holt, Rinehart and Winston, 1975), p. 127.
4. Vincent DeFrancis, *The Court and Protective Services: Their Respective Roles* (Denver: American Humane Association, n.d.), pp. 2-3.
5. Howard James, *The Little Victims: How America Treats Its Children* (New York: David McKay Co., Inc., 1975), p. 92.

# CHAPTER 2

# What is child maltreatment?

Child maltreatment is not a pleasant subject. No one enjoys thinking about the ways parents mistreat their youngsters. Few want to admit that people they know could maltreat their children; fewer still view themselves as potentially maltreating parents. Such attitudes have been responsible for the clouds of misinformation and emotionalism that surround the subject of child maltreatment.

The primary concern in dealing with the issue of maltreatment is identifying its young victims. Before this task can be accomplished, however, child maltreatment must be carefully defined and clearly understood. Professionals who deal frequently with children and citizens who observe them in more casual settings must recognize the conditions that constitute maltreatment.

## Child maltreatment legislation

One way to begin clarifying the subject of child maltreatment is to study laws pertaining to it. Because society is concerned with protecting children seriously threatened by their homes, legal definitions and provisions relate to severely maltreated children. During the last decade and a half, Congress and legislatures in all fifty states have enacted statutes designed to help identify severely maltreated children, care for their present injuries, and protect them from further abuse and neglect.

The Child Abuse Prevention and Treatment Act of 1974 is a federal law that provides a basic definition of child maltreatment:

The physical or mental injury, sexual abuse, negligent treatment, or maltreatment of a child under the age of eighteen by a person who is responsible for the child's welfare under circumstances which indicate the child's health or welfare is harmed or threatened thereby. [Public Law 93-247, 93rd Congress, Senate 1191, 1974]

Thus, federal law establishes three prerequisite conditions for child maltreatment: (1) that the maltreated individual be under eighteen years of age, (2) that the injury suffered be nonaccidental, and (3) that it be the care-taker (parent, foster parent, guardian, or baby-sitter) who inflicts the injury.

This federal law was designed not only to define maltreatment, but also to spur individual states to become more active in its prevention, identification, and treatment. One way to achieve this goal is to require or permit citizens who suspect that a child is being maltreated to report their beliefs to a governmental agency for investigation. All fifty states currently have child maltreatment reporting statutes they passed between 1963 and 1968. Although they are among the most frequently revised laws passed by legislators, their trend is toward a somewhat more sophisticated recognition of child maltreatment as a serious problem with which public and social agencies must reckon. Because they are state enactments, reporting laws vary considerably; therefore, it is necessary for concerned citizens to obtain copies of the statutes that pertain to them. There are, however, general characteristics that remain relatively constant among the laws of all fifty states.

While only forty-five states' reporting laws have separate sections defining child maltreatment, all statutes stipulate the kinds of treatment that must be reported to governmental agencies; therefore, in practical terms, each state law defines maltreatment within its jurisdiction. Four major maltreatment categories now exist in reporting laws. Physical abuse, or the nonaccidental injury of a child, presently is a reportable condition in every state. Physical neglect, the failure to supply the essentials of life to a child, including food, clothing, shelter, and medical care, must be reported in forty-seven states. Sexual abuse is a recent addition to maltreatment conditions that must be reported in thirty-seven states. Thirty-seven states consider psychological or emotional injury a form of child maltreatment. Although some states' laws include operational definitions or checklists of symptoms of reportable child maltreatment, most do not. Their language is often vague as it labels rather than describes child maltreatment.

When must a citizen report child maltreatment? As a general rule, state laws mandate that if a person has reason to believe that the treatment a child receives at home conforms to one of the defined categories of abuse or neglect, that individual must inform a governmental agency. The reporter need not have conclusive evidence; if there is reasonable cause to suspect that maltreatment is occurring, a report should be made. It is the job of the bureau that receives reports to investigate them and make the final decisions as to whether or not cases meet the legal definitions of maltreatment.

Just as there is variation among state reporting laws in regard to what constitutes child maltreatment, there is even disagreement as to who is a child. Although the 1974 federal statute defines a child as anyone under eighteen years of age, only twenty-six states have established that criterion.

Five states use the age of seventeen, eight states employ sixteen, one sets fifteen, and one state claims youngsters are no longer children when they reach the age of twelve. Nine states set no upper limit, but imply that any minor is protected under reporting laws.

Reporting statutes recognize that child maltreatment is not strictly a family matter, but rather a concern of the general population. All fifty states' laws stipulate professionals who are required to report their suspicions of child maltreatment. Typically, these include doctors, nurses, social workers, and police. In forty-two states, teachers and other school personnel are under mandate to report suspected cases of child maltreatment. In addition, day-care workers in thirty-two states have a similar legal obligation. In forty-four states, all citizens are either required or permitted to report; thus, every person in these jurisdictions has a legal responsibility to aid in the identification of maltreated children. In all fifty states educators are either mandated to report or permitted as citizens to express their suspicions of maltreatment.

Existing legal enactments give some indication as to the nature of child maltreatment, since they define it as a condition for which citizens have responsibility in the area of identification. However, legislation does not provide a comprehensive understanding of the variety of forms maltreatment can take. Even as this book is printed, child abuse and neglect statutes are being revised to reflect changes in public concern for and attitudes toward the maltreatment of children. Yet, parents do not read laws to determine how to mistreat their children. The negative effects of maltreatment on youngsters are not magically erased because maltreatment is illegal. Though legislation often denies its complexity, child maltreatment is a multifaceted phenomenon. It can be brutally obvious, as in the case of parents who severely beat or burn their children, or it can be more subtle, as when parents withhold any signs of affection and warmth from their offspring. Although only the brutally obvious incidents might conform to legal definitions of child maltreatment, the subtle incidents can have as deleterious effects on the health, development, and very existence of youngsters.

## Incidence of maltreatment

It is impossible to state with certainty the number of children who are maltreated each year in the United States. Most estimates are based on the incidence of serious cases reported to and confirmed by social workers, who refer to the state's legal definitions to determine if the care a child receives is maltreatment. Thus, because of the wide variance among states, parents in one jurisdiction could be found guilty of maltreatment, while adults in another who treat their children in an identical way may be found innocent of maltreatment. Also, not included in the figures are innumerable severe abuse and neglect situations that remain hidden from public view. Further, statistics do not deal with marginally maltreated children whose parents' treatment of them is harmful but not sufficiently detrimental to conform to legal standards of maltreatment. It can be assumed that this unreported group is so numerous that it would dwarf the number of reported cases by comparison.

The difficulty in determining the incidence of maltreatment is compounded by methodological inconsistencies. Some studies cite the number of families that maltreat, while others supply the number of children maltreated. Because there are many families in which several youngsters are abused or neglected, the magnitude of the problem of maltreatment is masked by referring to each family as one incident. An even more serious problem concerns arbitrarily selective studies that focus on only one aspect of maltreatment. Overwhelmed by the task before them, many researchers limit their definitions to "severe physical abuse." Thus, they include in their statistics the incidence of only one of the nine forms of maltreatment to which children are subjected.

In his book *Violence Against Children*, David Gil surveyed the 1967 and 1968 statistics of child maltreatment. In addition, he conducted a poll to discover the number of Americans who personally knew maltreating families. Projections based on his findings indicate that between 2.5 and 4 million children may be maltreated each year, though Gill believes his figures to be inflated.[1] Reevaluation of Gil's findings led Richard Light to conclude that as many as 1.7 million children may be seriously abused and neglected annually.[2]

A more recent survey conducted by the National Center of Child Abuse and Neglect reveals that approximately 340,000 children are physically abused and another 1.3 million are neglected yearly. This study confirms earlier findings that 1.7 million children suffer at the hands of their caretakers each year.[3] Since there are 68 million children in the United States under eighteen years of age, figures suggest that at least one in every forty children is a victim of child maltreatment.

It seems advisable to stop playing the numbers game and begin acknowledging that child maltreatment is alarmingly prevalent in America today. Attention must be focused not on academic issues involving its incidence, but rather on the parents and children whose daily lives it affects. Child maltreatment is not an abstraction to be dealt with by computers, but an intensely personal, individualized, and painful phenomenon that causes untold misery and the squandering of our nation's most valuable resource: human beings. Neither the legal statutes nor guesstimates on its prevalence define the complex nature of child maltreatment. Thus, let us turn our attention to the major categories of maltreatment to gain a clear understanding of its scope.

## Forms of maltreatment

Child maltreatment takes a variety of forms, for it may include any act or omission that adversely affects a child's development. Broadly stated, child maltreatment falls into nine categories:

1. Physical abuse
2. Sexual abuse
3. Physical neglect
4. Medical neglect
5. Emotional abuse
6. Emotional neglect
7. Educational neglect
8. Abandonment (the ultimate neglect)
9. Multiple maltreatment

### Physical abuse

Physical abuse is the most easily recognized and most often reported kind of maltreatment, for the marks of physical assault are visible on the child. It is frequently difficult, however, to ascertain how the child was injured, for many maltreating parents create stories to hide their culpability. Further, children are often reluctant to name their caretakers as their assailants; they remain silent either out of love for or fear of their parents. However, there are signs in physical abuse that suggest strongly that the injuries are parent inflicted. They include —

1. The identifiable imprint of an object on the skin (clothes hanger, belt buckle, electrical cord end, hand, teeth marks)
2. An injury that curves around the body because it was made by a flexible object (belt, hose, rope)
3. Injuries centralized on the face and head
4. Peculiarly shaped and sized injuries
5. Bruises of different colors, indicating injuries occurring over a period of time
6. Abrasions that are in various stages of healing, pointing toward continuing injury
7. Injuries on different areas of the body, suggesting the child has been struck from several directions
8. Burns of the following descriptions:
   a. Glovelike burns inflicted by immersion in hot liquid
   b. Circle-shaped burns on buttocks, caused by immersion in hot liquid
   c. Burns more severe in the middle, indicating that hot liquid has been poured on
   d. Object-shaped burns from such things as cigarettes, pokers, and cooking utensils

Other indications of physical assault constituting maltreatment may be gathered from observing children both with their parents and when they are absent. Physically maltreated children frequently are fearful of all adults, for they believe that any grown-up may attack them. They may be especially frightened and unresponsive in the presence of their parents. Some physically abused children, however, react in the opposite way: they are overly eager to win acceptance from adults by doing whatever they are told and even anticipate adult requests. These techniques of overcompliance have saved them pain in the past, and physically assaulted children often rely on their success.

When called upon to explain their child's injuries, maltreating parents use a number of tactics to hide their guilt. Some claim not to know how the child was hurt; others tell stories that are inconsistent with the injuries; still others change their explanations frequently; some place the blame on another, such as a playmate, sibling, or relative. Sometimes the parents' feelings of guilt are apparent through overreaction or obvious nervousness. Other parents appear angry and hostile toward their children and may verbally threaten either their health or life. Some maltreating parents bring a child to medical facilities for treatment when the injuries do not warrant it; perhaps they want someone to identify their problem and help them stop hurting the youngster. Other maltreating parents never take their child for medical care in the hope of avoiding detection.

Why do parents physically hurt their children? The California Department of Justice states: "The most common cause of inflicted physical injury is overpunishment which occurs when corporal punishment is unreasonably severe. This usually happens when the parent is extremely agitated or angry and either throws, or strikes, the child too hard or continues to beat him."[4]

### Sexual abuse

Sexual abuse may be viewed as a specialized form of physical maltreatment. It can be defined as any sexually stimulating act initiated by an adult and involving a child. Usually the adult is a male, and in approximately 90 percent of the cases, the child is a female. Most abuse involving boys is of a homosexual nature, and comparatively little is known about it. Sexual abuse involves children from infancy through adolescence; it runs the gamut from exposure, to fondling, to rape, and to incest.

It seems somewhat ironic that society cautions youngsters against sexual encounters with strangers but never warns children against the sexual advances of friends and relatives. Children are told repeatedly not to accept candy from strangers or to accompany them in cars. However, it is not the stranger children must fear most in terms of sexual abuse; people they trust are far more likely to be its perpetrators. Studies reveal that approximately 75 percent of sexually abusing adults are family members, people known personally to the child, or friends of the victim's family.[5]

Just as the public attitude is incorrect in regard to who commits sexual abuse, so it is inaccurate in its belief that the abuse occurs only once. Except in the cases involving strangers, there is rarely a single sexual encounter. Generally, sexual abuse becomes a pattern over an extended period of weeks, months, or years and is repeated with some frequency. The average age of the girl at the onset of sexual abuse is eleven years old. Thus, it can

be concluded that the vast majority of sexually abused children are enrolled in schools while they are being sexually victimized by adults.[6]

Until recently, sexual abuse remained the least mentioned form of child
maltreatment; it continues to be the most underreported kind of mistreatment to which children are subjected. Based on the findings of an American Humane Association study, Dr. Vincent DeFrancis concludes, "The
problem of sexual abuse of children is of unknown national dimensions,
but findings strongly point to the probability of an enormous national incidence many times larger than the reported incidence of physical abuse in
children."[7] Sexual abuse is laden with emotional impact because of the
personal nature of the attack. Much of it involves family members, and few
cultural taboos are more staunchly maintained than those against incest.
Not only is it illegal, but it is also immoral since it represents a violation of
normal family intimacy. Further, whether the sexual abuse involves a relative or a friend, it frequently occurs within the confines of the home. These
dual factors of social unacceptability and occurrence in private conspire to
lead family members to hide sexual abuse and outsiders to learn only rarely
of its existence.

Unlike victims of physical abuse, the sexually abused girl usually bears
no external marks of the maltreatment she receives. Frequently, the girl
undergoes a sudden behavior change when sexual abuse begins or when
she learns that not all children are treated by adults as she is. She may become withdrawn and fail to engage in acting-out behavior; she may cry often for no apparent reason and without offering an explanation; she may
turn suddenly hostile and present behavior problems; she may become extremely anxious when asked to undress for a school physical examination
or a physical education class. In older victims, pregnancy may result if intercourse occurs. At all ages, the female undergoes deep psychological and
emotional trauma caused by feelings of guilt.

Many sexually abused youngsters try to hide the reality of their maltreatment from others because they recognize that they are participants in
activities society bans. They submit to the sexual desires of the adult because of fear of physical punishment, threats of withdrawal of love, or because they want some external reward offered to them if they acquiesce.
Sometimes this secret burden becomes so great that the child feels she
must share it with someone. She may turn to a peer or a trusted adult outside her home for help. Such a plea for assistance cannot go unheeded.
Though it is a delicate subject that must be handled skillfully, sexual abuse
cannot be dismissed as too personal a matter to investigate. Suspicions of
sexual maltreatment must be aired and vigorously pursued in the hope of
saving the child from further victimization.

Sexual abuse not only violates child maltreatment laws, but it also
stands as a separate criminal charge. Because the abuser both has and acts
upon deviant impulses symptomatic of a complex of psychological prob-

lems, professional help must be provided for him. Frequently, his victim also requires supportive services to minimize the long-term detrimental effects of her experience.

### Physical neglect

Not all maltreatment involves active injury; the passivity of parents constitutes maltreatment as well. While abuse can be thought of as the actions of caretakers that harm children, neglect represents parental omissions that endanger the healthy development of youngsters. Though neglect is a less easily defined condition than abuse, it is no less deleterious to the welfare of young people.

The basic responsibilities of parenthood focus on fulfilling the physical requirements of children. It is a parent's obligation to provide a nurturing home environment in which a child can develop in relative safety. Physical neglect is characterized by failure to supply the necessities of life to a child. These essentials include food, clothing, shelter, general care, supervision, and reasonable protection from harm.

Physically neglected children can be identified in a number of ways. They are the youngsters who are hungry and may steal from others to satisfy their appetite. They may be thin because they do not get enough to eat, or they may be overweight because their diets rely heavily on starchy food. In either case, the nutritional state may be poor and can manifest this fact in frequent illnesses because of a lack of resistance to disease.

When parents fail to provide their youngsters with adequate clothing, physical neglect may be occurring. Children who wear light jackets when they should have heavy winter coats appear physically neglected. In such cases, parental disregard for the welfare and comfort of the child stands as the basis of neglect.

In other cases, children's clothing is adequate, but it is dirty, torn, and generally in poor repair. Perhaps the child wears the same clothes day after day without their being washed and mended. The family that can afford few clothes for a child is not necessarily negligent, for many loving families lack the financial resources to provide an extensive wardrobe for a youngster. However, when a child's clothing reflects obvious parental indifference to appearance and hygiene, physical neglect may be present.

Just as a child's clothing suggests parental failure to provide for general nurturance, so, too, does a youngster's ill-kempt body. Cleanliness is not judged by any absolute standards; yet, the child whose personal hygiene is so neglected that others do not wish to be near is an obvious case of lack of parental concern for that youngster's welfare.

Some ill-clad and poorly cared for children live in homes that are generally unsafe or unsanitary. Faulty wiring and nonfunctional plumbing suggest that the shelters their parents maintain are inadequate. In some homes the beds do not have sheets, dirty dishes are piled high, and insects and rats are prevalent. When parents do not exercise normal care in regard to the family's living quarters, children may be physically neglected.

Parents are expected to provide supervision for their immature off-spring; failure to do so constitutes physical neglect. If a primary school youngster returns from school to an empty house each afternoon, his or her parents do not meet their responsibility to see that their child is protected by adult watchfulness. When a seven-year-old is given charge of younger brothers and sisters in the absence of adult caretakers, the health and safety of the children are jeopardized.

Children are entitled to adult supervision and guidance not only within the home, but also in areas beyond its walls. Parents who do not know where their children are fail in their obligation to employ reasonable care in protecting the safety of their offspring. Assumed because of their ages to be mature and responsible, parents are expected to be vigilant and anticipate and forestall situations that potentially threaten the welfare of their young-sters. Parents who fail to fulfill these responsibilities neglect the most basic needs of their children.

In cases in which poverty is the cause of physical neglect, social ser-vices are frequently available to remedy the situation. However, physical neglect often exists because parents are either unable or unwilling to deal with the routine of daily life. In such cases the family is chaotic and lacks the discipline necessary to order and meet the physical requirements of its members. Dependent on their parents for nurturance, children suffer the brunt of adults' inability to supply the physical needs of the family.

### Medical neglect

Medical neglect can be considered as either a specialized kind of physi-cal neglect or a separate category of child maltreatment. It is defined as the failure of a parent to provide medical treatment for suspected or diagnosed physical conditions of a child except in those cases in which religious be-liefs proscribe a doctor's care. Educators presently monitor parental negli-gence in this area by requiring proof of immunizations before children can be enrolled in school. Further, periodic in-school medical screenings are designed as diagnostic tools to alert parents to the existence of conditions needing professional treatment. Parents who do not obtain medical assis-tance for their youngsters when it is indicated are medically negligent.

Observation frequently reveals the existence of medical neglect. Some children appear listless when they should be bright and active. Others have difficulty seeing the blackboard or hearing the teacher in class. A youngster may repeatedly complain of an ailment and, when asked if a doctor has been consulted, explain that his or her parents do not view the problem as warranting medical treatment. The child who is absent from school frequently because of illness, but whose parents never secure medical advice to keep the youngster well, suffers not only from a physical malady, but also from medical neglect.

It might be argued that medical maltreatment is not a product of parental negligence, but a reflection of economic status; however, cost cannot be used as a justification for medical neglect. In low-income families with limited financial resources, treatment is available at either low or no charge. In more affluent families, though it is costly, private treatment is an expense that can be absorbed either through health insurance or careful budgeting of family income. Thus, failure of parents to have a child's eyes checked or teeth filled cannot be attributed solely to monetary considerations.

Generally, medical maltreatment reflects either the indifference or inability of parents to direct their energies to the physical well-being and development of a child. It may be that within the busy lives of the adults, no time is allotted for attention to the child's medical problems. Obtaining medical treatment for a youngster involves establishing the appointment and arranging transportation to the doctor. For some parents this process seems overwhelming, for they have limited capacity to plan and carry through events on a schedule. Medical maltreatment may be a symptom of other kinds of neglect as well as an indication that the parents are unable to fulfill their nurturing roles.

### Emotional abuse

As maltreatment leaves the physical realm, it does not disappear; it merely becomes more pervasive and more nebulous and difficult to define. Emotional abuse involves actions by a parent that interfere with the healthy personal and social development of a child. Emotional abuse is noteworthy in that its effects are cumulative rather than isolated, and they eventually display themselves in the behavior of the child.

Many emotionally abusive parents hold unrealistic expectations for their children and communicate their standards in critical and demanding language. For example, some parents are so anxious that their child succeed in school that they apply tremendous pressure to the youngster to get high grades. Frequently, such parents ridicule the child when he or she fails to achieve the goals they have set; often, they demonstrate their disappointment through words and actions. These children come to believe themselves worthless because it is obvious to them that their parents perceive them in that way. Thus, the normal parent-child relationship of love and unconditional acceptance is transformed into an abusive one involving criticism and acceptance contingent on fulfilling impossible parental goals. These children are left with emotional scars both from being rejected and from concluding that it is their failures that make them unlovable.

Other parents see in their children elements of themselves they dislike;

therefore, they emotionally punish the child based on their projections of their own traits. The mother who has always feared her own sexuality may view the innocent actions of her daughter as seductive. She may so demean the child that she either embraces her mother's perception of her and becomes promiscuous or so studiously denies her sexuality that she is unable to establish healthy relationships with others.

Emotional abuse takes innumerable forms depending on the unique characteristics of family members and the dynamics of family relationships. The factor common in all emotional abuse cases is that parents hinder the personal growth of their offspring by speech and action. For example, when called to a conference involving the teacher and the parent, an emotionally abusive adult might say: "This boy is just plain bad. I can't do anything with him. He's a good-for-nothing, just like his father. Can't you people at school make him change? I've tried at home, but I gave up on him." The abuse takes its toll on the child and is most often manifest in behavior problems. Some children internalize their parents' neuroses. Others are convinced that they are worthless or bad and so act out behavior that confirms these judgments. Some withdraw from contact with others through excessive daydreaming in the hope of insulating themselves. They anticipate all interpersonal relationships to be as painful as those with their parents; therefore, they opt for isolation rather than risk further injury. Other youngsters become hyperaggressive and thus imitate their parents' attitudes toward them. In a group of psychologically healthy children the emotionally abused boy or girl is easily recognized.

Many emotionally abusive parents do not realize what they are doing to their offspring. Some are so narcissistic that they fail to see that they are actively involved in destroying the psychological and social existence of their youngsters. Others do not recognize that although children are resilient, they are also sensitive beings in the process of becoming. It takes some children years to recover from the emotional abuse they have experienced; as the population of mental hospitals and the suicide rate attest, many emotionally abused children never achieve normal psychological adjustment.

### Emotional neglect

Emotional neglect, like other forms of negligence, involves the failure to provide prerequisites for healthy child development through omission rather than through action. Emotionally neglected children frequently seem frail and unhealthy, for even though their physical needs are being met, they lack the emotional requirements for healthy growth. Every child requires a sense of emotional involvement with his caretakers; if parents do not provide it, the youngster is denied an ingredient for growth as basic as proper nutrition. Often, emotionally neglected children's behavior becomes delinquent because they have failed to receive the love, affection, and security necessary for the impulse control of antisocial acts. Because their need for attention is largely unsatisfied by their parents, emotionally neglected children seek out others who acknowledge their existence and make them feel important. Unfortunately, so starved are these children for notice that they frequently engage in misbehavior as the vehicle for gaining attention. Many adolescent girls who have been emotionally neglected turn to indiscriminate sexual activity in an attempt to receive the affection they so desperately need. Their male counterparts may turn to drugs, gangs, or vandalism to obliterate their pain, feel important in their own eyes, or vent their hostility toward society in general and their negligent parents in particular.

Emotionally neglecting adults are often indifferent to their children. Although they may provide the bodily essentials of existence, they fail to feel or show much concern for these youngsters or their activities. While the emotionally abusive parent's expressions of his or her feelings toward the child have a negative effect, the emotionally negligent parent's failure to exhibit either anger or warmth can be equally injurious.

### Educational neglect

Education is a process that begins in infancy and continues throughout life. Its formal phase occurs in schools where trained educators direct the learning of students. The informal education children receive from their parents is also an important part of their development. When parents fail to ensure that their children have opportunities to learn both in school and in the family, educational neglect occurs.

It is a parent's responsibility to see that his or her child attends school daily unless sick or unless some situation makes it imperative that the child be elsewhere. Educationally negligent parents do not fulfill this obligation. It is as though they do not care about the child's intellectual and social development. These parents fail to instill in their youngsters a respect for knowledge and an understanding that the learner must assume responsibility for his or her own education. Often these children fall into a pattern of nonattendance at school because their parents have little interest in their school activities. Sometimes parents insist that a child stay home from school to care for younger brothers and sisters. Adults' lack of concern about the educational growth of their youngsters makes it clear that they do not value education; thus, these children put a low premium on it as well.

Informal learning in the home is at least as important as the education a child receives in the classroom. In some families, however, children are not taught the basic skills of living, nor are they exposed to enrichment activities that broaden their knowledge and experience. The educationally neglecting home is barren of stimulation for the child because his or her parents take little interest in helping the youngster develop into a competent and well-rounded individual.

Educationally neglected children frequently have learning problems in school that either predate or are compounded by truancy. Normally their parents express little concern about their unsatisfactory progress. They do not help these children at home with studies, and they fail to ensure that they come to school regularly. Educationally neglected youngsters have few positive home experiences to share with classmates, for their families provide little opportunity for them to expand their interests and skills. Because they and their parents do not participate in activities as a group, these children may find it hard to work with others to reach a common goal. They may withdraw from the group or attempt to dominate it or divert it from its task. Thus, educational neglect blocks the full development of a child in terms of intellectual, social, and personal growth.

Not all educationally negligent parents are uninterested in their children. Many simply do not understand the importance of educational experiences, and especially of those in the home. Others rely on the school to provide for the total learning of a child and fail to recognize their responsibility in this area. Still others have low intellectual capacities themselves and are unable to offer much stimulation to their children.

### Abandonment

Perhaps the ultimate kind of child maltreatment is physical abandonment, for it stands as a total rejection of the parent-child relationship. Babies left in gas station restrooms and on doorsteps immediately come to mind. An older child may be put in the care of another adult under the pretense that the parents will soon return for the youngster. When they do not come to claim the child and make no provision for his or her continued sustenance, abandonment has occurred.

Abandoned children come to the notice of child protective services. They become wards of the court and are usually placed with willing relatives, in foster homes, or in care institutions. Rarely are they adopted, for there is always the chance that the natural parents will return to claim them.

Because abandonment represents the renunciation of the family unit, few palliatives can be applied. Attention must be focused on ascertaining the most satisfactory placement to meet the physical and personal needs of the child.

### Multiple maltreatment

Children in many families suffer from only one kind of maltreatment; however, other youngsters are subjected to several forms of abuse and neglect simultaneously. Although emotional maltreatment can exist in isolation, when physical abuse or neglect occurs, emotional mistreatment is almost certain to accompany it. The parent who beats a child is likely to verbally abuse him or her as well; the caretaker who leaves a youngster unattended for extended periods demonstrates through physical negligence that he or she is also emotionally neglecting this youngster.

Thomas Malthus's famous analysis of the manner in which population increases seems an appropriate parallel to the subject of multiple child maltreatment. Malthus noted that the number of people in the world does not grow arithmetically, but geometrically. Multiple maltreatment can be likened to population growth; one form of maltreatment is not simply added to another, but, rather, it is multiplied by it. Physical abuse plus medical neglect often equals permanent injury or death to the youngster. Physical neglect compounded by emotional neglect can produce a child much less able to develop normally than if he or she were the victim of only one form of maltreatment. A child's suffering increases geometrically as the kinds of maltreatment to which he or she is exposed increase.

Thus, the victims of multiple maltreatment experience a special kind of maltreatment that differs significantly from any of its individual forms. Because of its severity and complexity, multiple maltreatment is difficult to identify and resistant to change. Its symptoms often differ from those that are evident when any of the forms of maltreatment exists alone. Rather than being a rare phenomenon, multiple maltreatment is prevalent. A parent who is inadequate in one area of child rearing often has limited success in others. Thus, multiple maltreatment is an indication of serious problems experienced both by individual parents and by the family as a whole.

## Conclusion

Maltreatment can be broadly defined in terms of the law; it can be categorized. Examples of maltreating behavior can be supplied; anecdotes involving abused and neglected children can be retold; its incidence can be crudely calculated. Yet, there is something imprecise about child maltreatment. When does corporal punishment become physical abuse? At what point do the tender caresses between adult and child constitute sexual abuse? Where is the line between the family with poor housekeeping habits and physical neglect? What distinguishes calmness about childhood illnesses from medical neglect? What separates the disappointed parent with high hopes for his or her child from the emotionally abusive adult? Where is the boundary between allowing a child independence and emotional neglect? When does a parent's realistic acceptance of limited success for his or her child constitute educational neglect? The answer to these questions is that there are no answers. Just as all human behavior can be viewed as a continuum, so it is with child maltreatment. The extremes of healthy development and serious maltreatment are easily identified; however, the difficulty arises when judgments must be made on situations that fall somewhere in between.

Though the task of determining if maltreatment exists is difficult, it is far from impossible. When a teacher or concerned citizen sees the behavior of a child, attempts to understand it, and tries to learn conditions in the family that may be responsible for it, child maltreatment becomes a tangible subject, separated from intellectual activities that concern its precise definition. In abstract terms, it is hard to decide what constitutes child maltreatment; in practical terms, it is much simpler to identify a maltreated child.

Let us look at the case of a child any adult would recognize as maltreated. Her name is Madeline Handley. Of course, that is not her real name; yet, this youngster's story not only is true, but also is repeated so frequently in the lives of other children that it is terrifying.

### THE CASE OF MADELINE HANDLEY

Madeline entered the school in the first grade. Her ability level was classified as dull normal, and tests indicated her IQ to be in the low 80s. Bruises on the child from time to time signaled that she was being harshly punished at home by her mother. It was also revealed both by observation of her behavior and by investigation of her relationship with her parent that Madeline was being emotionally neglected. Her mother showed her little love and even less affection. Her physical needs were being met adequately, however, and Madeline came to school each day neatly dressed and well fed. Thus, Madeline was marginally maltreated both physically and emotionally, but her care did not conform to legal definitions of abuse or neglect.

Because of the lack of affection she experienced at home, Madeline responded hungrily to the attention she received at school. Teachers who showed her any love or caring became people to whom she clung. Under the watchful nurturance of school personnel, Madeline made good emotional adjustment to the classroom, worked reasonably well with her peers, and advanced slowly but steadily in her schoolwork. Her teacher was pleased with her progress and felt that Madeline's self-concept was developing relatively well despite the marginal maltreatment she received at home.

When she was in the third grade, however, something happened to Madeline. As if overnight, her energy level dropped significantly. When her teacher tried to show her affection, Madeline withdrew, fearful of the touch of an adult. Her moods alternated swiftly from withdrawal to aggressive hostility. Her interest in her schoolwork disappeared. Even Madeline's appearance changed, as she came to school in mismatched, wrinkled, sometimes dirty clothing. As she walked through the halls of the school, each step seemed an effort; on the playground, she isolated herself from the other children and showed no interest in playing.

The school's efforts to learn the reasons for Madeline's sudden transformation were unsuccessful. She confided in no one, and her mother claimed not to notice any change in the child. One day, her story was revealed.

Madeline's mother had a boyfriend who often came to the home. Sometimes he stayed with Madeline while her mother went shopping. When Madeline was nine, the man attacked her sexually. The act involved penetration and was repeated several times a week for months. Madeline told her mother of his abuse, but was instructed to comply with the man's demands and not to tell her story to anyone else. After a period of time, the man instructed Madeline to bring home some female playmates; it is unclear whether she understood why. One day, Madeline invited sisters who lived nearby home to play; one was a first grader, and one a second grader. The man grabbed the older child and began to sexually abuse her while Madeline held the girl's arms to stop her from struggling. The first grader was able to escape the house, find a policeman, and bring him to the home while the sexual abuse was still in progress.

Madeline is in the fourth grade now. No longer is she being sexually molested; yet, the effects of her ordeal persist. She sits and stares off into space as if in a trance. She not only has failed to make academic progress, but also has lost the skills she acquired earlier in her education. Madeline does not associate with the other children; she rarely plays even by herself. She isolates herself from adults, and even as one talks with her, there is the feeling that she only partially understands.

Is Madeline's case unusual? Unfortunately, it is not. Certainly, it involves maltreatment of a serious and legally punishable nature. Yet, when we look at this child's life, legislative definitions fly out the window because they seem irrelevant. It is the individual maltreated child who is important, not any contrived attempts to establish the total number of abused and neglected children. Although it is convenient to categorize the forms of maltreatment, such a strategy by itself does little to help the maltreated child develop a more normal life. Educators and other concerned citizens must focus on the plight of children as they have been victimized throughout history and are daily mistreated in our own society. Only then can we hope to help both the youngsters and their families to establish positive relationships.

### References

1. David G. Gil, *Violence Against Children: Physical Child Abuse in the United States* (Cambridge, Mass: Harvard University Press, 1970), p. 59.
2. Richard Light, "Abused and Neglected Children in America: A Study of Alternative Policies," *Harvard Educational Review* 43 (November 1974): 556-598.
3. National Center of Child Abuse and Neglect, *Child Abuse and Neglect Reports*, DHEW pub. no. 87-30086 (Washington, D.C.: U.S. Government Printing Office, June 1976), p. 3.
4. California Department of Justice, *Child Abuse: The Problem of the Abused and Neglected Child*, Information Pamphlet no. 8 (Los Angeles: California Department of Justice, 1976), p. 2.
5. Vincent DeFrancis, *Protecting the Child Victim of Sex Crimes* (Denver: American Humane Association, 1965), p. vii.
6. Vincent DeFrancis, *Protecting the Child Victim of Sex Crimes*, p. vii.
7. Vincent DeFrancis, *Protecting the Child Victim of Sex Crimes*, p. vii.

# CHAPTER 3

# Is child maltreatment increasing?

Most adults today perceive children as developing human beings who need help and guidance as they grow. Yet, children have not always been viewed with our culture's present sense of compassion and understanding. In fact, the acceptance of childhood and children is a relatively new social phenomenon. The deeper into the annals of history one looks, the more hideous the treatment children received. Moreover, there was little social outcry, for what would be labeled maltreatment today was considered standard practice in past cultures. Only within the last century has society recognized that children are people too, entitled to "life, liberty, and the pursuit of happiness" as well as to the active nurturance necessary to ensure these conditions. While the methods of child maltreatment have changed little over millenia, society's view of the elements that constitute maltreatment has been drastically altered. Yet, there remain some parents who fail to conform to contemporary society's conception of adequate child care; these are the maltreating parents of today.

## History's record on infanticide

Throughout the centuries, infanticide, or the killing of young children, was an established social custom practiced with great frequency in many cultures. It served as a method of population control, although war, famine, epidemic, and accident proved more effective in limiting the number of citizens. Since boys were viewed as useful in many societies while their sisters were not, female babies were often eliminated. According to the census figures in ancient Greece, for example, the ratio of male to female was four to one. Frequently only one daughter was spared in a family, while sons were rarely put to death. It has been speculated that the depopulation of Greece can be attributed directly to widespread infanticide practiced even by wealthy parents on their legitimate offspring.

The killing of illegitimate babies was commonplace in Western societies for centuries. In some societies it was against the law for an illegitimate child to be permitted to live; in other cultures the stigma associated with illegitimacy was so great that unwed mothers routinely eliminated the tangible symbols of their sinfulness. For the very poor, another mouth to feed could mean the difference between family survival and starvation for all; therefore, infanticide provided the course many chose. The practice remained prevalent well into the sixteenth century in Europe and even today is common in some isolated cultures.

In many societies, deformed children were put to death as soon as their imperfections were discovered. The Roman Law of the Twelve Tables pronounced illegal the raising of an impaired child. Following the beliefs of philosophers like Aristotle and Plato, the Greeks supported the elimination of weak babies so that only the strongest human specimens would survive. Similar practices were common through the sixteenth century in Europe; Martin Luther advocated infanticide of defective children because he considered them tools of the devil.

Infanticide viewed as religious duty was an established custom in many past societies. No sacrifice was considered more acceptable to the deities than the life of a newborn child. In ancient Palestine, sacrifice of the firstborn son was a common practice, although one officially unsanctioned by religious leaders. Infanticide is mentioned in the Bible as a technique used to thwart the fulfillment of prophecy. Pharaoh and Herod ordered the mass murder of male babies; Moses and Jesus Christ survived these purges to carry out the will of God.

The methods employed throughout history to accomplish infanticide include the drowning, burning, strangling or smothering, poisoning, beating, and abandoning of children. Generally, infanticide occurred without bloodshed, except for occasional ritualistic practices in which bloodletting was an important element.

When compared to its incidence in the past, infanticide is less prevalent in modern society. Except for the aberrant beliefs of fanatic religious cults whose practice of infanticide occasionally comes to light, religious fervor no longer leads to the killing of babies. Illegitimacy rarely elicits sentiments strong enough to warrant the deaths of infants born to unwed mothers. Although poverty still exists, our heightened sense of social responsibility to provide for the basic needs of all citizens eliminates the need for infanticide among the poor.

Infanticide does occur today, for it has been estimated that at least fifteen hundred children a year are killed by their caretakers; an additional fifteen thousand youngsters who survive parental attacks suffer permanent brain damage as a result of the brutality of adults directed against the children for whom they are responsible.[1]

## Physical cruelty to children

More numerous than the cases of infanticide throughout recorded time are the incidents of physical maltreatment ending short of death. The physical abuse to which children have been subjected throughout history is well documented. The Huns customarily scarred the cheeks of newborn males; Italians during the Renaissance often burned their children's necks with hot wax; in all ages, children were systematically maimed to make them better beggars.

In some cultures, children were jeopardized as a source of amusement for adults. In Europe during the sixteenth century, infants were used as playthings, thrown from one person to another. Woe to the child whose caretaker was a poor catch, for he or she might end up like the brother of France's King Henry IV, who fell to his death while being tossed from one window to another. Anthropological study of the contemporary Ik culture shows a society in which parents snatch the food from their offsprings' mouths and laugh when the youngsters burn themselves in fire. Thus, deliberate cruelty and the allowing of children to be injured to amuse adults exist even in the present day in some societies.

Accepted child-rearing practices of previous ages were often abusive. In such cases, children were the victims of the ignorance of their parents. For example, the custom of swaddling children was common for centuries throughout many parts of the world, including America. Children were tightly wrapped in cloth for their first year of life. Such treatment completely restricted their movements, sometimes cut off circulation to parts of their bodies, and often led to infections of the compacted flesh and to death. Washing young children in ice-cold water was a practice begun by the Romans and continued for many centuries with slight cultural variations. In some societies, children were rubbed with salt before being plunged into the frigid water; in others, youngsters were wrapped in cold damp towels before being put to bed. Though aimed at making children strong enough to withstand the physical hardships of life, such child-rearing procedures succeeded in killing many youngsters; only the hardy could survive them.

Another sanctioned practice of the past that exists even today in more moderate form involved the justification of physical abuse as punishment for the wrongdoing of children. In many cultures, children were viewed as little devils whose evil natures had to be beaten out of them. Biblical references to physical punishment are numerous and reflect social attitudes that persist to the present day. "The rod and reproof give wisdom, but a child left to himself bringeth his mother to shame (Prov. 29:15)" and "Withhold not correction from the child; for if thou beatest him with the rod, he shall not die. Thou shall beat him with the rod and shalt deliver his soul from hell (Prov. 23:13,14)," the Bible states. The *Bibliotheca Scholastica* of 1663 included perhaps the most famous pronouncement on physical punishment, "Spare the rod and spoil the child." Yet, in the past as in the present, parents have not always administered corporal punishment with an eye toward correction nor with moderation. Children have been crippled by their parents for minor or imagined wrongs; others have been mutilated by too-severe disciplinarians; still others have died as a result of beating, burning, and torturing supposed to make them better people.

For centuries, such physical excesses were accepted as parental prerogatives. Laws gave caretakers free rein in the treatment of their children. Because children were considered the property of their parents, the adults had license to do with their offspring as they wished. The Roman *Patria Postestas* empowered a father to sell or trade, abandon, torture, sacrifice, or kill his offspring with impunity. Further, because children belonged to parents, their servitude did not end when they reached adulthood, but continued whenever they were in the home of their parents. As Edward Gibbon wrote, "In the Forum, the Senate or the camp, the adult son of a Roman citizen enjoyed the public and private rights of a person; in his father's house he was a mere thing, confounded by the laws with the movables, the cattle and the slaves, whom the capricious master might alienate or destroy without being responsible to any earthly tribunal."[2]

As time passed and attitudes toward children became more compassionate, many societies passed laws against infanticide, but allowed parents to physically treat their children in any way they pleased short of causing death. Thus, the right to life became the only guarantee societies offered to their children, and even then it was severely limited. Government refused to protect a youngster from death but did agree to punish the assailant if the child died as a result of parental abuse.

Only recently have social attitudes toward physical abuse recognized that children have the right to expect to be protected from the inhumane treatment of their parents. The attention of the American public was first focused on the plight of children in the 1860s in the famous case of Mary Ellen of New York City. Though she was severely malnourished and beaten regularly by her adoptive parents, the authorities were powerless to act on her behalf. Well into the nineteenth century, children were totally at the mercy of their guardians because no legal statute empowered any governmental agency to interfere with the inner workings of the family to protect a child. It was the Society for the Prevention of Cruelty to Animals that finally succeeded in having Mary Ellen removed from her home. It argued that because she was a member of the animal kingdom, her case should come under the laws that prohibit cruelty to animals. It is a sad commentary on a society's attitudes toward children when it has laws to protect animals from maltreatment but fails to extend the same guarantee to its youngsters.

The case of Mary Ellen was an incident of obvious cruelty, wanton neglect, and inhuman abuse that shocked society into recognizing the existence of maltreated children. In response to the need to protect children from maltreating caretakers, the Society for the Prevention of Cruelty to Children was founded in New York in 1871, to be followed by other organizations with similar purposes throughout the United States.

Today, society no longer tolerates the deliberate cruelty to children that was commonplace in the past. Laws exist to identify the physically maltreated child; social services are provided to alter abusive family patterns; in extreme cases in which the life of the child is jeopardized, courts are empowered to order the child removed from parental care. Yet, physical abuse remains a serious problem in our society. A recent study of the incidence of physical abuse by Richard Gelles suggests the prevalence of physical violence done to children by their caretakers. Based on a yearlong survey, Gelles concludes that between 1.2 and 1.7 million children are kicked, bitten, or punched by their parents each year, while an additional half million are beaten up. Because his data are based on parents' self-admissions of physical violence against their children, Gelles warns that the incidence of physical abuse may be significantly greater than his figures indicate.[3]

## Child victims of sexual abuse

The phenomenon of sexual abuse has a long history. The Greek plays about Oedipus and Electra stand as proof that incest and other forms of sexual violation have existed for millenia. In ancient Greece and Rome, homosexuality was practiced with great openness. Young boys were frequently housed in brothels that catered to older men. Some more affluent patriarchs kept boy slaves for their exclusive sexual use. Often the walls of rooms were adorned with erotic paintings of nude children engaged in sexual activities.

Castration of infants or young children was practiced with some frequency because adults often found such children especially arousing. Many parents had little hesitation in mutilating their youngsters in order to collect the high fees that their young bodies commanded from the wealthy.

Not only did parents prepare and offer their children for the sexual pleasure of others, but also they indulged in sexual activities with their own children. The masturbation of young children by their parents was a common sexual practice in many cultures. Penetration and completed intercourse between parent and child were not out of the ordinary. Though such activities were frowned upon in some societies, little was done to halt incestuous relationships because it was believed that parents had absolute authority over their children.

By the eighteenth century, there was a reversal in social attitudes regarding the sexuality of children. Fanatic attempts were made to eliminate sexual impulses from and about children. Perhaps trying to deny their own sexuality or their erotic feelings for their children, adults led a battle to stamp out the natural curiosity of youngsters about their bodies. In some instances, children's genitals were cut off after they had been discovered exploring themselves. In the nineteenth century, clitoridectomies and circumcisions were performed without anesthetics to punish youngsters for their sexuality. Today, most parents recognize that the sexual curiosity of children is a natural ingredient in their development. Though many parents feel uncomfortable about the sexuality of their youngsters, few resort to the repressive torture methods common in the past.

Yet, sexual abuse is not an extinct phenomenon, but one that is still prevalent. Parents and caretakers who act out their sexual fantasies with children still exist. In Santa Clara County, California, a community with a population of one million, approximately six hundred cases of sexual abuse are confirmed each year. If we extrapolate from this number, it would appear that at least 100,000 children are sexually abused every year in the United States. If it is remembered that this figure is based solely on cases reported to and confirmed by governmental agencies, it seems reasonable to assume that the actual incidence of sexual abuse today is staggeringly high.

## Physical and emotional abandonment of youngsters

If infanticide is the ultimate form of physical abuse, abandonment can be considered the most severe kind of neglect. In societies accepting the right of children to life, abandonment, rather than infanticide, was a widespread practice. Often abandonment led to death if the child was not found and cared for soon after being deserted by his or her parents. Perhaps the two most famous abandoned children were the legendary founders of Rome, Romulus and Remus, whose lives were saved by a she-wolf who acted as their wet nurse and raised them to manhood. Another abandoned child was left in the bulrushes in the hope that his life would be spared; Moses grew up to lead his people out of bondage in Egypt.

In times of war, famine, and social dislocation, child abandonment was especially common. Parents who were unable to care for a child hoped that the youngster would be found by people who could and would provide a good home. Whether because the natural parents were too poor to supply the physical prerequisites of life or because they lacked the emotional maturity to accept and fulfill the responsibilities of parenthood, abandonment proved to be the choice of many adults for their children for centuries.

Society's obligation to care for abandoned children was established four thousand years ago in the Code of Hammurabi. Money was provided to foster mothers who took abandoned children into their homes to raise them. Frequently, however, the children were killed as soon as the foster parent received payment. It was not a humanistic love of life that prompted many women to take in abandoned children; rather, love of money often acted as their motivation. Early in the Christian era, during the reign of Justinian I, the first foundling homes were established as care institutions for abandoned children. Though the mortality was high in these facilities, the children they served surely would have died without them.

It is interesting to note that foundling homes were not established in the United States until the second half of the nineteenth century. Until that time, abandoned children were placed in almshouses for the sick and destitute. Wet nurses were hired to feed abandoned infants because there was no substitute for mother's milk available. Conditions in the almshouses were so deplorable and the mortality in them so high that few abandoned children survived. In response to these inadequate child-care facilities, the New York Foundling Asylum, the first in America, went into operation in 1869. Its success prompted first Philadelphia and then other cities to establish similar institutions to meet the physical needs of abandoned children.

The history of child-rearing practices reveals that for centuries, parents who were financially able abandoned their children to the care of others. In medieval Europe it was customary for the affluent to send newborns to nunneries, monasteries, foster families, or servants' homes for care. These children might or might not be visited by their natural parents from time to time. When the youngsters reached the age of three or four, they were allowed to return to their parents' home to be cared for by servants. Soon it was time for them to begin their education under the guidance of a private tutor at home or at a school operated by a religious order. Parents played little part in children's early nurturance; so distasteful was the task of raising small children that it was left to almost anyone who would take them for a price. Although the child's physical needs were supposed to be met by the substitute parents, children frequently died of malnutrition, infection, or accident that would have been prevented if the youngsters had been adequately cared for and supervised.

In the working class of the same time, children were literally bound into servitude through the apprenticeship system. In America and Europe, three- and four-year-olds were apprenticed to masters to learn trades. In return for their education the children were housed, clothed, and fed by masters who assumed all parental responsibilities for their upbringing. Many parents gladly abandoned their youngsters to the will and whim of masters. Such abdication of parental rights and obligations was viewed as a blessing by families on the thin edge of survival.

With the advent of the Industrial Revolution and the growing demand for labor it produced, children were abandoned to bleak, windowless factories or damp, dark mine shafts. The plight of child laborers in both Europe and America is infamous. Children as young as five were chained to their work areas to toil sixteen hours a day in the stifling heat of summer and the freezing cold of winter. When reform laws were passed in England in 1802, they limited a child's workday to only twelve hours and were heralded as the height of humane treatment. Reformers like Charles Dickens recognized that child workers had been abandoned by both their parents and their bosses; he took up their cause when children had few other advocates.

Although parents of centuries past viewed sending their children away, apprenticing them to tradesmen, and signing them on at factories as accepted practices of the day, their actions would fit modern definitions of abandonment. Even today, parents ship their children off to relatives or friends to be raised. Others leave babies and young children on hospital doorsteps and in shopping center parking lots. Some parents feel that because of their inability to fulfill parenthood's responsibilities, their children's prospects for a happy life are improved by abandonment. Others give little thought to the welfare of their children and abandon them because they are unwilling to meet their youngsters' needs.

Physical abandonment of children probably is not as common today as in the past. Yet, thousands of children are abandoned by their parents each year in the United States. If we add to this the hundreds of thousands of children whose physical and emotional needs are not being met by their parents and who thus may be considered abandoned even though they reside with their parents, the incidence increases dramatically. Research suggests that two million children each year are abandoned either by separation initiated by their parents or by physical and emotional neglect. Although parenthood has more practitioners than any other occupation, not all of them want the job; others are incompetent in the performance of their duties. In either case, their failure to live up to society's current expectations for parents indicates that child abandonment continues to stand as a serious threat to youngsters.

## Evolution of the concept of childhood

Yet another important historical element in the treatment children have received over the centuries stems from society's perceptions of childhood and children. In Western cultures through the Middle Ages the concept of childhood as a developmental stage of life did not exist. Children were viewed as adults of diminutive size. Numerous extant portraits emphasize this point; pictured are mother and daughter, father and son, with dress and demeanor identical between the two generations. Only the miniature size of the offspring distinguishes them from their parents. Thus, society possessed little tolerance for children's experimentation as a part of the process of growth.

In many cultures, children were viewed as evil little animals whose parents had the unenviable task of forcing them to repress and finally renounce their devilish, uncivilized natures. Little compassion was expended on children; in fact, adults seemed to fear the spontaneity and unpredictability of children, while they may have resented the care the youngsters required. Thus, anger and hostility characterized the attitude of parents toward their young in many cultures for centuries.

While the birth of a baby was heralded as a time for congratulation and celebration in many societies, the actual process of child rearing was often viewed as a chore, justified only because the useless child would eventually grow into a productive family member. The utilitarian philosophy that permeates social history emphasized that children were burdens to be endured only because of the eventual financial or social rewards they would bring to their parents.

In one of his most famous papers, "A Child Is Being Beaten,"[4] Sigmund Freud dealt with social and parental attitudes toward childhood. In it, Freud hypothesized that there is a universal unconscious wish to hurt children. He claimed that the impulse to destroy and the desire to nurture a child exist side by side in all adults. Recognizing the social unacceptability of this destructive tendency, Freud believed that parents bury it in the unconscious and deny its existence.

The phenomenon of myths and fairy tales that have been passed down from one generation to the next is an interesting one that yields some insight into adult feelings about childhood. Perhaps Freud's assertion that parents want to hurt children is supported by fairy tales, many of which recount the terrifying experiences of make-believe children. Rather than act out their feelings toward their children, parents may use myths to vent their sadistic impulses. The child whose bedtime story haunts his or her nightmares is not rare, for there is a threat implicit in myths: violence always waits around the corner for a child.

Viewed from another perspective, parents have employed fairy tales to control children. They threaten pain, suffering, and death to children, usually if the youngsters are bad, but often simply because they are children. Most frequently, adults are both the torturers and the rescuers in fairy tales; thus, parents emphasize the power of adults while they reinforce the helplessness of children. Parents tell their children by indirection that the youngsters had better conform to adult behavioral expectations or they may end up like the child in the myth, but without a grown-up to save them.

One of the basic fears of childhood is abandonment, and many fairy tales tell of children who are left by their parents or who wander away from adult supervision. Because children's gratification centers on the mouth and food as the fundamental element in survival, another anxiety common to childhood involves cannibalism. Fairy tales like "Hansel and Gretel" and "Little Red Riding Hood" incorporate these two phenomena. In both stories the children are bereft of parental protection; in practical terms, they are abandoned. The fate the children face is being devoured by evil creatures with proclivities for tender, sweet bodies. The youngsters are saved by kind adults who appear just in the nick of time. Both the children in the stories and those hearing the tales experience mortal fear for their lives before help arrives. Even today, parents subject their children to emotional stresses that both frighten children and convince them of their status as the victims of adults.

Yet, with the passage of centuries, much of the brutality that childhood encompassed has been eliminated. In previous eras when children were customarily mistreated, society did not censure those who abused or neglected their children. However, as our culture has evolved a more helping view toward childhood, those who violate its mores of child care stand out in stark relief. Perhaps maltreating parents today represent throwbacks to earlier ages; some parents are not entirely socialized to the role of parenthood as defined by contemporary standards. In addition, there remain prevalent social attitudes and conditions that foster child maltreatment and make its eradication difficult. It was not just our ancestors who were cruel to children in the dark pages of history, for children continue to be mistreated in large numbers. Perhaps society has not come as near to perfection as it believes. To understand the phenomenon of maltreatment, it is necessary to understand contemporary cultural attitudes responsible for its continuation to this day.

## Contemporary attitudes toward childhood and child rearing

For too long, society has perpetuated the myth of childhood as an idyllic state of constant happiness and continual contentment. Childhood has been romanticized as a carefree, golden time that ends all too soon when the burdens of the real world are foisted on the young adult. Yet, because all adults were once children, they should know the fallacy of this line of reasoning. The fears and frustrations of childhood are immense. Perpetuation of the illusion that children have no worries prohibits an objective analysis of the problems of children as they grow and develop. The society that fails to recognize the complexity of childhood and the dynamics of factors at work during it is unprepared to deal with the dilemmas that result from childhood.

America frequently considers itself a child-centered culture. It is true that childhood and the dependency it represents extend over a longer period now than at any previous time in the history of humankind. However, it can be argued that our society has made childhood a time of frustration by deliberately isolating children from contact with any but a few basic institutions, namely, the school, church, and family. Further, the myth of society's focus on childhood becomes clear when we recognize who the heroes of our culture really are. As Howard James puts it, "If we lived in a culture that really cared about children, then our schools would change, teachers and child-care workers would be more important than professional football players or golfers; we would replace the Miss America pageant and the Academy Award ceremonies with accolades for those who cared most about youngsters; social workers would work nights; and parents would stop treating their offspring like objects or pets."[5]

Just as society unrealistically idealizes childhood and falsely claims to center its attention on children, so it perpetuates the myth that parenthood is a fulfilling job all adults should accept willingly. To be sure, there are rewards that come to parents; however, the responsibilities of their tasks are at least as awesome. Further, parenting is not an innate ability possessed by all adults of the human species. Rather, it involves a set of learned behaviors dictated by society and not easily acquired. Although schools provide vocational training for most careers, until recently there were few educational mechanisms to teach adults the craft of parenthood. Not a state to be entered into lightly, parenthood is a long-term commitment to another human being that cannot be repudiated because the adult changes his or her mind. Unrealistic social attitudes toward parenthood minimize both its difficulties and its responsibilities; thus, they fail to prepare future parents for the demands they will face.

Social misperceptions of parenthood frequently hold that parents have autonomy in raising their children. One often hears expressed the feeling that parents can bring up their child any way they wish. The counterpart of this argument states that no one has the right to interfere with or criticize a parent's handling of his or her youngster. Law, custom, and common sense refute these beliefs, however. Parents cannot maltreat their children when such actions violate federal, state, or local statutes. Social mores mandate that an outsider can and should come between a parent and child when the parent is behaving in ways clearly contrary to the best interests of the youngster. The mere fact that a woman gives birth to a child does not magically ensure that she knows how to care for her offspring. Nor is it reasonable to assert that because all adults were once children, they know how to be good parents. Such a claim is as illogical as the assumption that because we were once students, we are all capable of being skillful teachers.

Closely related to the attitudes of Americans toward parenthood is the widespread support our culture lends certain child-rearing practices. The physical punishment of children by parents at home and teachers in school is sanctioned both by historical precedent and current social mores. Corporal discipline is viewed by many as a deterrent to the repetition of undesirable behavior. It is employed to make the youngster afraid to duplicate the actions that led to the punishment. Others in America perceive it as a useful teaching tool that conveys an object lesson, for it reinforces the position of children as subordinate to the authority of adults. One study of the prevalence of physical punishment in America reveals that between 84 and 97 percent of all parents employ corporal discipline at some time in their children's lives.[6] Further, the utilization of corporal punishment by schools strengthens its acceptance as a recognized part of child training. It is revealing that only three states, Maryland, Massachusetts, and New Jersey, have statutes or orders prohibiting its use in schools and other public institutions for children.

In addition, it can be argued that the use of corporal punishment encourages a tolerance for violence within American society. When parents and teachers show their disapproval through physical punishment, they indirectly teach the lesson that displeasure can be acceptably displayed through force. Children's emulation of parental behavior leads to the use of violence to solve differences of opinion, prove superiority, or assert control.

Although an occasional slap on the bottom in itself probably does not have negative effects on a child, some parents do not employ corporal punishment either infrequently or with moderation. They rely on society's acceptance of physical punishment to justify harsh discipline of their children. Many physically maltreating parents employ corporal punishment as a routine release for their frustrations rather than as an occasional technique to foster correction. Because social codes endorse the legitimacy of physical punishment of children, it is both frequently used and too often abused by those who fail to understand and observe the difference between discipline and maltreatment.

## The changing nature of the family in America

There has been much discussion over the past few decades concerning the evolution of the American family unit. Certainly, family relationships are presently in a state of flux, for while the family is asked to provide most of the economic, social, and emotional needs of its members, it is often unequal to the task. While many people adapt successfully to the changes occurring in American families, others find it difficult to adjust both to the general cultural climate and the specific demands on them within this fundamental social unit. The pressures of family life today manifest themselves in many forms, not the least of which is child maltreatment.

Alvin Toffler's *Future Shock* stated what most Americans have known intuitively for years: our world is changing so rapidly that it is often difficult for us to keep up with it. Too much change too quickly can lead to life crises in which people find it difficult or impossible to cope with the demands of their environments. Whether consciously or unconsciously, human beings employ adaptation, decision-making, and problem-solving techniques to deal with change. Yet, when the modifications life requires are so monumental or so numerous, the overwhelmed cannot regain equilibrium before the onslaught of more change. Such pressure situations often lead people into behavior they would not employ under less stressful conditions.

Not all people react negatively to large amounts of change. Just as there are people who can consume great quantities of food and not gain weight, so there are individuals who can adapt to significant modifications without noticeable disruption to their lives. However, because of the rate at which society is changing, those whose change metabolisms are slow are likely to experience serious problems when their mechanisms for dealing with fast-paced change prove ineffective.

The geographic mobility of Americans is legendary, with one of every five families changing residence each year. Though some move only down the street, many settle in areas far distant from their previous residences. Although the welcome wagon or friendly neighbors may greet the new arrivals, they are inadequate to meet the emotional needs of many families. Young couples often experience tremendous internal upheaval when they leave family, friends, and familiar surroundings to establish their households in new communities. Crisis situations that result from feelings of dislocation can lead to serious problems among family members. Because the offspring are at hand, they frequently take the brunt of parental frustrations caused by the geographic mobility of a family.

Geographic mobility is partially responsible for alterations in the patterns of social organization in America. The prevalence of the nuclear family can be seen as contributing to the continuation of child maltreatment. In the past, when two, three, or four generations lived in the same household or neighborhood, the extended family afforded support to young people as they undertook the adult roles of spouse and parent. Advice and comfort were available from trusted relatives whose life experiences provided possible solutions to problems being faced for the first time by younger family members. However, today's parents often live thousands of miles from other family members. When difficulties arise in marital relations or parental responsibilities, the adults in the nuclear family must attempt to resolve them without the assistance of relatives. This trial-and-error approach to family living can be destructive both to the individuals and the family unit involved.

Emotional isolation is related to geographic mobility as another commonplace of contemporary society. In many families, even if relatives are near young parents, there are barriers that prevent successful communication. The much-talked-about generation gap acts as a block between parents and their offspring who are just beginning their careers as parents. Further, society views independence as a valued quality that all adults must acquire. Because of the individualistic focus of our culture, young parents often consider it a sign of weakness if they ask for help from their own parents or admit uncertainty in rearing their children. Such attitudes discourage the continuation of close familial relationships into adulthood, while they demean the value of experience acquired through years of living and coping with the problems of daily life. Thus, parents who feel insecure in their roles as spouses and caretakers are encouraged by society to stand on their own two feet, make decisions independently, and live with their consequences, whether for good or ill.

A complement to the concept of separation from family is the dehumanization that has come to characterize social relationships in our increasingly urban, postindustrial society. It is becoming the rule rather than the exception for people not to know even their neighbors' names. They establish few supportive relationships that give them self-confidence in times of tranquility and comfort when life weighs heavily. Thus, adults have only their mates or children to turn to for companionship and confirmation of their worth. When family members cannot fulfill each other's needs, frustration, anger, and resentment often result.

In the past, intergenerational living patterns, established peer relationships, and even large family size gave parents opportunities for respite from their parenting roles. When mother or grandmother resided in the same household or when trusted friends lived nearby, mothers could put their children in the care of other women to escape temporarily the responsibilities of parenthood. When families had many children, an older brother or sister could supervise younger siblings while the parents pursued activities independent of their offspring. Now, as family size decreases, child care must be paid for. When a family has limited financial resources, rare, indeed, may be the occasions when a mother can hire a baby-sitter to tend her offspring while she rejuvenates herself with an excursion outside the home. Even the most devoted mother needs time for herself; even the most patient parents require time away from the children to refill their reservoirs of personal needs. Without experiences that recognize and meet the personal requirements of adults, parenthood can become a constant chore from which there is no relief.

Added to the geographic mobility and intergenerational isolation of modern American family life is the growing number of single-parent family units. In these families, one parent attempts to fulfill the roles of two. Statistics indicate that nearly 20 percent of all children in the United States live in households in which only one parent is present, and this percentage has steadily increased over the past few decades.[7] The three major contributors to the rising number of one-parent homes are the climbing divorce rate, illegimate births, and desertions.

Today, approximately 40 percent of all marriages end in divorce. One million divorces are issued each year, and many of these dissolved marriages involve children who become the responsibility of one parent. Parenting is a difficult task when it is shared by both husband and wife; when one must shoulder all its responsibilities while trying to deal with the emotional upheaval of a failed marriage, the burden can be unbearable.

The rate of illegitimate births in the United States has more than doubled in the past twenty-five years. Yearly, 350,000 babies are born to unwed mothers who must assume sole responsibility for their rearing. Many of these women are young; statistics reveal that one in ten girls becomes pregnant while still enrolled in school. For a parent who is hardly more than a child herself, child rearing can cause tremendous stress. Often it forces a young mother to assume adult responsibility before she has matured enough to cope with it.

In the past, husbands were generally guilty of deserting their families. Recently, however, there has been a significant increase in the number of female desertions. Runaway husbands and wives abandon both their marital and parental roles without making provisions for their families. If they think seriously about the welfare of their families at all, they assume that their partners will shoulder all family obligations. To the deserted spouse who feels betrayed by the removal of his or her partner from the home, single parenting can be a great strain.

In short, adults who must work, keep house, and care for children singlehandedly may feel unequal to the task. These parents may resent the youngsters because they are tangible signs of the failure and impermanence of the marriage or relationship that produced them. The nurturance they require, the limitations their presence places on social life, and the constant sense of responsibility they represent may lead single parents to feel completely overwhelmed. Because there is no mate present and few relatives or friends to turn to, the single parent may develop both hostility toward and disappointment with life.

Another trend related to the changing family structure over the past few decades has been the tremendous increase in the number of wives and mothers who work outside the home. The economic impact of working women has greatly increased the standard of living of many families. Further, it has produced a whole new industry: the child-care facility for infants and preschoolers.

A career can give a woman a new sense of worth and dignity. It can provide immeasurable satisfaction both monetarily and personally, while allowing a woman to appreciate the time she has with her family. Yet, working outside the home represents a hardship for some women. If they resent having to take employment, if they are too tired after work to deal with the demands of family life, if they feel overwhelmed as both breadwinners and child raisers, they may look for outlets to vent their frustrations.

A related tendency in family life in contemporary society concerns the amount of time and attention parents devote to their children. As the demands of jobs weigh heavily on both husband and wife, they spend less time playing, talking, and working with their youngsters. As adult lives become filled with social engagements, commuting, and work-related tasks, families participate in fewer activities together. Children are plunked down before television sets, the electronic, live-in baby-sitters of contemporary society.

It may be that because there is less contact between parents and children within families today, there may also be less physical abuse. Often, there is a correlation between the amount of time spent with a child and the incidence of physical maltreatment. However, in other families, an abusing parent need only see his or her offspring for a few moments before the onset of physical abuse.

Although the link between physical abuse and family interaction is open to speculation, there seems little doubt that minimized interaction between parents and their youngsters results in widespread neglect. Because parents entrust their youngsters almost from birth to the in-home amusement of television, many feel relieved of the responsibility to provide intellectual stimulation for their children. "Sesame Street" and "The Electric Company" are given total sway in the early education of many children. Further, if you have ever watched two young children sitting before a television set, it is clear that the amount of social interaction between them is negligible. If children are discouraged from playing with each other and adults take no interest in developing the skills of cooperation, patience, and fairness in their children through games, then the social growth of a child is being neglected.

Diminished contact between parent and child is likely to be responsible for the insecurity of a growing number of children in contemporary society. Because families participate in few activities together, rare are the opportunities for a child to be praised for completing a task well. For example, when families habitually ate meals together, the child could set the table and receive praise and affection for a job well done. Now, with fewer homes having dining rooms, and television trays replacing a central dining table, the opportunities for youngsters to work cooperatively with their parents, receive their appreciation, and view themselves as human beings worthy of parental love are greatly decreased. Thus, neglect of the basic needs of children can be viewed as a growing tendency within American society.

## Conclusion

In the final analysis, there is no scientific way to determine if child maltreatment is occurring with greater frequency today than in the past. Several related issues are clear, however. First, children have been the victims of mistreatment by their caretakers in all periods of the history of humankind. Because social customs and legal statutes have defined acceptable and unacceptable standards of care for children, the concept of what constitutes child maltreatment has evolved through the ages. Evidence clearly indicates that present social codes and legal enactments are more inclusive in their definitions of child maltreatment than at any previous time in history. Many kinds of child treatment that were considered customary in earlier eras are prohibited or strongly discouraged in contemporary America. Yet, child maltreatment exists today partially because of societal attitudes and conditions that foster it and despite laws and mores designed to eliminate it. It is the continuity of maltreatment that is significant rather than its absolute increase or decrease over time.

The problem of child maltreatment is only now beginning to gain the attention it must receive if real strides are to be made in the field. Involvement of the entire society is necessary to prevent, diagnose, and treat both the causes and effects of child maltreatment. It seems appropriate at this point to investigate the complex of personal and familial factors that are responsible for abuse and neglect by focusing on parents who maltreat their children.

### References

1. Ray E. Helfer, *The Diagnostic Process and Treatment Programs*, DHEW pub. no. 75-69 (Washington, D.C.: U.S. Government Printing Office, 1975), p. 22.
2. Edward Gibbon, *The Decline and Fall of the Roman Empire* (New York: Peter Fenelon Collier, 1899), pp. 352-353.
3. Richard J. Gelles, "Violence Towards Children in the United States" (Paper presented at American Association for the Advancement of Science, Symposium on Violence at Home and at School, Denver, February 25, 1977), pp. 16-18.
4. Sigmund Freud, "A Child Is Being Beaten: A Contribution to the Study of the Origin of Sexual Perversions," stand. ed. (London: The Hogarth Press Ltd., 1955), XVII, pp. 175-204.
5. Howard James, *The Little Victims: How America Treats Its Children* (New York: David McKay Co., Inc., 1975), p. 195.
6. Suzanne K. Steinmetz and Murray A. Straus, "The Family as Cradle of Violence," *Society* 10, no. 6 (1973): 50-56.
7. *Marital Status and Living Arrangements: March, 1976.* Current Population Reports, series P-20, number 306, U.S. Department of Commerce, Bureau of the Census (Washington, D.C.: U.S. Government Printing Office, 1977), pp. 6-7.

# CHAPTER 4

# Why do parents maltreat their children?

If child maltreatment were attributable to one characteristic common to all maltreating parents, it would be a relatively simple matter to eliminate. However, it is far more complicated than that. One parent maltreats his or her child, while another in virtually the same circumstances does not. The explanation for this situation lies in the multidimensional nature of child maltreatment. Abuse and neglect are not the results of single causes, but the outcomes of complexes of conditions; just as there are many forms of maltreatment, so there are many factors that can precipitate it.

Even though there are no simple causative relationships in the field of child maltreatment, a number of attitudes and conditions are more prevalent among maltreating parents than in the general population. These factors can act as clues to school and community personnel concerned about the maltreatment of children and committed to its elimination. It should be remembered, however, that a parent who exhibits one or even a number of these traits cannot definitely be labeled a maltreating parent; all that can be said with certainty is that he or she displays characteristics suggestive of parents who abuse and neglect their offspring. Further investigation, including study of the child, is necessary to determine if, in fact, the adult is a maltreating parent.

Because this chapter attempts to build a composite profile of maltreating parents, it seems necessary at the outset to explode the myths that have grown up to describe abusive and neglectful adults. Next, a review will be undertaken of traits and circumstances that prevail in families prone to maltreatment. They can be grouped under the following categories: (1) predisposing psychodynamic and character traits, (2) inadequate social learning, (3) dysfunctional family structure, and (4) environmental stress factors. Finally, we will examine some attitudes and behavior patterns that seem related to the particular form of maltreatment a parent employs. For example, physically abusive parents are often very different from emotionally neglecting adults. It is important that the teacher or community member recognize both the general signs of maltreatment and the specific clues suggestive of the type of maltreatment to which a family is prone.

**MYTH:** MOST PARENTS ARE INCAPABLE OF MALTREATING THEIR CHILDREN

The truth is that the potential for child maltreatment exists in nearly every adult. The only universal prerequisite for a parent to become maltreating is that there must be a child close at hand. All parents occasionally harbor negative feelings about their children. Rare, indeed, is the parent who can honestly say he or she has never been tempted to take out frustrations on a child. One often hears parents make statements like, "I was so angry I wanted to wring my kid's neck," or "I just want to get away from it all, leave the kids at home, and get out of the house." While other adults control such impulses, the maltreating parent acts out these emotions.

If responding honestly, most parents would admit that, given certain circumstances, they could maltreat their children. For example, when a job is lost, a marriage breaks down, friends are not near to give support, and a child seems demanding of attention, is it hard to recognize why a parent maltreats his or her youngster? Children are accessible; they ask more than the parent can supply; they will not fight back; they will not make a report to the police. Thus, the youngster is a convenient and safe target for parental anger. Although few would condone it, child maltreatment viewed in this light is an understandable occurrence. Although few want to acknowledge it, most adults possess the potential for child maltreatment.

**MYTH:** MALTREATING PARENTS ARE DERANGED DEVIANTS

Perhaps society takes comfort in the belief that only a mentally ill person could mistreat a child. Research suggests, however, that although severely disturbed people sometimes do maltreat their children, they represent only 5 to 10 percent of all abusive and neglectful parents.[1] Because mentally ill parents sometimes indulge in serious forms of abuse and neglect, including extended physical torture and deliberate starvation of their youngsters, their sensational cases often receive extensive media coverage. Yet, to characterize all maltreating parents as severely emotionally disturbed denies the fact that the overwhelming majority of parents who maltreat their children can be characterized as fitting broadly within the psychologically "normal" range on most emotional scales.

Many people find it difficult to face the fact that not all maltreating parents are raving maniacs whose sickness manifests itself in brutalization of their youngsters. Abusing parents can be churchgoers and community leaders; neglecting caretakers can hold good jobs and be friendly neighbors. They wear no signs that easily distinguish them from other adults. In short, maltreating adults are not as different from nonabusive parents as most people would like to think.

## MYTH: MALTREATING PARENTS DO NOT LOVE THEIR CHILDREN

Although they may not be able to display their love, most maltreating parents do care about the welfare of their children. Maltreating adults want to be good parents, but either they do not know how to perform their roles satisfactorily or personal, familial, or environmental factors interfere with good parenting.

It can be argued that it is precisely because their offspring are important to them that maltreating parents hurt their children emotionally and physically. To many adults, children are symbols rather than human beings. A young mother may see her child as a tangible sign of her worth; the youngster may represent the only person the mother has to whom she can give love; the child may be the sole supplier of the mother's emotional needs for love. In some families, children are expected to bind shaky marriages together; in other households, they are important signs that the family is a normal, functioning unit, conforming to social expectations. Thus, in many maltreating families the children are very much wanted, although for the wrong reasons.

Parents often feel guilty and ashamed about maltreating their children. They are afraid to ask for help and fearful of admitting their mistreatment when confronted. Yet, once their problems are faced squarely, a large proportion can be helped to improve family relations and show the love they feel for their youngsters.

## MYTH: ALL MALTREATING PARENTS ARE WELFARE MOTHERS AND UNEMPLOYED FATHERS

There has been much confusion about the issue of economic status as a factor in maltreating families. It should be understood that abusive and neglectful parents are of every socioeconomic level and are not limited to the ranks of the poor. The fact that a man earns $20,000 a year is not a guarantee that he does not sexually abuse his daughter; simply because a woman with small children cannot work and must live on governmental payments is not a sure sign that she neglects her youngsters. In short, maltreatment is not restricted to any economic bracket.

However, it must be noted that studies suggest that a disproportionate number of confirmed cases of serious child maltreatment involve low-income families.[2] In part, this finding results because the poor are more likely to come under the scrutiny of public agencies than the affluent. It cannot be denied that in our materialistic society, poverty places additional stress on parents. Oriented as America is to monetary success and a work ethic that views the unemployed as lazy and shiftless, the psychological pressures on the poor are tremendous. A man who cannot find a job may take his frustration out on his children; a woman who drinks heavily may not budget enough money to buy food for her youngsters. Poverty is but one factor that increases pressure on a family, thus raising the risk of maltreatment.

Further, it must be remembered that the apparent relationship between poverty and increased maltreatment is based upon evidence obtained from reported cases of child abuse and neglect. It may be that the affluent can hide maltreatment more successfully than their poorer counterparts. Private physicians traditionally have been more reluctant to report their suspicions of maltreatment than doctors in the public health clinics or hospital emergency rooms to which the poor are likely to bring their children for treatment. Further, social service workers who investigate maltreatment cases generally come from middle-class backgrounds, a fact that predisposes them to identify more closely with parents of that economic status. Therefore, they may be more likely to view as unfounded reports of maltreatment in middle- and upper-economic-level families, while they may confirm a higher proportion of reports involving parents of lower socioeconomic status.

Perhaps the most compelling evidence in regard to the relationship between poverty and maltreatment is that the vast majority of families of low socioeconomic status do not abuse or neglect their children, while some middle- and upper-income parents are maltreating. Thus, child maltreatment can be viewed as a generalized social problem rather than a condition linked causally to one economic subgroup.

**MYTH:** SOME RACIAL AND ETHNIC GROUPS ARE MORE LIKELY TO MALTREAT THEIR CHILDREN THAN OTHERS

Just as there is no direct causal relationship between economic level and maltreatment, so there is none in regard to ethnicity. Maltreating par-

ents are black, white, yellow, and red; Protestant, Catholic, Jew, and athe-
ist. No cultural group in American society has a monopoly on child maltreatment.

Yet, as poverty produces stress with which a family must deal, so minority status in American society places psychological and physical pressure
on parents. The man of whatever race who feels locked out of a job because
of racial considerations may maltreat his children; the woman whose income level places her in a marginally livable public housing ghetto may
abuse or neglect her youngsters. Ethnicity may compound the factors that
dispose a parent to maltreatment, but it is not causally related to it.

Some people claim that certain groups in America have established cultural patterns that border on maltreatment. While it is true that child-rearing practices differ among ethnic groups, all conform to socially acceptable
standards of child care. Thus, it is false to maintain that maltreatment is a
product of race or ethnicity within American society.

> **MYTH:** ALL MALTREATING PARENTS MARRIED YOUNG AND HAD
> CHILDREN SOON AFTERWARD

Maltreating parents are of all ages. Some are young and marry because
of pregnancy. Others marry later in life and wait several years before having children. The characteristic they share is not chronologic age, but the
inability to deal positively with their children. Emotional immaturity and
life circumstances predispose parents to mistreat their offspring, rather
than any constancy in physical age.

> **MYTH:** MOTHERS ARE MORE LIKELY TO MALTREAT CHILDREN
> THAN FATHERS
> **ALTERNATE:** FATHERS ARE MORE LIKELY TO MALTREAT CHILDREN
> THAN MOTHERS

Research suggests that the incidence of maltreating parents of each sex
is almost even. Approximately half of all abusive and neglecting parents
are men, while the other half are women. Common sense would indicate
that because our society both teaches and condones violence in men, they
would be more likely to physically abuse children, while women would
more frequently be neglectful; however, no clear-cut evidence substanti-
ates this intuitive belief. It also stands to reason that the parent who spends
more time with a child is more likely to maltreat him or her; research suggests that this may well be the case.[3] A more recent study indicates that

parents tend to maltreat children of their own sex; mothers abuse and neglect their daughters more often than they maltreat their sons.[4] Though the evidence is somewhat inconclusive, it suggests that child maltreatment is not causally linked to the sex of a parent, for both men and women mistreat their offspring.

**MYTH:** MALTREATING PARENTS ARE COMPULSIVE LIARS INCAPABLE OF TELLING THE TRUTH

Because our culture expresses shock and anger when maltreatment is uncovered, parents are reluctant to admit that they abuse or neglect their youngsters. Because the adults often feel guilty about their treatment of their children, they attempt to hide it both from society and themselves. Because severely maltreating parents are subject to criminal prosecution, they often deny their culpability. Yet, they can be helped to confront their problems and inadequacies. Often, when they recognize that the efforts of others are meant to be constructive rather than accusatory or punitive, they discard the lies they have used to insulate themselves and respond positively to assistance.

Although some maltreating parents make up stories, assume outraged stances, take defensive positions, and distort the truth to protect themselves, deception is not an inherent part of their characters. Rather, it is a protective device they feel compelled to employ. When it is shed, the road from maltreatment to improved family relations often stretches before the maltreating family.

**MYTH:** MALTREATING PARENTS DESERVE TO BE PUNISHED, FOR THEY CANNOT BE HELPED

Some severely abusive and neglectful adults should be incarcerated for their brutality; there is little hope they will ever be adequate parents. Yet, the fact remains that most maltreating parents can be aided to become acceptable parents through the efforts of those who care about both children and adults. If the ultimate goal of those concerned with child maltreatment is to assist the family in becoming a functional unit, then a therapeutic, rather than a punitive, attitude must be adopted. Perhaps our society relies too heavily on punishment, while it ignores remediation and rehabilitation. Punishment is a shortsighted approach to maltreating families that is often the result of indignation rather than genuine concern.

Social attitudes toward maltreating parents are changing slowly to recognize that the vast majority of abusive and neglectful parents are not monsters, but people with problems. Most maltreating adults should not be punished, but supported and encouraged. A punitive approach to parents who maltreat their children may cause the temporary cessation of neglect or abuse, but it does not resolve the underlying factors responsible for maltreatment.

> **MYTH:** THE BEST WAY TO HELP A MALTREATED CHILD IS TO REMOVE HIM OR HER FROM THE HOME

In serious cases of child maltreatment in which the physical welfare of the child is severely jeopardized, taking the child from the family and placing him or her in a care facility is a course of action necessary to ensure the youngster's safety. In less dangerous situations, however, separating a youngster from parents and siblings can be a needlessly traumatic experience for the entire family.

Perhaps if adequate provisions for institutional child care existed, removal from the home would be a more acceptable alternative for maltreated children than it is at present. However, abused and neglected children are frequently housed in overcrowded, sterile environments with youngsters who have been declared delinquent. In foster homes, children are discouraged from establishing close relationships with their surrogate parents because the placements are supposed to be short term. Often, however, they are not, for nearly three quarters of all maltreated children removed from their homes never return to them.[5]

When a child is taken from home, too often his or her case is nearly forgotten. Because the youngster is no longer in jeopardy, social service workers turn their attention to more immediate family crises and may devote only minimal effort to helping the parent bring about changes required before he or she can be reunited with the youngster. Thus, the child and parent who love each other despite maltreatment remain unable to fulfill each other's needs because of the separation.

In the vast majority of cases, both child and adult benefit if the youngster's welfare can be closely monitored while the family remains intact. The best remedy for child maltreatment is to eliminate it by helping the family develop new patterns of interaction. The interests of all its members are served best when the family is strengthened as a unit of mutual support and caring.

## Psychodynamic traits of maltreating parents

An individual is largely the product of childhood experiences. Within the family exist all the basic relationships and responsibilities that later life holds in slightly different forms. Whether a person is successful in adult roles is dependent largely upon how well family life has prepared him or her for them. Thus, a number of characteristics of maltreating parents are developed in their childhoods by unsatisfactory family relationships. Evidence indicates conclusively that a predisposition to child maltreatment is an intergenerational phenomenon taught by one generation to the next.

The basic bond between parent and child is normally established soon after birth. While it is no longer believed that mothering is an instinctual drive, it does appear that the physical closeness of mother and offspring as well as acceptance of the dependent needs of the infant by the mother are important ingredients in establishing what may be called the parenting bond. If a mother fails to assume responsibility for her child and shuns a close relationship with her offspring, the child suffers. When the youngster grows to adulthood and becomes a parent, the failure of bonding between mother and infant that the child experienced may repeat itself; thus, the lack of intimacy between parent and child affects yet another generation. Sometimes this phenomenon is called a "faulty mothering imprint"; others call it "abnormal rearing"; still other writers refer to it as a "poor parenting model." Regardless of terminology, it describes one of the basic characteristics of maltreating parents: the inability to view the child as a needy person dependent on the adult.

In addition to and partially because of the unsatisfactory bonding between parent and child, many maltreating parents experienced abuse or neglect at the hands of their parents when they were young. It seems natural to ask why a formerly maltreated parent would mistreat his or her child. Would not a person who was abused, harshly punished, or neglected as a child do all possible to save his or her offspring from the same kind of pain? Many parents do just that; determined not to repeat the pattern they endured, they avoid the very techniques their parents employed with them. However, other formerly maltreated children internalize characteristics of their parenting models so completely that their behavior toward their children is almost a carbon copy of the mistreatment they experienced as youngsters.

If evidence is necessary to substantiate how much parents are influenced by the treatment they received when they were children, consider the findings of Richard Gelles, who conducted a study of forms of violence within families: "Whether an individual uses his hand, a belt, a curtain rod, or a yardstick [in punishing his child] is greatly determined by how he was hit as a child and what techniques were deployed by his parents on each other and on the children. When respondents stated how they hit their children and then later in the conversation, discussed how they were treated by their parents, the instruments were sometimes identical."[6] Further, the offenses for which parents punish children are generally those for which they were chastised as youngsters. Therefore, it appears that both the crime and punishment are determined by intergenerational influences.

Thus, the psychodynamics of abusive and neglecting parents reflect their inability to relate positively to their children because of the manner in which they were raised as youngsters. Frequently, maltreating parents have negative self-concepts, and it is common for them to project their dislike of themselves onto their youngsters. "Seeing the baby who is attacked as another edition of one's own bad self is characteristic of the abusing parent."[7] This unconscious defense, known as projection, gives the adult justification to maltreat the child. For example, a father can rationalize that he is attempting to correct defects in his youngster when he beats the child for spilling a glass of milk. In reality, he may be expressing the self-loathing he developed as a child when he was told repeatedly that he was clumsy.

Another manipulative psychological tool maltreating parents frequently employ is called role reversal. Parents who did not establish a close bond with their parents or were maltreated as youngsters or whose parents projected their feelings about themselves onto them failed to receive the nurturance they needed. Throughout life, these people look to others to supply their desires, usually with limited success. When they become parents, they misperceive the parental role and demand that their children fulfill their needs. The youngster is expected, in effect, to parent the parent. Oblivious of the needs of their children, maltreating parents are consumed with yearning for someone to take care of them. Of course, the child is doomed to fail as emotional supplier; parents often react with renewed abuse or neglect prompted by feelings of being betrayed by their offspring.

Closely tied to role reversal is the inability of maltreating parents either to recognize that children have special needs or to fulfill them. Even if adults do not demand that youngsters parent them, they are often unable to understand what they should do for their youngsters, for maltreating parents frequently do not view their offspring as children. Some see the youngster as an independent human being who is expected to be self-sufficient. Others perceive their offspring as objects of little importance who are nonthreatening as long as they demand nothing from the adult. In short, maltreating parents often have little realization of the unique needs of youngsters and of their responsibilities as parents to meet those needs.

## Character traits of maltreating parents

Maltreating parents often find their lives filled with frustration because they have difficulty finding satisfaction. Seldom are they content; rarely are they happy; infrequently do they feel pleased with themselves. Because their parents often were demanding and unpredictable, the offspring never developed trusting relationships with them; therefore, they find it hard to establish sincere friendships throughout life. This sense of social and emotional isolation is often overwhelming, and though the parent may realize help is necessary, he or she is fearful of opening up to possible rejection by requesting it.

One of the personality traits most closely connected with maltreating parents is immaturity, a sweeping term that is frequently ill defined. Emotionally immature people find it difficult to deal positively with reality; they may fantasize about the way they wish life to be and grow depressed when they are unable to attain their goals. At work, for instance, immature people may believe themselves worthy of promotion and complain bitterly when they are passed over, never recognizing that they lack the qualifications for the more responsible job. Immature adults are frequently tense and anxious because they never seem to achieve what they want; they may become hostile and sullen as their dissatisfaction with life grows. They do not recognize, however, that failures are products of personality and that responsibility must be assumed for them. Although everyone experiences anger and disappointment, most people find constructive outlets for these emotions. The immature parent, however, may take out hostility on his or her mate and children. While the healthy adult might swing a golf club to vent aggression, the immature parent may swing a fist at his or her child.

Immature adults are frequently self-centered and unable to recognize anyone else's needs. Therefore, they are happy only when people are concerned about their desires. They gain little satisfaction from giving of themselves to others; therefore, they find it difficult to establish mutually satisfying relationships. This vicious cycle of egocentrism and isolation is self-perpetuating, for one factor compounds the other until the immature adult is shut off from people and becomes completely self-absorbed.

Because of their unrealistic views, ever increasing sense of hostility, and complete emotional separation from others, immature parents are powder kegs waiting to explode. They often appear impatient and impulse ridden. Their behavior is frequently erratic and overreactive. In short, there is an unpredictability and instability about immature adults that marks them as potential or actual perpetrators of child maltreatment.

## Inadequate social learning

Some parents fail to gain enough knowledge about children to avoid maltreatment. These adults do not understand what society deems as normal child-rearing patterns. Because they are unaware of techniques that facilitate the growth of children, they hamper their youngsters' development out of ignorance rather than as the result of personal psychodynamic factors. In a very real sense, these maltreating parents are too ill informed on the subject of children to be good parents.

Some parents who know little about children are of low intelligence. The adult who is marginally mentally retarded has difficulty handling many of the routine tasks of life. He or she may need help reading a job application or have difficulty tallying a time card. In fulfilling parenting roles, one low-intelligence parent may not understand the importance of good nutrition in the physical development of his or her youngster while another may fail to realize that children need intellectual stimulation to help them learn and grow. Although low-intelligence parents are often loving and nurturing and do the best job they can in raising their youngsters, in some cases it is not good enough.

It is not only marginally retarded parents who maltreat their youngsters because of ignorance; many parents of normal intelligence fail to learn the skills necessary to function in society, and these shortcomings spill over into the home. A father who has never internalized the habit of hard work may lose one job after another because his employers will not tolerate his lack of diligence. The frustration and insecurity he feels when out of work may manifest themselves in his home life both in marital disputes and child maltreatment. Or take the case of a mother whose sense of time and punctuality do not conform to society's standards. Perhaps the baby-sitter must leave at 3:00 PM, but the mother does not return home until after 6:00 PM. Thus, for three hours the children are neglected by being unsupervised. When failure to meet parental responsibilities becomes a pattern, child maltreatment exists.

Often, maltreatment results directly from a lack of adequate parenting skills. There is no sense that tells parents intuitively how to care for a child's physical, emotional, and psychological needs. For the adult who has not taken a parenting course or been around young children, parenthood can be a myriad of uncertainties and mistakes, with the child as victim. How warm should bathwater be for an infant? How frequently should diapers be changed? At what age should a youngster be taken to the dentist? How much sleep does a child require? What distinguishes a spanking from a potentially dangerous beating? The adult who has little familiarity with the routine tasks of child rearing is predisposed to child maltreatment because of lack of knowledge; when he or she becomes a parent, previous inadequate learning in this field may well result in child maltreatment.

The task of parenthood is a difficult one, for the adult must not only understand the daily care a child requires, but also the developmental stages through which the youngster progresses. The parent who does not realize that it is normal for young children to assert their independence by saying no to practically everything may interpret the child's behavior as willful disobedience and apply punishment accordingly. Further, many parents hold unrealistic expectations for children by demanding that they behave in more mature ways than their ages allow them. The mother or father who expects to toilet train a child at ten months of age, and such cases are not rare, soon learns that the youngster does not regulate this function adequately. The uninformed parent may believe the child stubborn and uncooperative; he or she may beat the child in an attempt to make the youngster behave in the desired manner. Yet, it is the parent who is at fault in such a case and not the child, for the adult acts as though the child were older than he or she actually is. Because the parent is unaware of child developmental processes, he or she may expect the child to act as a much older child would and may become maltreating when the youngster does not live up to unrealistic parental standards.

Because of their lack of knowledge about children, maltreating parents frequently view their youngsters as peculiar and different from other children. This phenomenon is often tied to parents' demands that their offspring accomplish tasks for which they are not developmentally prepared. For instance, parents may consider their two-year-old clumsy and uncoordinated because the child cannot catch and throw a ball with proficiency. In other cases the child's normal progress is viewed as deviant. For example, a child may be progressing normally in school, but is perceived as stupid by his or her parents for not learning as quickly as they would like. In either circumstance, parents often justify their attitudes and actions toward youngsters with the rationale that because they are unusual, they cannot be treated like other children. Because their parents see them as different, these youngsters are often in line for harsh physical punishment, neglect, or emotional abuse.

This discussion of inadequate preparation for parenthood points up the fact that even though lack of social learning stands as a chief cause of child maltreatment, it may well yield to remediation more easily than any of the others. It is far simpler to teach adults techniques of good parenting than it is to compensate for the maltreatment they received as children. It is easier to present parents with positive alternatives to child maltreatment than it is to restructure families to remove destructive elements responsible for abuse and neglect.

## Dysfunctional family structure

The relationships that exist within a family can be positive or negative, constructive or destructive. In all families, members look to each other for fulfillment of their emotional needs; when they fail to provide the nurturance required, child maltreatment may occur. For example, the husband and wife who have stopped communicating with each other may take their marital frustrations out on the child. The father who makes up excuses to stay out of the house may overreact to the crying of his youngster when he is home. The wife whose husband demands that she stay at home to care for the children may neglect their well being to spite her spouse.

Frequently, abusive and neglecting homes are highly charged emotional environments. The smallest disagreement may develop into a screaming and shoving match in which the children become pawns in their parents' struggles or are totally forgotten because of the adults' preoccupation with themselves. Sometimes the parents are so involved in punishing their mates that the children become the weapons they use against each other. For instance, if a mother believes that her husband loves their daughter more than she, the child may be maltreated in the mother's attempt to win back her husband's attention and affection. If a father feels that his son takes his mother's side in arguments, he may abuse or neglect the child to punish both his spouse and his offspring. Thus, children often become the victims of family struggles that primarily concern the adults.

Often in maltreating families, one parent is authoritarian, while the other remains dependent and passive. The domineering mate tolerates no interference with his or her position as autocrat of the family. This situation is generally acceptable to the spouse who is unwilling or unable to make independent decisions. In such families the authoritarian is the more likely physical or emotional abuser, while the more passive partner stands by and allows or tacitly encourages the maltreatment. In effect, the spouses support each other's opposite positions; yet, such a relationship is far from healthy. It represents a destructive bond that keeps both adults from developing into mature marriage partners and good parents.

In other maltreating families the partners have poor problem-solving skills; thus, they find it difficult to analyze situations, view alternatives, and select solutions that offer the greatest benefits and fewest drawbacks. Often, they discount the importance of problems in the belief that if they ignore them, the difficulties will go away. Because of their inability to reach and act on reasoned conclusions, the parents often react impulsively. When the spouse or child is at hand, both become likely targets for the irrationality of the maltreating adult.

Just as many maltreating parents feel isolated from friends, so they may feel cut off from meaningful communication with their partners. As the sense of isolation grows, it can be overwhelming. Because the parent cannot share hopes, fears, and failings with his or her spouse, such feelings build up to the point at which they manifest themselves in child maltreatment. The child becomes the victim of a marriage that fails to be any more than a living arrangement, for it is devoid of all mutuality and, therefore, is dysfunctional.

Thus, child maltreatment is often attributable to the dynamics of a family rather than to the unique characteristics of the maltreating parent. To end maltreatment in such cases the relationships that exist in the family unit must be abandoned or restructured. The family members must be helped to identify the sources of conflict and resolve them in the most mutually satisfying ways. Such changes in family functioning aid parents in dealing with each other and their offspring.

## Environmental stress factors

Poverty, unemployment, underemployment, minority status, or insufficient education can be seen as elements that affect a parent's self-concept and his or her ability to perform the parenting role adequately. Such environmental stress factors often combine with the psychodynamics of the individual to result in child maltreatment. Other conditions that may precipitate child abuse or neglect include alcoholism, drug addiction, marital difficulties, recent relocation, the absence of the spouse, or the arrival of a new baby. All these circumstances place added strain on a parent and may weaken his or her ability to deal rationally with other family members.

Research into incidents of child maltreatment suggests that typically a crisis occurs not long before the onset of abuse or neglect. Perhaps it is a trivial upset, as when a child is late for dinner or when the washing machine breaks down; perhaps it is a significant event like the abandonment of the family by the father or the birth of a baby. In any case the crisis can be viewed as a stress factor that triggers maltreatment.

It should be understood, however, that environmental stress factors do not cause maltreatment; rather, they act as immediate forerunners to it. To a parent already predisposed to child maltreatment, a crisis is the final straw that leads to abuse or neglect rather than a single event solely responsible for it. For example, when an alcoholic mother beats her child because the youngster has disobeyed her, the child's behavior can be viewed as the immediate precursor of maltreatment. Yet, the actual reasons for abuse are probably more closely tied to the psychodynamic factors responsible for the woman's dependence on alcohol than to the action of the child. Thus, though it may appear that one situation is responsible for the maltreatment, it is far more likely that a complex of personal characteristics are at the heart of the abuse.

As the incident included above demonstrates, environmental stress factors cannot be viewed in isolation; eliminating crises even if that were possible would not completely erase the prospect of maltreatment in a family's structure. A three-pronged approach of helping people to handle the stressful situations of life more successfully, while directing attention to the characteristics of both the individuals and family unit involved, holds the greatest promise for dealing positively with the maltreating family.

## Differences between abusing and neglecting parents

Whether a parent abuses or neglects a child is tied closely to the characteristics and circumstances of the adult and of the family in which he or she lives. Although no rigid dichotomy can be presented to distinguish between caretakers who abuse and those who neglect, there appear to be some significant differences between the parents who display these behaviors. A knowledge of these general tendencies may be useful to the educator or community member committed to discovering maltreating parents and helping them become positive forces in the lives of their children.

Abusive parents are generally more volatile and impulsive than neglecting parents; further, parents who abuse their youngsters are more conditioned to violence than their neglecting counterparts. Often, the abusive parent was abused as a child, while the neglecting adult lacked the emotional or physical support every youngster has the right to receive. Therefore, abusive parents have been prepared by their childhoods to expect adults to actively mistreat children, while neglecting adults have learned patterns of parenting that include the omission of reasonable parental provisions. Abusive adults tend to be more possessive of their children than neglecting parents. Frequently, abusive parents view their children as competitors, while neglecting ones have a difficult time considering their youngsters important human beings.

Parents who physically or emotionally abuse their offspring are often anxious when they must deal with problems involving their children. If called to a conference with a teacher, an abusive parent is likely to be defensive and ill at ease. Because abusive adults are often hypersensitive to criticism about their parenting practices, they frequently reject offers of advice and assistance related to their dealings with their children. Often they have unrealistically high expectations for their children and are totally unaccepting of the limitations of their youngsters. To abusive parents, a mistake or an error is a catastrophe rather than a natural and inevitable part of living. Further, abusive parents fear spoiling or coddling their offspring; thus, they often overreact when they must handle a minor problem involving their children. Tied to their feelings that a child must be dealt with firmly is the belief that physical punishment is a positive child-rearing practice. Often, the physically abusive parent defends his or her attacks on the child with great vehemence; this too-staunch insistence of the value of corporal punishment may indicate that he or she uses the child as a pawn to discharge aggression.

In the case of sexually abusive parents, the father generally assumes a dominant role in the life of the family. The mother is passive and often has conditioned her daughter to be accepting of other people's demands on her. Sometimes the mother knows of the sexual abuse, but does nothing to stop it because of fear, shame, or relief that her husband does not bother her sexually. Frequently, the family is an isolated unit with few friends. In many sexually abusive families the father restricts the outside activities of his daughters to keep them from telling others of their maltreatment. To the rest of the world the sexually abusive family may look stable and responsible; yet, the veneer of concern and closeness is designed to insulate it from detection.

The neglecting parent is often poorer than his or her abusive counterpart, although neglect cannot be linked causally to economics. While the abusive parent often has a rigidly compulsive life-style, the neglecting adult may lack daily routine in his or her unstructured life. Further, neglecting parents often demonstrate a poorly developed sense of responsibility in all aspects of life. They may view their children with hostility as unlovable individuals without giving any explanation or may simply appear indifferent to the youngsters. The needs of the children, either physically or emotionally, may not be apparent or important to them. They discourage the dependence of the children, for they desire to escape responsibility for the welfare of their offspring. Just as they find it difficult to become involved with their children, so they remain isolated from people in general; they lack friends and often do not belong to either formal or informal social groups.

## Conclusion

Maltreating parents are adults with problems rather than inhuman monsters who delight in hurting their children. They are people who have problems that affect their ability to be good parents rather than hopeless mental and social misfits. Although they often deny it, they are adults who need help to learn adequate parenting skills to allow their children to develop normally.

To understand why a parent abuses or neglects a youngster, we must take time to study both the maltreating adult and the family unit of which he or she is a part. Frequently, maltreating adults were conditioned to abuse or neglect as children; sometimes they possess personality traits that predispose them to hurt their children. Often, they have failed to internalize the values of the general society in regard to children and child rearing; sometimes the structure of the family unit precipitates mistreatment. Frequently, the frustrations of daily living combine with other factors to lead parents to abuse or neglect their youngsters.

Maltreating adults can be helped to become good parents through the concerted efforts of school and community members who empathize with both the parents and children in maltreating families. Yet, as important as it is to recognize maltreating parents and their needs, it is their children with whom we must be primarily concerned. Let us turn our attention now to the victims of abuse and neglect: the children we see daily.

### References

1. Blair Justice and Rita Justice, *The Abusing Family* (New York: Human Sciences Press, 1976), p. 47.
2. David G. Gil, *Violence Against Children: Physical Child Abuse in the United States* (Cambridge, Mass.: Harvard University Press, 1970), pp. 110-113, 138.
3. Gil, *Violence Against Children*, pp. 115-118.
4. B. Johnson and H. A. Morse, "Injured Children and Their Parents," *Children* 15 (1968):147-152.
5. Naomi Feigelson Chase, *A Child Is Being Beaten: Violence Against Children, An American Tragedy* (New York: Holt, Rinehart and Winston, Inc., 1975), p. 158.

6. Richard J. Gelles, *The Violent Home: A Study of Physical Aggression Between Husbands and Wives*. Sage Library of Social Research, volume 13 (Beverly Hills, Calif.: Sage Publications, Inc., 1972), p. 176.

7. Brandt F. Steele and Carl B. Pollock, "A Psychiatric Study of Parents Who Abuse Infants and Small Children," in *The Battered Child*, ed. Ray E. Helfer and C. Henry Kempe, 2d ed. (Chicago: The University of Chicago Press, 1974), p. 11.

CHAPTER 5

# How can you identify a maltreated child?

Maltreated children come in all sizes, shapes, and colors. Some are bright and do well in their studies, while others struggle to learn. Some plead for the attention of their teachers; others appear to be socially well adjusted; still others withdraw in the hope that their presence will escape notice. Some maltreated children are well dressed and seem well cared for; others show by their appearance that the treatment they receive is shabby. In short, some maltreated children openly wear the scars of their parents' inability to nurture them satisfactorily, while others carry less observable signs of inadequate parenting.

The caution that has been expressed repeatedly in this book is reemphasized here: although a child may display symptoms that conform to maltreatment, the educator or interested community member must not reach a premature conclusion that the child is maltreated. A wide variety of circumstances may be responsible for marks on a child's body indicative of physical abuse or for behavior patterns suggestive of neglectful parental care. Suspicions must be investigated through conferences with the youngster, the parents, and previous teachers, as well as through school records that catalogue the family's history. Only when school personnel have gathered substantial information on the family and its internal functioning are they in a position to assess if a child is being maltreated at home.

In some cases, maltreated children tell an adult they trust about the conditions under which they live. Generally, however, abused and neglected youngsters remain silent about the treatment they receive from their parents. Therefore, the concerned citizen or educator must observe the behavior children exhibit for signs that suggest maltreatment is occurring. One way to help concerned citizens identify maltreated children is to establish broad categories based on the kinds of behavior abused and neglected youngsters most frequently display. Two factors must be borne in mind, however. First, because of the uniqueness of each individual, two children may react in opposite manners to the same parental behavior. Second, because of the complexity of each human being, a youngster can be expected to display a wide range of behaviors. Despite these limitations, it is possible to categorize children's behavior in reference to observable clues suggestive of abuse and neglect. Such general guidelines can aid the concerned adult in identifying maltreated children.

## General guidelines for identifying maltreated children

### The aggressive child

All children want their own way from time to time, but the aggressive child consistently disrupts others in a quarrelsome, bullying manner. Often aggressive children start fights over trivial issues. They may be defiant, domineering, and totally unconcerned with anyone else. They have learned that they receive attention from both peers and adults when they cause trouble. In cases in which the parents pay little heed to their youngster, even notoriety is attractive and desirable to a child. In families that neglect the establishment of standards of acceptable behavior, children often do not understand that their rights do not extend to interfering with those of others. Aggressive children often blame peers or adults for their own misconduct, destroy physical objects that do not belong to them, and express extreme dislike for most of the people with whom they come in contact. They are not very likable primarily because they do not have good feelings about themselves.

Aggressive children often resort to physical means when they become angry. Sometimes, they have learned this pattern of behavior from abusive parents who express themselves with physical punishment when they are displeased. Like their parents, aggressive children have little self-discipline to enable them to control their impulses to act against those who anger them. Rarely are aggressive children happy, for they must continually seek ways to exert dominance and release pent-up emotion.

### The show-off

Many classrooms contain children who are extremely extroverted and outspoken. They raise and wave their hands frequently when volunteering to answer a question. In fact, they volunteer even without knowing the answer to the question being asked. Often, they cannot wait to be recognized by the teacher, but call out answers and are unable to be quiet until it is their turn to speak. Sometimes, they appear hyperactive and physically restless. So anxious are they to be the center of attention that they rarely give others a chance to speak. When they express an opinion, they hold it dogmatically and will not admit that any other view could be valid. Often, they have a number of friends and do relatively well in athletics, for the aggressiveness they project is appropriate to sports competition.

In many cases, extremely outgoing children receive little warmth or attention at home. Their parents pay little attention to them. Perhaps they show by their actions or words that they prefer a brother or sister to the extroverted child. In such cases, the youngster adopts outspoken behavior in an effort to compete for a fair share of praise and love. In other families the parents may encourage the child to believe that he or she is and should be the center-ring attraction in all gatherings. Often, however, the child assumes an outgoing posture to mask insecurity and feelings of inferiority. Frequently, the reinforcement the youngster has received is inappropriate to his or her accomplishments, for the child may either be praised excessively for small tasks or receive no notice for significant successes.

### The disobedient child

A child who purposely breaks the established rules of school and classroom is both a concern and a problem for school personnel. He or she may be insolent and impolite, respond to others defensively, and continue to argue until everyone else has stopped. Often, such children pretend not to hear instructions given to them as they pursue behavior or activities opposite to those desired. Disobedient children struggle against authority sources in an attempt to wrest power from them. Often, they goad teachers or principals into threats and actions that the adults would be wiser to avoid, for such children are infuriating with their insolence and defiance. Disobedient children are rarely happy; often, they seem preoccupied and worried.

Children who receive little positive reinforcement at home often disobey to gain attention. They have learned that their misdeeds make people notice them. For some youngsters, misbehavior brings status with their peers; so hungry are they for admiration that they seek it by being disruptive and "tough." It sometimes seems that they measure their worth by the number of public reprimands or the amount of punishment they receive. For such children, disobedience seems a compulsion that must be pursued.

A child's lack of respect for authority may be tied to parental attitudes held and expressed in the home. In other cases it develops as a result of inconsistent discipline within the family. If parents accept disobedience today and punish it severely tomorrow, the youngster learns that adults are often capricious in exercising their power. Further, parents who pay little attention to a child encourage him or her to struggle against them. Defiance is the one way the child can gain their notice. Although this child wants parental love and affection, he or she prefers anger and punishment to total indifference. For other children, disobedience is acting-out behavior. When parents tell or show a child repeatedly that he or she is bad, they often convince the child of their judgment. In such cases children may internalize parental concepts and assume behavior that confirms their parents' evaluation of their worthlessness.

### The child who lies, cheats, and steals

Most children tell lies from time to time; however, to some youngsters, lying is a way of life. An insecure child may tell a grand tale about his or her family or an activity in which he or she claims to have participated to gain others' attention or admiration. At other times a child lies to escape punishment when his or her wrong has been discovered. Such falsehoods may reflect a deeper hostility the youngster feels toward parents, teachers, or peers.

A child who cheats, whether in schoolwork or at play, sometimes feels that the means he or she uses to succeed are immaterial. Either because familial expectations are high and the child fears not living up to them or because adults have taught him or her by word and example that dishonesty is acceptable, the youngster assumes a pattern of behavior in which "getting away with things" becomes of primary importance.

The desire to avoid detection may carry over into the area of theft. Children sometimes steal items even when they have no use for them. Often, they have little respect for property or for the concept of rightful ownership. Perhaps they feel that objects are available to them for the taking. Sometimes, youngsters steal to receive attention; often, they want to be found out so that someone will notice them.

Frequently, the child who habitually lies, cheats, or steals is supplied with little supervision or concern at home. His or her parents may take no action to correct the youngster's behavior, and this fact confirms to the child that they have few positive feelings about him or her. In other families, dishonesty is condoned and encouraged as an expression of the parents' hostility toward society and frustration with life. In both cases, parents neglect their obligation to train their children to be the best citizens possible.

### The child nobody likes

Some children are more popular than others; yet, often there is one child in a classroom nobody likes. This child is sullen and depressed. Sometimes, he or she wanders around the room restlessly. This may be the child who waits until no one is around, destroys a book or breaks a vase, and then blames the act on someone else. This child claims that others single him or her out and are unfair. Frequently, the child brags about himself or herself and past accomplishments. Often, he or she is jealous of other people and wants to degrade them. Such a poorly adjusted child cannot participate smoothly in group activities, for he or she is unable to devote effort to the accomplishment of a shared goal. The child may be absent from school more often than most children and may complain about hating school, teachers, and classmates.

Simply stated, socially maladjusted children do not know how to establish healthy relationships with other people. Their home environment may include little warmth from parents who share their inability to develop healthy associations. Often, such families live isolated lives and participate in few activities together; therefore, the children fail to learn the skills necessary to act in concert with others. Further, the basic reason why others do not like these children may be because they are not very fond of themselves; thus, their poor self-concept makes them act out behavior that alienates peers and adults. Because the socially maladjusted child both feels and is rejected by others, he or she remains incapable of forming relationships that would improve his or her self-image.

### The ill-kempt child

The child who comes to school daily in soiled, torn clothes, who needs a bath, and whose hair is stringy and dirty can be easily identified in a classroom. His or her slovenly appearance may be tied to a general lack of care about table manners, the neatness of assignments, and the quality of schoolwork.

The dirty child often comes from a home environment in which standards of cleanliness are ignored. Perhaps washing facilities are absent or inadequate at home. In other cases an ill-kempt appearance may be indicative of a lack of adult supervision. Parents may be absent from the home most of the time and leave the child virtually on his or her own. In other cases, parents simply do not care about the child. Because these youngsters do not feel valued, they take little pride in themselves or their work. Thus, their appearance and school assignments reflect their poor image of themselves as they confirm by other people's reactions to them that they are not very desirable or worthwhile human beings.

### The listless child

Youngsters who have little energy and even less ability to concentrate on studies miss out on some of the most valuable learning experiences of life. They are slow in completing tasks, wait for someone to help them rather than try to solve problems on their own, and often do not want to do anything but daydream. They may slouch in their seats, fail to hand in assignments on time or at all, and seldom volunteer to do or say anything. While it may appear simply that they are lazy, there are more likely explanations for their behavior.

Listless children may be physically neglected at home. Their nutritional needs could be neglected, or it is possible that their parents pay so little attention to them that they stay up late watching television. They may be medically neglected and have a physical condition that needs treatment by a doctor. In other cases parents and teachers set standards of achievement for the child that are unrealistically high. Therefore, the child becomes so frustrated that he or she stops trying to succeed. The opposite may be true, for the child may be capable of more challenging work than anyone believes and may become bored by the elementary nature of assigned tasks. Often, the listless child receives little parental praise or attention for accomplishments, while excessive criticism is heaped on him or her for failings. To minimize parental rebukes, the child may simply leave all tasks incomplete.

### The careless child

This youngster hands in messy papers, makes many errors on schoolwork even when he or she knows how to accomplish it correctly, allows his or her desk to become disorganized, and frequently complains of losing articles. The youngster's shirttail may be continually sticking out, and his or her hair uncombed. This disarray does not particularly bother the youngster, for he or she has learned to accept it. Careless youngsters frequently appear unconcerned with the details of living and express this attitude when attempts are advanced to make them be more careful.

The lack of structure a careless child demonstrates can be the product of a home enviornment that places little value on neatness and lacks a sense of routine and order. Perhaps the younster's parents expect little in this regard, and so the child stumbles through each day in a disorganized way. In other families, excessive pressures on a child are responsible for the adoption of an "I don't care" attitude toward life. Since the child cannot meet all parental demands, he or she gives up trying to satisfy any of them.

### The accident-prone child

Youngsters who frequently injure themselves, stumble, fall down, or run into others are injury prone. They hurt themselves in situations in which other children rarely do. In physical activities they display poor motor coordination and seem always to be bumping into things. It seems that the injury-prone child does not know the boundaries of his or her body and has difficulty controlling it.

In some cases the injury-prone child may have an organic dysfunction or disease that needs professional care. When health factors can be ruled out, accident-prone children frequently are hungry for the attention they receive whenever they are injured. Some accident-prone children have learned that while their parents generally ignore them, they give them sympathy when they are hurt. This same desire for concern, affection, and caring is sought in school from teachers and classmates. Some children who feel they must excel in all undertakings feign injuries as an excuse for their inability to succeed in physical activities. The child who fails to perform well in a group activity at recess may claim that his or her poor performance is due to an injury suffered during the game. Other children with low self-esteem have little regard for their own safety and hurt themselves because they do not exercise proper care to keep themselves from harm. Their actions may stem from unconsciously self-destructive motives.

### The fearful child

On the other end of the behavior spectrum from the aggressive youngster is the fearful child. Fearful children appear anxious and uneasy. They
may show extreme emotional instability, for minor events often throw
them into a panic. Because they are afraid of being criticized and terrified
of failure, they take few risks. Such youngsters require continual reassurance that their actions are acceptable. Often, they are "clinging vines" who
latch onto anyone who shows a caring attitude toward them.

The fearful child is sometimes the product of a neurotic home in which
parental insecurities and doubts are openly communicated to the youngster. Sometimes, fearful children have justification for their fright, for
many of them receive frequent harsh punishment from their caretakers.
They have learned to be skeptical of grown-ups and to avoid situations in
which they may incur adult disapproval. Some fearful children live in unpredictable home environments that have little consistency and few cer-
tainties on which they can rely. In other families, while the parents do not
actively encourage the fears of their youngsters, they do nothing to alleviate them. Often, they ignore the child's insecurity and provide little attention or affection to convince him or her of their love.

### The shy child

A shy child differs from a fearful child in that his or her fear centers on
contact with people, while a fearful child's anxiety has more generalized
sources. The timid child has great difficulty carrying on a conversation; often, he or she speaks in a soft voice; sometimes, the child has a speech im-
pediment. Frequently, timid children sit quietly with lowered head in an attempt to avoid drawing attention to themselves; usually, they have few
friends. The shy child may not receive much attention from teachers
because he or she rarely performs any troublesome act. Yet, his or her
problems are real, for the shy child has difficulty making decisions about
even the most trivial matters and seldom defends or expresses himself or
herself.

Some timid children's parents share their shyness. In other families the
child becomes timid because his or her parents are excessively critical.
Thus, because the child fears failure, he or she rarely ventures into areas
that are unfamiliar. Parents who expect no less than perfection from their
youngster and express this standard either verbally or through actions in-
hibit the child so greatly that he or she fears attempting any task. Further,
timid children sometimes come from physically abusive families in which
parents administer harsh punishment for even the slightest wrongdoing.
Parents or teachers who force shy children into the limelight often do more
harm than good, for the youngster may retreat even further from adults.
The child's self-confidence and courage must be developed by small incre-
ments over an extended period.

### The withdrawn child

Withdrawn children isolate themselves both from people and from the world in general. They avoid contact with peers and adults by cutting themselves off from reality. They appear tense, nervous, and unhappy. Often, they wear a vacant expression that suggests they have entered mentally the world of daydreams. Withdrawn children are easily discouraged, and even small events unreasonably hurt or upset them. They rarely express feelings about any issue because they fear ridicule and feel that their opinions are worthless. The withdrawn youngster may make tentative attempts to get in contact with other people, but they often end in outbursts of anger, hatred, or fear. In schoolwork the withdrawn child is easily frustrated and abandons tasks he or she finds difficult after only a little effort. The child may sit in the back of the room or in a corner in which he or she feels insulated from intrusions by others.

The withdrawn child is often frightened of people because of unsatisfactory experiences suffered in the past. His or her parents may be unpredictable; thus, the child arranges his or her life to be as inoffensive as possible. In some families parents who make extensive demands on their youngsters force their offspring into withdrawal. The child is bullied and responds by turning inward. In other homes the parents may be unable to establish positive relationships with others, and this trait is learned by their children. The withdrawn child frequently lacks love, affection, and praise. Because the child experiences many failures and few successes, he or she sets up firm defenses for self-protection.

### The emotionally unstable child

Some children are volatile and unpredictable. Often, they get extremely agitated and appear worried and preoccupied. Their insecurity often manifests itself in their inability to learn, for emotional factors interfere with their achievement. Further, the emotionally upset child frequently can perform a task successfully today, but will fail at it tomorrow. He or she is often defensive as if looking for a fight; his or her general attitude toward life is negative. Often, the child has symptoms that suggest hypochondria, for he or she complains of illness when physically fit. His or her defensiveness, tenseness, and unpredictability win few friends.

The emotionally unstable child often receives little attention or affection from his or her parents, who fail to meet the youngster's emotional needs. Perhaps the parents are rarely home and do not provide adequate supervision and psychological support. In families with several children the emotionally disturbed youngster may experience difficulties in dealing with siblings. In such cases parents remain unaware of the problems or incapable of resolving them. The emotionally upset child sometimes is under tremendous pressure from exacting parents. Because the child is emotionally inadequate to either absorb or defend himself or herself against their excessive expectations, the youngster may react with rapid changes in mood and extreme displays of emotion.

### The low-achieving child

Some children of average intelligence learn more slowly than others. They have a short attention span and are easily distracted from their schoolwork. Their achievement level is generally below that of the rest of the class or below their potential. Some slow-learning children withdraw from classroom activities; others become disobedient or disruptive as if to distract attention from their failures in the academic realm. The low-achieving child rarely completes assignments and seldom volunteers, even for tasks not involving schoolwork. He or she feels insecure and unsure both when new learning is occurring and when previously mastered material is involved.

Some slow-learning younsters have brain damage that impairs their rate of learning. Others have specific learning disabilities that make achievement more difficult. Still others may be physically neglected, and their slow achievement may be related to poor nutrition or insufficient sleep. Some slow learners are ill frequently and may have medical problems that their parents neglect. In other families, slow rates of achievement may be attributable to educational neglect in which parents fail to provide their youngsters with a stimulating environment that encourages their natural curiosity. Slow learners must receive encouragement and satisfaction as they tackle tasks at which they can succeed; if they meet only failure, their already slow rate of learning may decrease even more.

### Summary

The categories delineated in the preceding pages are not mutually exclusive. The aggressive child may also be disobedient and may cheat, steal, lie, and show off. The shy child may display fearful, withdrawn, and accident-prone behavior. Children demonstrating any of the behaviors may be slow learners. Further, it is important to remember that the marginally maltreated child may exhibit none of the patterns of behavior discussed here; he or she may appear perfectly healthy. On the other hand, children who are not being mistreated at home may display any of the behaviors for reasons unrelated to maltreatment. The purpose of this chapter is not to provide an absolute standard against which to measure a child for maltreatment, but rather to advance a flexible tool based on behavioral clues that suggest that a child needs attention.

## The "child factor" in child maltreatment

Much research has attempted to discern if there are conditions that make one child more likely to be the victim of maltreatment than another.

Such an inquiry does not try to prove that the child causes his or her own mistreatment, nor does it indicate that he or she "deserves" it. However, a growing body of evidence suggests that because of a variety of factors related to the child, most of which are beyond his or her control, some children are more likely to be abused and neglected than others.

Women often experience more difficulty during one pregnancy than during others; their hostility toward the child, therefore, may begin even before birth. Further, almost from the moment they are born, some children are more demanding of parental attention than others. Only hours after birth, doctors and nurses can often identify a "difficult" infant who cries more violently and is less easily comforted than other babies. Some infants have mild dysfunctions of the central nervous system that lead to poor eating habits, frequent choking, fussiness, or extreme passivity and unresponsiveness. Although these babies seem perfectly healthy, they possess disorders so minor that even physicians cannot identify them. Yet, to a mother whose child caused problems during pregnancy and is difficult to care for after birth, any subtle difference from other children may single the child out for abuse or neglect.

Another factor that seems to make some youngsters more likely victims of maltreatment than others is prematurity. Because babies born before full term are usually separated from their mothers shortly after birth for intensive care, mother and child are robbed of the first few days of life together when the bonding relationship is normally formed. Without this crucial stage the mother may be unable to establish a healthy nurturing attitude toward the child.

During pregnancy and early childhood most parents fantasize about what their children will be like and what part the youngsters will play in their lives. Parents whose perceptions of a child are distorted or whose expectations for him or her are unrealistic are likely to be extremely disappointed, frustrated, and angered when the youngster is not all they had hoped.

Not only may unfulfilled expectations lead a parent to maltreat a child; also, the developmental stages of life often precipitate abuse and neglect. A parent who enjoys a child during the passivity of infancy may be totally frustrated by the same child as a toddler when he or she grows in independence and exerts some autonomy. Thus, it is not so much the child as the stage of growth that leads to his or her maltreatment.

Further, research suggests that at least in regard to physical abuse there is a correlation between the age and sex of a youngster and the likelihood of maltreatment. While in preadolescence boys are more frequently abused than girls; in children over twelve, girls are more often the victims.[1] It has been hypothesized that young girls are viewed as more conforming and compliant than boys; therefore, less physical force is used with them.

However, as boys grow older and gain physical strength equal to or greater than their parents', the incidence of physical maltreatment for sons decreases. On the other hand, as girls undergo the maturation processes of adolescence, parents sometimes impose tight restrictions on their daughters. Their anxiety concerning their daughter's possible sexual relationships can result in violent conflicts and physical force used to enforce parental control.

Every adult who works with children has encountered youngsters who seem to provoke hostility, aggression, and frustration. These children are infuriating or, at the very least, extremely irritating. It is difficult to determine what came first in such cases: maltreatment by the parent or provocative behavior by the child. In some physically maltreating families the child identifies with the parent who abuses him or her by becoming aggressive and hostile. In other families the child invites punishment to receive parental attention. In still other homes it seems that parents subtly encourage their offspring to engage in behaviors to which the parents can respond with abuse or neglect. Perhaps as justification for their parental behavior, or because the child internalizes the adults' negative perceptions of him or her, child and parent jockey themselves into positions in which maltreatment is likely to occur.

There is little doubt that there is a relationship between mental retardation, brain damage, and child maltreatment; the exact nature of the connection is at question, however. Some research suggests that retarded children are more likely to be abused than youngsters of average intelligence.[2] However, other experiences suggest that a child's retardation does not cause abuse, but often results from it. Because many abused and neglected children who function at low rates make remarkable gains in learning after the maltreatment is eliminated, it appears that their retardation may be causally related to maltreatment.[3]

From the educator's perspective the fact that an unusually high proportion of mentally retarded children are maltreated must be viewed as significant. It is to these high-risk children that special attention should be given to discern if they are being abused and neglected at home.

## Conclusion

Maltreated children manifest a wide variety of behavior patterns. Some are easy to identify; others are more subtle. Yet, when we remember that children are a teacher's stock in trade and that understanding is an educator's basic tool, it is clear that personnel within the school who have been trained to recognize the signs are well suited to identify maltreated children.

Deciding upon the action that should be taken after the abused or neglected child is spotted is at the heart of the subject of child maltreatment. In the next chapter we will explore briefly both formalized and innovative programs that have been developed to help the maltreating family.

## References

1. David G. Gil, *Violence Against Children: Physical Child Abuse in the United States* (Cambridge, Mass.: Harvard University Press, 1970), pp. 102–104.
2. A. Sandgrund, R. W. Gaines, A. H. Green, "Child Abuse and Mental Retardation: A Problem of Cause and Effect," *American Journal of Mental Deficiency* 79 (1974):327–330.
3. Harold P. Martin, "Which Children Get Abused: High Risk Factors in the Child," in *The Abused Child: A Multidisciplinary Approach to Developmental Issues and Treatment,* ed. Harold P. Martin (Cambridge, Mass.: Ballinger Publishing Company, 1976), p. 30.

CHAPTER 6

# What is presently being done to help maltreating families?

At the present time most services in the field of child maltreatment are targeted to identify children who are experiencing continuing serious abuse or neglect. Few programs, public or private, are designed either to help the marginally maltreating family or to prevent abuse and neglect before they occur. This chapter reviews the status of maltreatment programs in an effort to establish the range of services presently available in most communities, the potential of some innovative programs being offered experimentally in localized areas, and the needs of potentially and actually maltreating families for which no programs currently exist.

Two philosophies vie for dominance when the question arises, "What should be done with maltreating families?" The approach that has held near-total sway in the past is punitive: maltreating parents should be punished for what they have done to their children. This perspective advocates the removal of all maltreated children from their homes and the criminal prosecution of their parents. The punitive attitude toward abuse and neglect is based largely on emotional reactions, for child maltreatment is a subject charged with strong feelings. Incidents of maltreatment remind parents of the impulsive desires to hurt their children they may have felt but have managed to control. Perhaps because of guilt at having wanted to abuse or neglect their youngsters and relief that they restrained themselves, people's most sanctimonius and self-righteously judgmental attitudes are leveled against maltreating parents. In another sense the punitive approach to maltreating parents is both glib and facile, for it allows society to make abusing and neglecting parents the scapegoats for its shortcomings. Further, it ignores the larger issues of remediation and rehabilitation that should be the ultimate goals of any rational approach in dealing with those who violate our culture's standards of adequate parental behavior.

Punishment as the cure-all for maltreating parents is a shortsighted approach emotionally, socially, and economically. First, it fails to consider that except in the most extreme cases of serious abuse or neglect the child may be far happier staying with his or her parents than being separated from them. Even in families with severe problems the love between parent and child is often strong, and the stability and security it offers invaluable to both parent and offspring. Removal of a child to foster care or to an institution often means the severence of any emotional bond for the child. As Dr. Vincent DeFrancis writes: "Because it is easier to place a child than it is to pour into his home the social services which could stabilize family life, far more children are separated than should be. In the process, the right of a child to be with his natural parents and siblings is overlooked, or it is disregarded as unimportant."[1] Thus, when the punitive approach to maltreatment is followed, both the emotional and social roles of the family unit are all but destroyed. Further, if the parents are prosecuted, they wear that stigma as well as a criminal record for the rest of their lives. In such cases the possibility of establishing a healthy family environment is diminished even further. From an economic standpoint, imprisonment and government-supplied child care are expensive alternative living arrangements costing thousands of dollars a year while restricting the productivity of the incarcerated adult.

A second approach that is being adopted to deal with child maltreatment involves employment of therapeutic techniques to undo the damage to the child and help parents learn constructive ways to deal with their youngsters. The focus in this philosophy is on improvement of the lives of the child, parents, and family as a social unit. Often, this approach involves a coordinated effort to provide complementary services to all family members, utilizing the range of sources of assistance available within the community. The ultimate goal of the therapeutic treatment approach is not only to guarantee that abuse and neglect will not be repeated, but also to help the members of the family perform positive roles in each other's lives.

Since its dual concerns are the child and the parents, the assistance-oriented philosophy recognizes that while not all families can become functional units, most can be aided in this regard. Supporters of this approach to child maltreatment believe that the best interests of all family members are served when agencies pool their resources to analyze the total needs of a family and provide services to supply them. The therapeutic approach to maltreatment is gaining support throughout the United States, and it is fast replacing the punitive philosophy as the dominant attitude in America today. Elizabeth Philbrick sums up the case for aiding maltreating families when she writes, "Economically, as well as socially, does it not make sense to help parents become better parents while their children are still with them, instead of trying, post facto, to provide substitute parents while putting the pieces of the broken home and broken people back together again?"[2]

## Parents' responses to the discovery of their maltreatment

Because of the legal and social sanctions against child maltreatment, parents confronted with the facts of their abuse or neglect are frequently hostile and uncooperative. This reaction is familiar to many who work in the child maltreatment field. Some parents initially display antagonism, evasiveness, and defensiveness. They deny they have problems that need solutions and claim that their treatment of their children is both warranted and proper.

Often, parents' defensive reactions to the suggestion that they are maltreating their youngsters are rooted in past relationships with people. Because some parents have received little support and much criticism and coldness from others, they expect everyone to respond to them in this way. The hostility many maltreating parents display to offers of assistance often discourages the would-be helper. Those who work with maltreating parents must be careful not to misinterpret the generalized anger, frustration, and fear of a parent as a personal attack, but must understand it as a defense mechanism employed to insulate the parent from pain. In many such cases the parent wants help and knows it is needed, but is unable to ask for or accept it openly.

On the other hand, some maltreating parents appear docile, cooperative, and overly eager to admit their maltreatment when confronted with it. In fact, they are overly compliant with the wishes of others, having learned throughout life that by appearing to do what people ask, they save themselves much criticism and pain. These anxious-to-please parents look too good to be true to a person concerned with maltreatment, and often they are, for although they seem to abandon their abusive or neglectful patterns of behavior, too often little significant change takes place. Instead, parents say what they think the worker wants to hear so that he or she will believe progress is being made. It is easy to be deceived by the overly compliant parent who makes the worker see his or her efforts as unerringly successful; yet, it is well to be skeptical of substantial life changes that are claimed to have occurred in a miraculously short time. Such parents must be given the self-confidence and unconditional acceptance they need to understand that genuine growth and not a pleasing facade is the ultimate goal of assistance in the area of child maltreatment.

Yet a third group of parents knows that it needs to modify its child-rearing practices and earnestly seeks to do so. While such adults may at first exhibit hostility or indulge in denial, internally they recognize the need for change. These parents are more amenable to assistance than either aggressively hostile or overly compliant parents, for they have fewer defenses that must be dismantled before they can accept help. It should not be assumed, however, that dramatic changes will occur overnight even in these willing parents; just as their abusive or neglectful patterns of parental behavior have developed over a long period, so it takes an extended period of retraining for them to adopt constructive methods to deal with their children.

## Federal efforts in the field of child maltreatment

The Child Abuse Prevention and Treatment Act of 1974 established an office under the Department of Health, Education, and Welfare known as the National Center on Child Abuse and Neglect. The functions of NCCAN are fourfold:

1. Demonstration programs have received grants through NCCAN to develop and test methods of preventing, detecting, and treating child maltreatment. A number of plans focus on the formulation of comprehensive programs of maltreatment identification and reporting, improvement of investigative procedures in alleged cases of maltreatment, and employment of teams of professionals to treat the troubled family as a unit.
2. Research on the causes, prevention, and treatment of child maltreatment has been funded through NCCAN. Such topics as the relationship between alcoholism and maltreatment, the incidence of maltreatment among military families, and social stresses as predisposing factors in abuse and neglect are being studied to broaden the field of knowledge within the area of maltreatment. In addition, researchers continue to assess the actual incidence of maltreatment nationwide, undoubtedly a figure far greater than the number of cases reported annually to public agencies.
3. NCCAN has made training available to workers whose responsibilities include providing services to maltreated children and their families. In addition, it has funded the creation of materials to increase the public's awareness of maltreatment and of citizens' obligations to report it. In this regard, NCCAN supports state efforts to establish centralized maltreatment registries to which all suspected cases of abuse and neglect are reported. The central registry ensures that uniform procedures will be followed in the investigation of each report. Further, it acts as a record of prior reports made in regard to a particular family; thus, it divulges a pattern of parental behavior toward children.
4. NCCAN maintains a central clearinghouse of information on publications and programs on maltreatment throughout the United States. This information is available to workers in the field of child maltreatment upon request.

In another federal effort, Title XX of the Social Security Act authorizes and partially funds protective service agencies for children through state and local bureaus. These agencies, including hospitals, police, courts, and social service departments, are charged to report suspected cases of maltreatment with which they come in contact, investigate cases of abuse and neglect reported by others, and plan and provide treatment for maltreating families. It is rare for these departments to take any action until a crisis has occurred in the home and maltreatment has reached life-threatening levels. Instead, they must wait until maltreatment is reported to them or is discovered in the course of unrelated investigations. For instance, when police are called to inquire into a loud domestic argument, they may uncover child maltreatment as they gather information regarding the original complaint. In another example, parents may bring a child to a hospital emergency room with a broken arm. In the course of the physical examination the doctor may discover evidence of prior injuries in various stages of healing that suggest that the youngster is being maltreated. Such cases are then referred to the appropriate social agency for investigation and disposition.

## Protective services

When a person has reasonable cause to suspect that a child is being maltreated by his or her caretakers, this person is required by law in most states to report his or her belief to the protective services division for investigation. Called Child and Family Services in some areas, the Child Welfare Division in others, or Health and Rehabilitative Services in still other states, these publicly supported government agencies are staffed with social workers whose responsibilities include checking reports of maltreatment and planning programs of action to deal with abusing and neglecting families. The usual procedure followed in evaluating reports of maltreatment includes visiting the home, talking with both the parents and children, and interviewing neighbors in an attempt to discern if the charge of maltreatment is founded. With evidence based on this inquiry the protective services worker may recommend that the case be closed because the suspicions of maltreatment are unsubstantiated, conclude that moderate maltreatment is occurring and advise that the family receive assistance, or determine that such serious abuse or neglect is involved that the child should be removed from the home and his or her parents' case turned over to the courts for criminal prosecution.

It is easy to understand why many of the reports of maltreatment made to protective service agencies are judged to be groundless. Certainly, some reports have no basis in truth; they may be made by disgruntled relatives who want to hurt the family. Other cases may involve marginal abuse and neglect that is not of a serious enough nature to conform to legal definitions of maltreatment and allow social workers to intervene. In other cases maltreatment may be hidden from the investigator by the family, which denies any wrongdoing. Since protective service agencies usually operate only during weekday business hours and are unmanned in most communities at night and on weekends when maltreatment occurs with greatest frequency, the social worker may be too late in entering the case to uncover a pattern of maltreatment. Further, except in cases involving observable physical injury or neglect, the protective service worker often finds it difficult to assess the risk to the child by continued exposure to his or her parents. As a result the vast majority of confirmed cases involve physical abuse or physical neglect. Because of the subjectivity of identifying emotional or psychological neglect and because of the social taboos surrounding incest in sexual abuse cases, many reports of these kinds of maltreatment are judged by social workers as unsubstantiated. In addition, it must be kept in mind that the investigation of maltreatment cases is only one of many responsibilities of a social worker whose average work load may consist of sixty to one hundred cases a month. As a result the protective service worker often has neither the time nor the knowledge to investigate each reported case of child maltreatment with the thoroughness it requires.

When a report of child maltreatment is confirmed by protective service investigation, one of three courses of action is normally taken. In the most severe cases, juvenile or family court proceedings are initiated immediately to remove the child from the home and place him or her in either an institution or a foster care facility. In such cases the parents are often indicted and tried on criminal charges arising from their maltreatment. A second, more temporary, procedure involves the hospitalization of physically abused and neglected children. In some cases it is unclear if a child's physical condition is the result of maltreatment; placing the child in the hospital allows time for further investigation of the case without exposing the youngster to possible risks within his or her home enviornment. This course of action does not require court involvement, but it does afford protection to the child. The third and most frequently employed alternative in dealing with confirmed cases of maltreatment is to allow the child to remain in the home while providing both protective supervision and assistance through social agencies that have frequent contact with the family and that evaluate the child's safety on an ongoing basis.

In cases in which the child is not endangered by remaining with his or her family, social workers attempt to provide the kinds of assistance that the parents need to abandon the maltreatment of their youngsters. Some communities enlist the aid of visiting homemakers who work with parents on improving their domestic and organizational skills. Other areas employ public health nurses who show parents how to care for their offspring. In other communities maltreated children are enrolled in publicly supported day-care centers to allow the parent to take a job or to have time away from the children. However, most social service agencies lack comprehensive treatment and follow-up programs to bring about substantial change in the maltreating family. As Vincent DeFrancis of the American Humane Association concludes, "But most disturbing is the fact that *no state* and *no community* has developed a child protective service program adequate in size to meet the service needs of all reported cases of child neglect and abuse."[3]

There are a number of reasons why social agencies often fail in their dealings with maltreating families. First, there is little data available to help agency planners develop programs that have a high probability of success. Often, because of financial constraints, programs are begun and abandoned before their effectiveness can be evaluated. Further, though a social worker may genuinely want to help a family, he or she may be unfamiliar with the dynamics of child maltreatment, and a twice-monthly appointment with the family may accomplish little. As Douglas J. Besharov, Director of the National Center on Child Abuse and Neglect, writes:

> The goal of an effective child protective process is an individualized treatment plan for the endangered child and his family. A visit to most child protective agencies, however, quickly dispels this idealistic notion. In too many communities there is a devastating lack of services—a lack of sufficiently qualified child protective workers, social workers, psychologists, psychiatrists, and of all sorts of diagnostic and treatment services. Furthermore, the agency's inability to deal with the underlying familial, social, cultural, and economic forces that shape the individuals and families it seeks to help is a fundamental and inherent weakness in the process. Child protective workers are forced to make do with woefully inadequate, outdated, and inappropriate services and facilities.[4]

Thus, although child protective service agencies attempt to help maltreating families, so great are the demands on their personnel and so inadequate the programs they employ to initiate and continue treatment of the family that it is impossible for social services to meet the multiple needs of maltreating families.

## Group therapy

One of the most widely used treatment modalities in the field of child maltreatment is group therapy. Such sessions are generally guided by a social worker, psychologist, or psychiatrist familiar with the dynamics of child maltreatment and cognizant of both the most typical needs and individual concerns of parents who abuse and neglect their youngsters. Group sessions allow parents to share their innermost fears and frustrations with others whose experiences have been parallel. Because the group members are in various stages of development toward being good parents, they learn both from others' admissions and successes.

Not all group therapy in the field of maltreatment is targeted toward adults. Some programs provide therapy for maltreated children and their siblings, for abuse and neglect affect all family members even though their ramifications may be greater for one child than for others. In these sessions youngsters air their frustrations about their parents as they come to understand that they need not always be the victims of adults. Just as maltreating parents often must improve their self-images to avoid repeating a pattern of pain for their children, so the youngsters must accept that they are worthwhile individuals who are not deserving of maltreatment but who are entitled to a full and happy childhood. Group sessions for maltreated youngsters attempt both to help the children understand themselves more fully and to gain some insight into the dynamics that have led their parents to maltreatment.

In cases involving severe psychological disturbance, individual therapy may be indicated either for a parent or a youngster. When satisfactory progress is made in these more intensive sessions, the patient is often prepared to join a group in which he or she can interact with others who understand maltreatment from firsthand experience.

There are some drawbacks to group therapy, however. It is not a treatment form that is successful with all parents and children. Some individuals find it hard to relate to others and refuse to be drawn into active participation within the group. Others fail to see that there are similarities between themselves and other group members. In some cases maltreating parents attend therapy sessions because they feel obliged to do so and not because they are serious about changing their patterns of parental behavior. This factor is especially prevalent in cases in which the court or protective service personnel link attendance at group therapy sessions to the return of a maltreated child to his or her home. Under these circumstances the maltreating parent may go through the motions prescribed for him or her with little commitment and even less change.

Individual therapy is an expensive and time-consuming process. It often does not yield significant results for months or even years. Patients who participate in it cannot expect miracles, nor can they hope to have all their problems solved by the psychologist or psychiatrist. They must understand that it has taken them a lifetime to become the individuals they presently are and that it will take long, painful hours for them to uncover and recognize why they act and react as they do.

## Family life education

Family life education is employed both as a preventive and as a treatment element in regard to child abuse and neglect. As a preventive tool it has the advantage of being able to reach large segments of the general population, with particular emphasis on high-risk individuals, including teenage parents and unwed mothers. Offered through the community adult school or through the public school, parenting courses concentrate on healthy child development; thus, they attempt to eliminate unrealistic parental expectations for children. Further, discipline techniques are explored that offer viable alternatives to harsh punishment. In more general terms, examining elements of family living, learning to cope with stress and crises, and understanding interpersonal relationships are topics frequently incorporated into the family life education curriculum.

In 1972 the Office of Education and the Office of Child Development of the Department of Health, Education, and Welfare began a nationwide program to prepare teenagers for the job of parenting. Called Education for Parenthood, this project suggests a curriculum that may be employed in secondary schools, while it urges voluntary organizations to involve prospective parents in programs concerned with child development. Young people are not only provided with classroom instruction about child rearing, but also are given practical experience working with children at day-care facilities, head start centers, and nursery schools.

Perhaps the best known parenting course offered nationally through workshops is Dr. Thomas Gordon's Parent-Effectiveness Training, or PET. Through lectures delivered by group leaders, a manual for parents included in the course fees, and discussions that arise from participants' concerns, parents learn alternative methods of dealing with the complex task of child rearing. Other programs similar to PET are offered privately through community colleges, civic organizations, and social service agencies.

A number of communities and agencies have begun parent education groups for maltreating adults as a treatment tool. In these classes the curricula are frequently flexible to allow for discussion and analysis of the problems that are most important to group participants. Topics for discussion range from discipline for children, the needs of youngsters for affection and love, motivating factors responsible for children's actions, to the training of youngsters to assume responsibility.

Maltreating parents often have difficulty handling meal planning, food shopping, cleaning, clothes repair, and similar household tasks. Their inability to deal with such mundane tasks reinforces their feelings of worthlessness and sometimes leads inadvertently to neglect. When such problems are aggravated by poverty, they can become a persistent source of frustration stemming from feelings of inadequacy. Some communities have classes on domestic skills for maltreating parents, while others employ visiting homemakers who teach the parent skills ranging from how to bathe the baby to how to establish and stick to a budget. These homemakers offer concrete assistance to maltreating adults that results in observable changes in the parents' lives and surroundings. In addition to their educational function the homemakers help break down the sense of isolation and inadequacy common to many maltreating parents.

## Crisis hot lines

A crisis hot line is a service available to potentially and actively maltreating parents in a number of communities. The most successful hot lines operate around the clock, 365 days a year. Manned by listeners who understand the dynamics of child maltreatment and are aware of community resources to deal with it, a crisis hot line offers an opportunity for parents to break through feelings of isolation when they fear they may hurt their children. Callers can remain anonymous and, therefore, have no fear that police officers or social workers will appear at their door. However, if a parent wants to identify himself or herself in a plea for help, volunteers and paid professionals should be available to begin treatment immediately.

Most successful hot lines are administered by a professional social worker or psychologist. Many are publicly funded, while others are operated by nonprofit organizations or community action groups. The hot line must be well integrated with other community services or it becomes merely a phone number to call to let off steam. While this cathartic function is important, it is equally vital that hot lines operate as the first step in a treatment program for potentially maltreating parents, with access to complete information on sources of assistance for parents.

As with many child maltreatment programs, crisis hot lines frequently devote a great deal of energy to obtaining sufficient funding to continue their work. Further, there must be enough publicity of the existence of the hot line so that maltreating parents know the service exists. Those who handle incoming calls must be perceptive listeners and nonaccusatory questioners to ascertain the status of children in the home – whether they have already been maltreated or whether the parent fears he or she may hurt the child in the near future. A staff of consultants must be available to deal with families in need of help whenever they call, for desperate people cannot wait hours or days for assistance to arrive. A poorly run hot line can do great harm, for the parent who feels denied help when he or she calls sees the the hot line as yet another source of frustration and may take out this anger on the child.

## Multidisciplinary treatment model

Because of the lack of comprehensiveness of many of the programs instituted under the auspices of child protective service agencies and by private sources, an attempt has been made to create a plan that utilizes the special skills of professionals from several different fields. This approach to the maltreating family acknowledges the multidimensional nature of maltreatment, that there is no single universal cause for all abuse and neglect, and that there is no one kind of family in which maltreatment occurs. This multidisciplinary team strategy is sometimes referred to as the Denver approach to treatment and was originated in large part by Dr. C. Henry Kempe and Dr. Vincent DeFrancis, two leaders in the field of treatment for families in which abuse and neglect are present. Although the model differs somewhat from plan to plan, it generally includes one team member from each of the following job categories:

| | |
|---|---|
| Protective services worker | Public health nurse |
| Hospital social worker | Lawyer |
| Family physician or pediatrician | Law enforcement officer |
| Psychologist or psychiatrist | Team coordinator |

The team is involved both in the diagnosis of maltreatment and in assessment of the ways to meet the needs of the maltreating family through an implemented treatment program. The team begins its work when a report of suspected maltreatment is made and usually continues close contact with the family for three to nine months if the family responds positively to treatment.

Although not all members of the team may be needed to deal with each confirmed maltreatment case, each is available to cooperate with the team when his or her services are required. Further, because maltreatment is frequently preceded by a crisis that may occur at any time, members of the team are accessible to the maltreating family around the clock.

Long-term treatment for many families within the multidisciplinary approach frequently involves group therapy for parents in which they discuss with other maltreating parents their fears and reactions when dealing with their children. Guided by a psychologist, psychiatrist, or trained social worker, group membership helps break down the sense of social isolation common to many maltreating parents. Further, it demonstrates to them that other parents experience similar problems in regard to their children. Some parents need more intensive help in working out their problems than group therapy can provide; for them, individual sessions with a psychiatrist or psychologist may be employed as a treatment mode. Sometimes, maltreating adults are encouraged to attend parenting courses that educate them to a variety of domestic skills and alternative methods of handling children.

A second important element in the long-term treatment of maltreating parents involves helping the adults feel happier about themselves. They must learn that other people can be trusted and that it does not show weakness to ask for help from others. Further, parents must understand that they are worthwhile human beings who are both deserving of praise and of self-respect. Such attitudinal changes can be achieved through a number of techniques. The treatment team can help the family acquire a telephone to establish contact with the outside world. Transportation can be arranged so that the parents can have some healthy experiences beyond the four walls of their home. A public health nurse or parent aide can go to the home regularly to help the parent learn how to organize and accomplish domestic chores. Such in-home contacts offer both practical assistance and healthy interpersonal relationships for parents whose needs in both areas are great.

A third element in a multidisciplinary approach to treatment of parents who abuse and neglect their children centers on strengthening the marital relationship. It is common for maltreating parents to have unsatisfying marriages as a symptom of their generalized inability to deal successfully with other people. Marriage counseling may be necessary to reestablish a couple's relationship on a healthy basis of mutuality. Even though only one parent may actively maltreat the child, both adults should be involved in all aspects of the treatment to learn alternative ways to deal with family members. Most workers in the field of maltreatment agree that it is generally preferable to try to reconstruct a marriage rather than abandon it, just as it is more desirable to restructure the attitudes in the home so that the child can remain with the family rather than be removed from it. In some cases, however, divorce or separation is inevitable, and when appropriate, this fact must be acknowledged.

The multidisciplinary team recognizes its responsibility not only to maltreating parents, but also to their abused and neglected children. These youngsters also need treatment to counteract the detrimental effects of their maltreatment. Sometimes, older maltreated children participate in group therapy sessions in which they share their feelings about themselves and their parents. Younger children often benefit from nursery school or day-care attendance that provides them with needed social contact both with children their own age and with nonmaltreating adults. Sometimes, older maltreated children participate in group therapy sessions in which they share their feelings about themselves and their parents. Sometimes, play therapy is indicated for a child whose normal development has been severely retarded by the effects of maltreatment. Temporary or long-term foster care may be necessary for children whose homes are not safe; however, the goal of the multidisciplinary approach to treatment is to reunite the family as quickly as practicable. It is interesting to note that some multidisciplinary teams now evaluate nonmaltreated siblings in maltreated families. Such an analysis can provide insights into differences among children and aid in the selection of treatment approaches for family members.

Many maltreating families can be significantly aided by an individually planned, carefully structured, and well-executed treatment program. However, parents with severe mental illnesses are difficult to treat, as are parents who are fanatic in their justifications for their child-rearing practices. Further, some parents who fit neither category simply do not respond positively to present treatment programs. It is estimated, however, that between 70 and 75 percent of maltreating parents can be significantly aided by the team approach to treatment.[5]

Unfortunately, too few communities offer their citizens the benefits of a multidisciplinary team approach to deal with child maltreatment. First, such plans are expensive to operate because of the number of highly trained professionals required. Second, this approach is dependent on cooperation among several discrete governmental agencies; such willing teamwork is too often the exception, while competition and needless duplication of services are too frequently the rule. In short, the team approach to treatment is implemented only in those communities that recognize both the magnitude of maltreatment and its multidimensional nature; such enlightened areas remain all to rare.

## Current treatment programs

### Comprehensive Emergency Services

In 1972, Nashville-Davidson County, Tennessee, set up a twenty-four hour a day program called Comprehensive Emergency Services (CES) for Children in Crisis. Its thrust involves speedy mobilization of community resources to aid neglected and abused children who are endangered in their homes. Its basic elements include a public awareness program to alert the community both to the problem of child maltreatment and to the sources of assistance available. An around-the-clock answering service exists to receive reports of suspected maltreatment and to dispatch immediately social workers to investigate the allegations. Depending on the outcome of investigation, a number of services are employed. When children must be removed from their home, emergency foster homes and group homes exist to accept them. When parents are absent from the home, a trained caretaker is prepared to enter it to care for the children; when parents lack the skills to care for their home and children, a competent homemaker can go and assume the necessary duties. In cases of fire or other catastrophe, families can be housed in emergency shelter as a unit. When children are brought to a hospital for treatment, a trained team of doctors and nurses familiar with the symptoms of maltreatment goes into action. In addition to these emergency services the CES plan provides for coordination and follow-up of cases that require long-term treatment.

The Comprehensive Emergency Services for Children in Crisis program has served as a model in the field of multidisciplinary community projects throughout the United States. Its success is measured in large part by a decrease in the number of children who are separated from their families and an increase in the number of reports received. The strength of the program rests in the coordination of various community agencies that can be mobilized depending on the individual circumstances of a case. The CES program recognizes that child maltreatment is not merely a legal or medical problem; instead, it arises from interrelated causal conditions that require varying kinds of remediation.

### Project Protection

Montgomery County, Maryland, a suburb of Washington, D.C., has one of the highest median incomes of any community in the United States. The educational level of its residents is also well above average. Could child maltreatment exist in this enlightened, affluent community? The brutal death of a nine-year-old girl at the hands of her parents spurred the community to action. County health, social service, and law enforcement agencies, as well as the school district, joined together to initiate a comprehensive community plan for dealing with child maltreatment. The protective services and public health agency personnel were significantly increased to a level adequate to investigate reported suspicions of maltreatment. In addition, a multidisciplinary treatment team was formed to study each confirmed case and plan a program suited to the unique needs of that family.

Project Protection is the Montgomery County school district's component of the community approach to child maltreatment. Begun in 1974 with federal funding, Project Protection is a three-pronged approach to child maltreatment. First, a policy statement on maltreatment was developed that sets guidelines concerning what constitutes child maltreatment. Also, this statement explains procedures for teacher reporting of suspected cases and advocates that if a teacher is in doubt, he or she should report for the sake of the child.

The second and largest phase of this project involves staff development. Training sessions for teachers are held during regularly scheduled faculty meetings to acquaint teachers with the signs of maltreatment as they may be manifest in the classroom. Further, teachers are reminded of their legal obligation to report suspected abuse and are given training sessions on how to report, what happens during report investigation, and what kinds of services are available within the community to aid families in which child maltreatment is confirmed. In addition, student assemblies, private school faculties, PTA groups, and other community organizations are encouraged to request informational programs for their members, and thousands of people have been reached through these media. It is recognized that coupling heightened awareness of maltreatment in both educators and the community is an important step in fighting maltreatment.

The third phase of Project Protection involves incorporating information on maltreatment into the school curriculum. In courses and units designed to prepare students for parenthood, children learn about healthy child development – an important factor – since maltreating parents frequently have unrealistic expectations for their children. The topic of violence is discussed in regard to social attitudes that condone it generally and support its use with children in particular. The importance of learning to cope with stress and crises makes up another part of preparation for parenthood since crises often precipitate child maltreatment. In addition to these areas of study, students learn of the community resources available to aid both the maltreated child and the family.

In 1971, twelve cases of suspected maltreatment were reported in Montgomery County; in 1974, over two hundred cases were forwarded to protective services for investigation.[6] The increased incidence of detection is heartening; even more encouraging is the potential for prevention that such a program suggests. Help through the schools may identify marginal cases before they become serious incidents of maltreatment; education on parenting may teach future parents positive ways to deal with their own children.

### Project THRIVE

In 1975 the National Urban League established a child maltreatment resource project called Project THRIVE. Funded by a federal grant, Project THRIVE operates in Indianapolis, Indiana, and Columbus, Ohio, providing supportive assistance to groups and institutions concerned with the issue of maltreatment, especially as it relates to black families. Its services include developing and disseminating information on child maltreatment to nontraditional agencies such as churches and settlement houses. In addition, its staff serves as consultants to law enforcement and social service agencies by explaining procedures to families and advising them of resources and alternatives available to them within the community. Concerned with the unique position of the black family in American society, Project THRIVE attempts to supplement existing services to maltreating families while it keeps intact the cultural characteristics of the family in the lives of blacks.

### The Parent Resource Center

The Parent Resource Center in Orlando, Florida, is a private, nonprofit organization concerned with a variety of services designed to strengthen family relationships. Its major thrust is toward improved parent education, and its classes, workshops, and seminars include prenatal, maternity, and neonatal care patterns, parent discussion groups, and playshops in which parents learn to make toys of household objects. In addition, an Infant Enrichment Laboratory helps parents learn about their newborns, while the Parent/Child Cooperative School provides parents with direct participation in the education of their preschoolers.

One of the most innovative services sponsored by the Parent Resource Center is its Cousins Respite Care Program. The center trains paid caretakers to provide for the needs of mentally, emotionally, or physically handicapped children so that parents can leave the youngster in capable hands while they pursue activities outside the home. This service, in which caretakers enter the home and temporarily relieve the parents of the continuous care such special children require, seems significant in regard to child maltreatment, for research suggests that exceptional children constitute a high-risk group in regard to abuse and neglect. Parental knowledge that help is available when the constant pressures of care for a handicapped child become overwhelming seems likely to decrease the incidence of maltreatment; thus, the cousins program can be viewed as a preventive scheme for a specific target population designed to head off abuse and neglect before they occur.

### Parents' Center Project

The Parents' Center Project for the Study and Prevention of Child Abuse is the creation of a small private social agency in Boston. Begun in 1968, the Parents' Center Project accepts physically maltreating families on a referral basis from child protective services. The project has two basic goals: to help the preschool child develop as an individual at a day-care facility and to aid parents through its Parents' Group to learn to care for their children lovingly.

Though the Parents' Center Project is not large, it suggests that a two-pronged approach to treatment of the maltreating family is feasible. Rather than concentrate solely on children or parents, the Parents' Center Project aims to offer treatment to both until they reach the level of growth at which they can deal with each other constructively. It should be emphasized that this program deals only with child maltreatment involving physical abuse and excludes all families in which other forms of maltreatment occur.

### Extended Family Center

The Extended Family Center in San Francisco was established in 1973 as a three-year demonstration project with support from the Office of Child Development. Like the Parents' Center Project, the Extended Family Center offers day-care facilities to help maltreated children develop to their potential and group parent sessions that break isolation and help adults learn good parenting techniques. The Extended Family Center employs formerly maltreating mothers to work with adults. These mothers help facilitate communication and trust between the parents receiving treatment and the professional staff. In addition to group therapy, parents also attend occupational therapy sessions that are used as a way to measure treatment progress. As parents begin to complete projects, as they reluctantly and then enthusiastically tackle new tasks, their self-esteem and ability to cope with life are seen to improve. These are good signs that the parents may be better able to perform their parenting roles in the future than they have in the past.

### Parents Anonymous

Parents Anonymous is a self-help program with hundreds of chapters throughout the United States and Canada. Its cofounders were Jolly K., a maltreating parent, and Leonard L. Leiber, a protective services worker. Together they helped organize groups of maltreating parents who knew they needed assistance in dealing with the pressures of parenthood. The parent groups meet frequently under the guidance of a professional to discuss their situations and share techniques that have been successful for them in regard to their children. Maltreating parents learn that they are not the only people in the world who have ever taken their frustrations out on their children. Through group contacts, parents come to feel accepted as people and begin to lose their self-loathing, while their self-images improve as they receive reinforcement from others.

Through a grant from the National Center on Child Abuse and Neglect, Parents Anonymous established a twenty-four-hour toll-free telephone system available to any parent throughout the nation who feels overwhelmed and wants to talk. Both Parents Anonymous groups and the crisis hot line offer empathic listeners for parents who need to know that someone cares.

### Santa Clara Child Sexual Abuse Treatment Program

The Santa Clara Child Sexual Abuse Treatment Program in San Jose, California, was the first comprehensive service designed to aid both the sexual offender and his young victim. The program offers counseling and therapy for both children and their parents. Most of the victims are girls who need to be relieved of the guilt they feel because of their abuse and the subsequent breakup of the family unit. Daughters United, the therapy group for victims, allows the girls to deal openly with their feelings and work out many of the emotions that might otherwise lead them to promiscuity, drugs, and early marriages or to run away. Parents United, the adult group for both offenders and their wives, attempts to have the parents take responsibility for the abuse as a mutual problem often stemming from basic marital stress or incompatibility.

The goal of the Santa Clara Child Sexual Abuse Treatment Program is to eliminate both the maltreatment and its causes, thus allowing the family to remain intact. Most clients spend between six months and one year in the program; follow-up studies reveal that the incidence of recidivism is very low. Its success has stimulated other communities to develop similar programs.

### Family Stress Center

The Family Stress Center in Chula Vista, California, is a community-based program that attempts to expand and improve the comprehensive nature of services to maltreating families. Partially funded by the YMCA, the Family Stress Center has as its dual purpose the prevention of neglect and abuse and the amelioration of the consequences of maltreatment. Its efforts in the field of prevention include a hot line for parents under stress, parenting classes, public awareness activities, couple and family counseling, in-home services of parent aides who show parents how to deal with the routine tasks of domestic life and child rearing, crisis nursery facilities, and in-home baby-sitting services.

In the area of treatment for abusing or neglecting families the Family Stress Center works in careful coordination with other agencies operating in San Diego County. The center is prepared to intervene in crisis situations within maltreating homes, provide medical care for a child, or refer the child to protective services if he or she is endangered in the home. Long-term treatment for maltreated children involves attendance at the Family Stress Center's child-care facility for preschoolers, play or individual therapy as required, and specialized assistance from professionals in such areas as physical or speech therapy.

Parents are afforded individual, couple, and family counseling as appropriate, education services on child rearing, crisis nursery facilities, day care for their children, transportation to and from the center, and homemaking services and baby-sitting as needed. Further, the Family Stress Center is aware of and utilizes facilities provided by both private and public agencies within the community to supplement the services it offers.

## Conclusion

In the past few years there has been increased awareness of and concern for the maltreating family as a unit with multiple needs. In response a number of programs have been developed to provide varying kinds of assistance to eliminate abusive and neglectful parenting patterns and replace them with constructive techniques that foster positive family relationships.

However, efforts on the federal, state, and local levels through social service agencies remain inadequate to deal with the multidimensional nature of child maltreatment. Although community-based programs have been instituted to supply services not previously available, most are limited in their effectiveness by being localized; others are hamstrung by perpetual financial insecurity that threatens their existence. Further, so busy are such workers in dealing with the crush of maltreatment cases reported to them that there has been only token development of programs aimed at the prevention of abuse and neglect.

Some tentative movements have been made to involve schools in communitywide responses to the problem of child maltreatment. Montgomery County Maryland's Project Protection, discussed in this chapter, represents such an effort. In other areas, state commissions of education attempt to provide guidelines for local school districts to employ in regard to maltreatment. For a variety of reasons such recommendations are frequently ignored or so drastically altered as to be impotent.

The involvement of schools and their personnel in preventing child maltreatment, dealing with it in cases of marginal abuse and neglect, and reporting incidents of serious maltreatment while providing services for families stands as the missing link in the chain of maltreatment programs now available in most communities. The trends in the field during the past decade suggest that in the next few years, schools and educators throughout the country will be asked and then required to assume responsibility as the front-line force in a concerted effort to eliminate child maltreatment. It is time for schools and teachers to begin to accept the silent challenge of the abused and neglected children they claim to serve.

## References

1. Vincent DeFrancis, *Termination of Parental Rights: Balancing the Equities* (Denver: American Humane Association, 1971), p. 9.
2. Elizabeth Philbrick, *Treating Parental Pathology Through Child Protective Services* (Denver: American Humane Society, 1960), p. 1.
3. Vincent DeFrancis, *The Status of Child Protective Services: A National Assessment* (Denver: American Humane Association, 1971), p. 9.
4. Douglas J. Besharov, *Child Abuse and Neglect Reports*, DHEW pub. no. 76-30086 (Washington, D.C.: U.S. Government Printing Office, February 1976), p. 15.
5. Ray E. Helfer, *The Diagnostic Process and Treatment Programs*, DHEW pub. no. 75-69 (Washington, D.C.: U. S. Government Printing Office, 1975), p. 41.
6. Diane D. Broadhurst, "Project Protection: A School Program to Detect and Prevent Child Abuse and Neglect," *Children Today*, May-June 1975, p. 25.

# CHAPTER 7

# How can teachers help maltreated children and their families?

If each school were to establish a comprehensive program to identify maltreated children and to offer maltreating parents services to learn positive ways to deal with their children, the incidence of child abuse and neglect would decrease dramatically. Yet, for a number of reasons, many schools are reluctant or unable to establish such a program on a school-wide basis. Perhaps the principal is not committed to the task of school intervention in cases of maltreatment; he or she may feel that there are more pressing matters that demand the school's attention. It may be that teachers are unwilling to become involved to the extent necessary for a comprehensive plan to be effective. In some communities, parents vehemently deny that maltreatment exists in their neighborhood and remain unsupportive of school efforts to become involved in dealing with maltreated children and their families.

Is there then no alternative to school-wide commitment in the field of maltreatment? Such a conclusion denies the potential for constructive action that an individual or small group of teachers within a school can exercise. Either alone or in partnership with others, teachers have provided the impetus for many innovative programs that later have become widespread and accepted practices. The same can be true in dealing with maltreated children and their maltreating parents.

Evidence supporting the need for involvement of teachers in the lives of maltreated children is compelling. The terms *abuse* and *neglect* scare some people; yet, it must be remembered that these conditions exist not in the abstract, but as factors that affect children with whom teachers deal daily. Because of the nature of existing programs, only the most severely maltreated youngsters currently receive any assistance, either because cases are not reported to social service agencies or because treatment and follow-up projects are inadequate. And what of the large number of marginally maltreated youngsters for whom no laws provide protection? The message is clear: teachers must begin to identify and work with maltreated children and their parents as part of their professional obligation to meet the needs of each youngster in their charge.

Schools have long understood that the home is an important agent in the life of each child, either for good or ill. Presently many teachers work routinely with parents to facilitate the growth of children. Others are reluctant to involve parents in the school's efforts to aid its students. For both these groups of teachers, identifying and dealing with maltreating families offers tremendous potential for some of the most gratifying professional experiences any teacher can have.

## Identifying maltreated children through existing evaluative procedures

How can a teacher use the existing facilities and procedures of a school to spot children suffering from maltreatment? Much of the data that researchers have brought to light may be employed as a starting point. For instance, it is well to keep in mind that the incidence of maltreatment among special education students is far higher than in the general population; thus, a teacher concerned with abused and neglected children should be especially cognizant of the possibility of maltreatment among these exceptional children. Research also suggests that economic factors are tied to maltreatment, at least in a contributory way. Children whose families suffer various kinds of deprivation deserve careful analysis to determine if poor parenting behavior results in maltreatment.

Whether aware of it or not, teachers are involved in a five-step process when dealing with children: analyzing the needs of a youngster, planning a course of action to meet those needs, implementing the individualized prescription, evaluating the success of the plan, and monitoring the progress of the youngster on a continuing basis.

Shortly after the opening of school each year, teachers begin to identify a variety of individual differences in children in regard to both academic performance and behavior. Teachers plan and carry out individualized academic programs and appropriate interactional techniques to maximize intellectual and personal growth for each youngster. Yet, despite the best efforts of teachers, many children do not succeed at satisfactory rates; others make normal gains but do not achieve as well as they might. It then becomes the teacher's task to learn of the factors that hamper the youngster's development and to attempt to eliminate or ameliorate them.

The teacher must consider a number of explanations for a child's inadequate progress:

1. Is the problem a result of the child's handicap, either physical or mental?

2. Is the problem a product of the classroom or school environment?
3. Is the problem induced by the circumstances of the child's family life?
4. Is the problem a consequence of maltreatment within the home?
5. Is the problem multifaceted?

### Preliminary analysis

Preliminary analysis often points clearly to one factor as responsible for a child's unsatisfactory progress in school. For instance, if the youngster complains that he or she cannot see the chalkboard, it seems advisable to have the child's vision checked. In other cases, when test scores indicate learning disabilities or low intelligence, the teacher must modify academic expectations for the youngster. In many instances, however, a student's lack of growth requires more in-depth investigation to uncover causal factors.

For many children the school itself may impose barriers to satisfactory progress. Some children find the program of instruction inadequate to meet their needs despite many efforts to individualize it. The result is that children experience considerable frustration that can retard growth as it leads to serious acting-out or withdrawal behavior.

### Classroom management techniques and school-wide policies

Another factor that cannot be ignored involves classroom management techniques. Teachers and schools sometimes are responsible for creating or at least aggravating some of their most serious problems. For instance, a high frequency of negative comments from a teacher is reinforcing, albeit negatively, to children striving for attention. Although the teacher may believe his or her remarks are correcting student behavior, frequently they encourage children to be more disruptive. On a recent visit to a classroom I heard a teacher say to a youngster, "You will regret the day you were born!" This threat was followed by, "How dumb can you be?" Children can sense when a teacher does not like or accept them even through more subtle statements than these. Like all human beings, children respond negatively to people who are unaccepting of them. Furthermore, youngsters learn that their misbehavior brings them recognition from adults as well as status from their peers. To the child who receives little attention at home, even negative reward is appealing. Thus a teacher's attitude toward youngsters can foster misbehavior and resentment while it hampers academic growth.

Just as the negativism of an individual teacher can interfere with the development of young people, so school-wide policies can be detrimental to youngsters. Corporal punishment often aggravates the conditions it is employed to eliminate. It teaches that power and not respect, force and not reason, hold sway in dealing with people who displease us. Fear of physical punishment causes many children to withdraw, stifles their creativity, and robs them of the opportunity to learn self-control and self-discipline. Further, research indicates that children who are physically punished have lower achievement and IQ test scores than children who receive other kinds of discipline. In short, the evidence is compelling for the elimination of corporal punishment from all schools. If such a course of action is not taken school wide, however, an individual teacher can decide both not to employ corporal punishment and to protect his or her students from it.

Thus, teachers who rely on verbal abuse or physical punishment are sometimes responsible for interfering with the development of their students. More educationally sound classroom-management techniques include involving students in the establishment of rules and the consequences for breaking them, setting up procedures to provide feedback to children prior to imposing consequences, rewarding positive behavior, helping children explore their values, feelings, and actions, allowing youngsters to learn on their own from their mistakes, and planning and structuring classroom activities to maximize effectiveness. The teacher who provides structure, consistency, and loving concern eliminates many discipline problems within the classroom while greatly facilitating learning.

### Family and home environment

Many children's problems in school stem from their family and home environment. A child whose family has recently or frequently moved may need special assistance to adjust to the new community. The child whose family has just been enlarged by the arrival of a baby brother or sister often experiences a period of regression while attempting to redefine his or her role within the family. In some cases a family may not be meeting the physical or emotional needs of a child; still other homes are physically, sexually, or verbally abusive. How can a teacher concerned with the optimal growth of every youngster learn if home factors are at the root of a child's lack of development?

### The child

Substantial information on each child enrolled in a school is contained in the school records. Certainly, a teacher should consult this information as soon as he or she becomes concerned about the progress of a student. The child is another revealing source. Not only does the child's performance on tests and behavior in class tell the perceptive teacher a great deal about the youngster, but also the child can provide a great deal of factual data about his or her life. Further, brothers and sisters reveal large amounts of information that aid the teacher in understanding a child.

Verbal children who want to interact with the teacher are particularly willing to share their experiences; a great deal of insight can be gained by the teacher while listening to a child. Young children are especially anxious to talk about themselves to their teachers. Wise teachers make time available to learn as much as possible about the children in their charge.

An anecdote seems appropriate at this point. A teacher recently told me of an incident that occurred in her class several years ago. A youngster approached her desk and matter-of-factly announced, "It's a good thing my father is in jail now or else he would have got my other sisters pregnant too." Investigation initiated by the teacher through a social service agency revealed that sexual abuse had been occurring within this family for nearly a decade. The oldest girl in the family had been impregnated by her father when she was thirteen years old, and the pattern of physical intimacy was being repeated with an eleven-year-old daughter. Because the youngster felt close enough to his teacher to expose this family secret and because the educator recognized her responsibility to report this incident to the governmental agency designed to investigate it, help was forthcoming for the family. The father was prosecuted for his actions and received extensive counseling after his release from jail. He was able to reenter the family, and to date there has been no repetition of his incestuous behavior. Thus, a student's comment to a responsive adult aided a family to become a functional unit and saved all its members from continued long-term injury.

Needless to say, this story is a dramatic one, and few teachers may ever be confronted with such a blatant confession of maltreatment within a family. Yet, many of the small incidents children recount to their teachers create a composite picture of marginal abuse or neglect. In this way the teacher is aided in understanding the circumstances of children's lives.

### Children's reactions to the principal

One technique I found useful as an elementary school principal in helping teachers assess the children in their charge was employed on the very first day of school each year. When visiting kindergarten and first grade classes, I would introduce myself as the principal and ask, "Do any of you know what the job of the principal is?" Spontaneously and without hesitation, four or five children would call out in chorus, "You beat us when we're bad." Interestingly, the school had banned the use of corporal punishment, so the youngsters' response could not be attributed to the tales of older brothers and sisters. These children's belief that the principal whips children was a clue to the harsh physical punishment they had received at home and to their parents' threats that the school doled out the same penalty for misbehavior. Further, it is noteworthy that the children already viewed themselves as "bad." So conditioned were they to punishment that they did not say "if" they misbehaved they would be punished, but rather "when." Already they possessed a fatalism about themselves and the way they would be perceived and treated by adults. Such encounters with children can be almost as revealing of situations in the child's life that impede healthy development as direct statements. The teacher who is concerned to know more about a child than his or her score on a particular test must make use of all avenues of information to gain a complete picture of a youngster.

### Class discussions

Another way teachers can learn about the youngsters in their care is through class discussions. Activities designed to encourage children to talk about their feelings and concerns are growth experiences for children and enlightening times for teachers. Many teachers use word or phrase activities to help youngsters explore their attitudes and values. One teacher I know was able to learn a great deal about children by presenting them with open-ended statements like, "When I think of mother, I _____" and "Daddy is _____" Over the course of two or three such sessions a revealing pattern emerges of youngsters' attitudes toward their families and themselves.

### Assessment: observation and hypothesis

In the early stages of assessment it is often advisable to ask a colleague to observe the classroom to provide some objective information. The data derived from conferencing on such observations often affords new insights to the teacher. For instance, the observer may discover basic interactional patterns within the class that the teacher was too involved to notice. In other instances an observer offers the teacher an opportunity to test his or her perceptions against those of another person. This process of feedback can lead to confirmation of the teacher's original analysis, modification based on added information, or outright rejection.

After initial assessment of the needs of the children in a classroom, teachers can begin to formulate plans specifically designed to be most beneficial to each individual. In cases in which family factors are believed to be impeding the growth of a youngster, the teacher may wish to confirm a hypothesis before taking action on it. In such instances individual conferences with children can be structured in line with the teacher's tentative judgment of the youngster's problem and its source. A few examples may clarify this point.

### Individual conferences

A teacher I know believed it likely that one of her students was harshly punished at home. She hypothesized that his bullying, physically aggressive behavior stemmed from the marginally abusive treatment he received from his parents. She engaged in a dialogue with the child to test her theories:

> *Mrs. Jones:* Charles, you are not following the rule about not hitting other children. What is your reason for this?
> *Charles:* The other kids bother me.

> *Mrs. Jones:* What are you supposed to do when someone bothers you?
> *Charles:* Tell you.
> *Mrs. Jones:* What do you do if one of your brothers bothers you?
> *Charles:* Hit him back.
> *Mrs. Jones:* What do your parents do when you misbehave at home?
> *Charles:* My mother yells at me, and my father whips me.
> *Mrs. Jones:* When you do good things at home, what do your mother and father do?
> *Charles:* I don't know. They buy me things or take me places.
> *Mrs. Jones:* What else do your parents say or do when you are good?

This line of questioning is geared to assess both the amount of physical punishment and of reward the youngster receives at home. It must be remembered that children's responses will not always be totally accurate; yet, in most cases they reflect the child's perception of how the parents deal with and feel about him or her. It is the youngster's view of their treatment of him or her that is both important and revealing.

Another teacher had a student who came to school in dirty, uncared-for clothing. The teacher suspected that the child was marginally neglected physically and was not receiving the love and affection she needed to develop normally. The dialogue in this case went as follows:

> *Mr. Green:* Jenny, who helps you get washed and dressed in the morning?
> *Jenny:* Nobody. I do it myself.
> *Mr. Green:* You looked very nice in that blue dress you had on last week.
> *Jenny:* Did I?
> *Mr. Green:* Yes. At your house, who does the chores?
> *Jenny:* My mother has been sick since she had the new baby. She does some things but she gets tired. I cook the meals.
> *Mr. Green:* Is your mother happy that you help her?
> *Jenny:* I don't know.
> *Mr. Green:* How does your mother show you she is pleased with you?

In this case the teacher wants to test his hypotheses about physical and emotional neglect. One such conference in private with a student may be insufficient to confirm or reject his suspicions. In this instance it is unclear whether or not there is a father residing with the family, how long the mother has been ill, or if the illness of the mother is a rationalization the child adopts to protect her from criticism. Certainly, even this short private conversation suggests that the teacher is justified in continuing his inquiries until he can amass sufficient information upon which to base a sound judgment of the source of his student's difficulties.

## The child study team

Once a teacher has gathered data on children experiencing difficulty in terms of educational, social, and emotional growth, the most profitable strategy on which to proceed to help a youngster is the child study team approach. This approach is concerned not only with maltreated children, but with all youngsters who are having trouble achieving to their potential. The team approach offers teachers the chance to receive feedback from their colleagues. Ideally, four or five teachers who work with children of similar ages may compose a team. A group leader should be selected to co-ordinate the activities of the team. In many schools, groups that fit these criteria presently exist as committees that evaluate youngsters for placement in exceptional child programs, guidance committees, or team teaching groups. It is the goal of the child study team to help teachers plan and carry out the best kind of individualized program to assist each child.

Social workers and mental health personnel have learned that the best way to get advice from their colleagues is to place all the information they have gathered into a compact presentation. Most teachers have little experience with organizing the data they acquire on a youngster; in this regard they can learn from the social worker's format. The child study team should establish a procedure by which teachers can come before the team to present case studies of the youngsters they work with who need help. Other team members assist the teacher in evaluating the evidence presented, suggesting possible causes for the youngster's difficulties, and planning strategies to eliminate them.

A case presentation begins with factual data on the child, including name, age, and physical description. Next, the teacher briefly expresses the nature of his or her concern. If the educator believes that the child's home environment is contributing to the problem, this opinion should be expressed at this time.

All acquired background on the youngster should be summarized so that team members have a perspective on the case. Information should include the youngster's performance on IQ and achievement tests, past performance in school, and attendance patterns. A detailed medical report should be included, especially if there is evidence of physical abuse or medical or physical neglect. Next, a complete social history of the child and the family should be recounted. This part of the case presentation may review previous anecdotal evaluations by teachers, past parent-school contacts, information on the size and age composition of the family, its economic status, where and with whom the child has lived, and any other pertinent data. Also, it may be advisable to indicate how well the targeted child is developing in comparison to siblings who have been or presently are enrolled in the school. If additional data have been gathered on sibling relationships, it may be included at this point. In short, any information on family dynamics over time that has been learned either directly from the child or from other sources should be presented at this stage.

In regard to the child's present status, detailed reporting of social, emotional, and academic performance should be reviewed. Included here may be samples of the child's work, observation reports by a colleague who has watched the child in the classroom, and brief anecdotes on his or her behavior. The teacher should next review the steps he or she has taken to date to deal with the child and evaluate their level of success.

Based on the accumulated evidence, the teacher next states his or her tentative conclusions concerning the nature of the child's problems and their probable causes. At this point, the rest of the child study team becomes involved in discussing the case with particular reference to the causes of the child's difficulties and ways to ameliorate them.

Two kinds of recommendations are normally put forth as a result of a case presentation. First, team members discuss and decide what steps can be taken within the school to deal with the youngster's problems. This in-school approach may call for a cooperative effort by many of the teachers and special service personnel of the school, but it does not require that parents play any role. The second kind of recommendation a child study team often agrees on includes a strategy for parental involvement. Depending on the case, a single parent-teacher conference may be sufficient to bring to the attention of the parents the school's concern for the child. In other cases more extensive school-home contact as well as the involvement of community and social service agencies may be required. It is the nature of the individual case that determines the strategy recommended for solving the unique problems of the youngster.

The case presentation process in conjunction with the child study team approach offers a number of benefits and comparatively minor detriments. It requires a teacher to learn a great deal more about a child than he or she might otherwise, for many sources must be investigated to gather all the data the child study team needs to understand the case. The team offers the teacher worthwhile feedback on his or her analysis and efforts to date, as well as new approaches that may be used in the classroom, alternative strategies to develop home contacts, and a sense of confidence through the group decision-making process. The only disadvantage of the case presentation format is that the process of information gathering is time consuming because of its thoroughness. Certainly, this investment of time and energy is a small price to pay when compared to the benefits that children can ultimately reap from the process.

A word of caution should be added here. If case presentations are poorly prepared or if teachers are unwilling to accept the tentative recommendations of the child study team, the entire process breaks down into a series of unproductive, frustrating sessions. It is for this reason that the role of the team leader is crucial, for he or she can work with teachers before they present cases so that they are aware of both the level of preparation required and the cooperative element implicit in the team approach. Poorly handled, the child study team degenerates into a nonfunctioning unit; well managed, it can be a potent force for the improvement of the lives of youngsters.

Teachers also need to be alert to the issue of confidentiality relative to school records. Recent federal court rulings have stipulated that a child's cumulative record is open for the parents' inspection. If information acquired during the process of investigation were placed in a child's record, it potentially could be embarrassing and even damaging to the child, the family, and school personnel. The wise educator not only understands the tentative nature of his or her analyses, conclusions, and plan of action, but also takes the necessary precautions to share such information only with people who need to know about it. Further, the educator maintains child study team records in a location separate from cumulative records so that access to them can be limited. This is not to say that the case data is kept secret from the family involved or from the educators who try to assess the child and parents. Yet, because of the unofficial nature of such evaluative information and the somewhat speculative character of its contents, it seems necessary to protect both the child and the family from the public exposure of such data and at the same time shield educators from charges of impropriety.

The case conference presentation that follows should be useful to persons involved in the implementation of this process as part of their maltreatment prevention program.

---

## SAMPLE CASE CONFERENCE PRESENTATION

**Physical description**

Billy Jones is seven years old, male, white. His build is slight, his skin is very pale, and he has about him the gaunt look of malnutrition. On his left arm are three marks: two bruises and a sore. All three appear to have been recently acquired.

**Major concerns**

Billy worries me for the following reasons:
1. At lunchtime he frequently asks for a second helping and, when asked about his large appetite, explains that he does not eat breakfast at home.
2. He is listless in class and often just wants to sit during recess. Billy has fallen asleep on three different occasions in the last month.
3. Billy's schoolwork is below average and more appropriate to a first grader than to a child in the second grade.
4. The marks on Billy's arm give me some concern. The sore continues to ooze. I wash and bandage it daily because he is receiving no treatment for it at home. Billy explains the injuries as the result of a fall he took last week. He says his parents say that bumps are a part of growing up and that they will heal soon.
5. Billy has worn only two different shirts all year, and often his clothes are dirty.
6. Mr. and Mrs. Jones, Billy's parents, have failed to respond to either of the two letters I wrote to them explaining that Billy needs a good breakfast daily. I would call the home, but they have no telephone. From my observations and discussions with Billy I believe his parents are neglecting some of his basic needs, specifically in regard to medical care, clothing, and food.

**Background information**

Billy has been in attendance at our school since the beginning of this school year. The records indicate that the Jones family moved here from Opelika, Alabama, during July and that Mrs. Jones registered Billy on the first day of school. The records from Opelika indicate that

---

*Continued.*

Billy received C and D grades and behaved well in class. The comment on the permanent record folder states, "Billy gets along with the other children, but needs lots of encouragement to finish his work." His medical records indicate that all required immunizations have been completed and that no major illnesses or injuries are present. His achievement tests, administered in April of last school year, indicate readiness level in mathematics and reading. No IQ test data is available. Last year Billy attended school 123 days out of the required 180 days and was promoted to the second grade. He did not attend a public or private kindergarten. This year he has been absent 14 days out of the first 45-day marking period, but not for more than 3 days at any one time.

### Social history

I have not had personal contact with Billy's parents but have asked Mrs. Auburn, the school secretary who registered Billy, what she can recollect from that experience. Mrs. Auburn clearly recalls that Mrs. Jones was not able to read all the directions on the registration sheet and asked for assistance. She also indicates that Mrs. Jones was "sloppy" in dress, seemed unsure of herself, and had difficulty managing the other children in her family. Billy was present at the registration and was asked to take care of the younger children by Mrs. Jones. Mrs. Auburn also remembers that the children were not very clean and were not wearing shoes. She did not remember whether there were two or three other children, but a review of the records indicates three younger siblings: John, age 4; Mary, age 3; and James, age 18 months. The only other relevant information that I have been able to acquire relates to the father's work. He is listed as a day worker; the mother is not employed. Records do not indicate their educational attainment.

### Present performance

The summary statements presented in earlier sections of this review are indicative of Billy's present performance. Academically, he is achieving on the readiness level in reading and making progress in math. At the beginning of the year he could not count past nineteen or recognize letters in the alphabet other than those in his name and then only in sequence. He can now count to 100 and recognize fourteen letters in the alphabet. He also has acquired a word recognition ability with four words other than his name. His writing is poor. He cannot write on lines nor recollect letters from memory. He can write the numbers 1 to 20 from memory but inverts the numbers 2, 3, and 5.

Socially, Billy seems to be fairly well accepted by the other children. He never bothers other children and tries to be friends even though a few of the children have made fun of him because his clothing was torn on several occasions. Also, when he came to school one cold day without a coat, some of the children kidded him. Billy simply walked away, hung his head, and was upset for about 30 minutes. Afterward, he went back to his work as if nothing had occurred. The children also have teased him about sleeping in class and have called him "slow poke" because he does not get his work done on time.

Emotionally, Billy seems fairly well adjusted. In light of the criticism from other children, he seems to withstand it much better than other children with whom I have worked. He does not get upset when I correct his work but tries to do better. I have also noticed that he responds more positively to the children and me after lunch than in the morning when he seems to be dragging himself to class and that while comments are made to him that cause him to be upset and withdrawn in the morning, the same comments made after lunch do not elicit withdrawal. Instead, he seems to ignore them.

Mrs. Gray has observed him on two 15-minute occasions, one in the morning and once in the afternoon. She reports on his listless behavior in the morning with little accomplished during a group writing lesson, but his more attentive behavior with greater accomplishment after lunch.

---

### SAMPLE CASE CONFERENCE PRESENTATION—cont'd

**Actions**

Actions taken by me to help Billy can be summarized as follows:

1. I realized that my comments to Billy needed to be made in private because the other children were picking up on them.
2. I have given him candy on two occasions in the morning and have noticed that his activity level and work performance increased considerably.
   ave given him a little more individual attention than the other children, and he seems have responded to this treatment.
4. I have begun to establish a warm relationship with Billy. On three days he came to me and asked for some more candy, and he has also requested my assistance with his work.
5. For now, I believe that I have made some progress with Billy in his work and will begin to emphasize his achievements to the other children so that negative criticism from them can be reduced.

**Tentative conclusions**

1. Billy is not getting adequate care at home, particularly in areas of medical treatment, sufficient food in the morning, and the appropriate clothing, particularly on cold days.
2. Billy appears to be of average or low-average intelligence, as evidenced by the fact that he responds reasonably well to the teaching of new information. If in attendance for one week without a break, he makes substantial progress.
3. Because Billy responds much better socially, emotionally, and academically after lunch or on the occasions when given food in the morning, it is likely that the lack of breakfast is affecting his performance.
4. Billy appears to have a reasonably good self-concept. He accepts criticism and rebounds well from such treatment by the children.
5. The Joneses are either unaware of or not able at this time to care for the needs of the child.

**Recommendations**

1. Because the relationship with Billy is developing along positive lines, it is desirable to discuss with him a little more about his family. Focus particularly on the breakfast situation; who gets up when he does, if it is possible for Billy to make his own breakfast, etc. Also, ascertain the reasons for his absences.
2. Continue to provide individual attention and reshape peer attitudes.
3. Send positive notes, with accompanying work papers, to parents and invite parents to school as an open invitation.
4. Make a home visit after school to establish relationship with the parents. This effort should be a preliminary introduction and a rapport-building session that could be followed up soon after by a parent visit to the school.
5. Discuss with Billy his medical experiences, particularly times when he has gone to the doctor, and the reasons for his visits.

---

Ideally, the above case study would be prepared one week in advance for distribution to the study team. The team, in turn, would review it, be prepared at the next session to question the presenter, and assist in the development of recommendations for the treatment plan. This procedure, with the inclusion of student work samples and other relevant documents like letters sent to and from parents and teachers' observation reports, would save substantial time during the case conference presentation. An alternative plan is, of course, to read and distribute the materials at the time of presentation.

For organizational purposes, it is also desirable to ask questions of the presenter in some kind of systematic manner. That is, questions about the child's physical description should be entertained first, followed by "concerns." If the case is presented at the meeting, it is desirable not to interrupt the presenter until he or she has completed each individual section. Questions relevant to that section would be entertained at its conclusion. It is also desirable to have a person take notes in regard to additional information that should be acquired. This procedure will allow the presenter to maintain full attention to the case.

An acceptable alternative is to allow the presenter to complete the entire case presentation before entertaining questions. The approach selected will depend on the ability of group members to use time well, for if they get bogged down with one section, the case may not be fully covered.

Well-organized teams with strong leaders who know what to do in advance and are well prepared ought to be able to handle two cases an hour. If a case is not prepared in advance for study by the other team members, it is likely that it will take an hour to present and discuss.

## Implementing a two-pronged approach in helping maltreating families

The recommendations of the child study team are designed to assist the child both in and out of school. Modifications in a teacher's expectations for a youngster may have to be made as a result of a thorough investigation of his or her difficulties. In addition to varied teaching techniques that the child's unique circumstances require, the teacher may find that he or she must adopt new methods to deal with the social and emotional aspects of the child. Perhaps the teacher must show the child a great deal of affection and attention to convince the youngster of his or her worth; it may be that the child requires structured activities with built-in rewards to encourage him or her to carry a task to completion. There are many techniques with which most teachers are familiar that can be called upon, depending on the needs of the child.

Concurrent with adaptations in the experiences the child receives in the classroom, the teacher should initiate contact with the youngster's parents. At this stage, it is well to review all that is known about the family, its knowledge of and attitude toward the school, and any previous experiences school personnel may have had with the parents. This information is crucial in assessing how receptive parents will be to overtures from the teacher.

Before any attempt is made to contact parents, each teacher must evaluate his or her counseling and conferencing skills, for the teacher who is unfamiliar with or insecure in the area of good human relations has little chance of enlisting the cooperation of parents. The effective teacher-counselor should be able to—

1. Establish rapport with parents
2. Listen to feelings as well as to words
3. Encourage parents to clarify their feelings
4. Keep conferences on task
5. Show empathy for both the parents and the child
6. Communicate feelings of openness, trust, and confidentiality
7. Recognize his or her own feelings and nonverbal clues while dealing with parents
8. Assess the point beyond which the parents' cooperation will be lost

This list represents only the minimum requirements of a successful counselor. Certainly, these items are not skills peculiar only to practicing psychiatrists and psychologists, for they are basic to the effective administrator and teacher as well. Perhaps they can best be summed up as a caring attitude that is sensitive to the needs of the people involved and to the dynamics of the individual situation.

A parent-teacher conference is not a rarity for most teachers; indeed, parents have less experience with conferences than do teachers. Yet, even though many school districts require periodic parent-teacher conferences either at report card time or as circumstances dictate, few teachers have been trained in conferencing skills. Thus, conferences have become whatever the teacher believes they should be. In too many cases they are held only when a child's academic performance or behavior is so deficient that the teacher feels he or she must inform the parents and get them to exhort their child to do or be better. Under such circumstances many conferences are doomed to failure even before parents and teachers sit down to meet.

Why do parent-teacher conferences fail? Often, the cause is related to a mutual sense of guilt felt by teacher and parent. Sometimes, teachers feel that a conference is an admission of failure and a desperate call for help. In such situations they often become defensive as they try to shift responsibility from themselves to the parents. Parents counter with their own defenses, claiming that the teacher is not doing a good job. Often, parents leave conferences with such hostility and frustration that when they get home, they harshly punish their youngster, either with heavy restrictions or severe whippings. In such cases not only does the parent resent both the teacher and the school, but the child also becomes hostile toward both his or her teacher and parents. It must be remembered that most teachers and parents are making honest attempts to help children grow and develop normally, although they do not always succeed. It does little good to play either the " 'It's your fault'—'No, it's your fault' " or the " 'Well, you're the teacher. Do something'—'Well, you're the parent. Do something' " game in conferences.

In a well-run conference the teacher must act as a guide. He or she must be cognizant of the needs and frustrations of the parent. Further, the teacher must be willing to share both a sense of frustration with the present situation and his or her commitment to its improvement. It is through the establishment of a cooperative positive relationship that conferencing can be successful.

The productive conference results in a plan of action acceptable to both parent and teacher aimed at furthering the welfare of the child. Because the successful conference is a cooperative venture, the teacher must be careful to be nonaccusatory, nonjudgmental, and as nondefensive as possible. If parents exhibit defensive or aggressive behavior, the skillful teacher must attempt to quiet their fears and avoid responding in kind. In short, the successful conference is dependent on both good human relations skills and sound communication techniques that develop a sense of shared responsibility and commitment.

### Preparing for a parent-teacher conference

Having assessed his or her counseling and conferencing skills and having investigated the parents' attitudes toward both self and school, the teacher is ready to consider the advisability of scheduling a parent-teacher conference. Because many parents' contacts with the school are infrequent, the prospect of a conference with their child's teacher is a threatening one. Parents whose children have academic or behavior problems automatically react negatively to the thought of a school conference because they anticipate being told once again how poorly their youngster is doing and, by extension, how inadequate they are as parents. Under such circumstances of dread and defensiveness there is little point in setting up a parent-teacher conference; indeed, it might actually make matters worse. Therefore, it is advisable to employ strategies to predispose parents to view contacts with the school in a positive light.

The process of readying parents for a teacher conference should ideally begin long before presentation of the case to the child study team. A variety of techniques are employed by resourceful teachers who realize that a greater investment of time in these all-important preliminary stages not only will save time later, but also will increase the chances of success while decreasing the amount of frustration. The key to predisposing parents to think positively about the school and teacher is a caring attitude for the child that is communicated to both the youngster and the parents. Even an inadequate parent appreciates knowing that a teacher finds things to praise in his or her child, for the parent is gratified and feels worthwhile when hearing positive comments about his or her youngster.

There are a number of effective strategies teachers implement to enlist parental support for the school. Notes sent home with a child on a regular basis telling of his or her successes in school are greatly appreciated by parents. These letters may mention concerns for future progress and often include an open invitation to the parent to contact the teacher. Early in the school year some teachers telephone parents to introduce themselves and express their willingness to be in contact with the parent. Much can be learned from the parent's tone and responses in such calls. Other teachers encourage parents to participate in school activities, either in the classroom or on field trips. Such invitations are extended in the spirit of cooperation, and it is important that no attempt be made to coerce the parent to comply.

Some teachers follow up their initial parent contacts with visits to the home if parents seem amenable. This face-to-face encounter is designed to establish rapport and allow parent and teacher to become better acquainted. In this nonthreatening, familiar environment, parents often feel free to discuss many details of their parenting duties, and much of the family's social history can be supplemented through such meetings. Often, parents discuss their child's medical history, and this information may clarify an apparent maltreatment situation. For instance, minimal brain damage may result from difficulties during pregnancy, delivery, or shortly after birth; dysfunctions such as hyperactivity may cause the same behavior as maltreatment. When the organic origins of these conditions are uncovered through information supplied by the parent, the suspicion of maltreatment can be discarded. Other teachers inform parents either in person, by telephone, or by letter that they are assessing all students and would be glad for the opportunity to learn of any factors the parent believes would assist in the evaluation. In effect, all these techniques are preliminary contacts designed to make parents view the school as a place concerned with the welfare of children. Their secondary function is to provide the teacher with a sense of what the family is like, how it fulfills its nurturing roles for the child, and what strategies may be employed to help the school and home work together for the benefit of the youngster.

### The parent-teacher conference

Much of the information gathering and all the preliminary contacts with the parent are designed to make the parent-teacher conference a positive experience, with rewards for the parent, teacher, and child. The conference should begin on a friendly note in an attempt to establish rapport between teacher and parent. It is well in the early stages of the meeting to emphasize positive aspects that will build the confidence of the parent and eliminate his or her defensiveness. If the child did a good job on an assignment or was helpful in class that day, the teacher might recount that anecdote. If the parent is on time for the meeting, the teacher can comment on how much he or she appreciates punctuality. If the teacher has had little success or opportunity to make contact with the parent and to establish a warm relationship, this initial session may be devoted to those ends. It may also be used to acquire needed background information on the child and the family.

Assuming that the parent and teacher have communicated before, the next part of the conference should be devoted to identifying and clarifying the joint concerns of the parent and teacher in regard to the child. The teacher must learn the parent's view of the problem, level of concern about it, and willingness to attempt to ameliorate it. At this stage it seems well to seek information on parent-child interaction, forms of discipline employed, and the extent of positive rewards and affection given to the child. Simultaneously, the teacher gathers data on parental needs, level of frustration, and receptivity to assistance. Frustration and receptivity may be assessed indirectly from statements the parent makes about the child or other family members and nonverbal clues he or she emits concerning patience and openness and through the intuitive sixth sense that tells us what people are feeling regardless of their words or the pose they adopt.

Because the teacher must establish a basis of mutuality with the parent if the conference is to be successful, much time must be spent exploring the willingness and the capability of the parent to change. Alternative methods of dealing with specific situations can be discussed. Often parents have good ideas in this regard and are more willing to try them because they thought of them. The teacher can also recommend some specific steps the parent can implement immediately on a daily basis. For instance, he or she can suggest that the parent set aside a few minutes at the same time each day to spend with the child alone. The teacher can help the parent locate the time of the day that is normally uncommitted to other activities and can suggest pasttimes such as playing a game or reading a book that parent and child can participate in together. It is important that the parent commit himself or herself to implement these suggestions; otherwise, the conference time may have been wasted.

After parent and teacher have finished their discussion, it is generally a good idea to bring the child into the conference. It is important that the child understand that the teacher and parent are concerned about his or her welfare and are not sharing any secrets. The teacher can summarize what he or she and the parent have discussed and explain that the parent, teacher, and child are going to work together to improve the areas of the youngster's achievement or behavior that need to be worked on. As with the parent, it is important that the teacher acquire a commitment from the child to work on a specific aspect of behavior. For instance, if the child hits other youngsters, the teacher may derive a statement from the youngster saying he or she will try to avoid that behavior in the future. At this point, it is time to terminate the conference.

Thus, it is apparent that the skills needed in conferencing are not beyond the realm of teachers but do require a great deal of sensitivity. Some teachers already use a system not unlike the one outlined above; for them, conferencing is a challenging and rewarding experience. Others have little experience in this area and need many sessions of role playing before they are adequately prepared for such interaction. In either case, conferencing is a crucial part of any teacher's effort to help maltreated children and their families. To understand more fully the process of a conference involving parent, teacher, and child, let us trace the progress of an actual case involving a child we shall call Sally Smith.

## THE CASE OF SALLY SMITH

Sally is in the second grade, and this year is her first in this school. Her family moved during the summer so that her father could take a better job. Sally has two older brothers and a baby sister. Records from the school she previously attended show her to be of average intelligence but below average achievement. Her attendance was generally good, although she was absent on four separate occasions for a week or longer. Sally is a fearful child who shies away from adults and from larger and older children. The few friends she has made are in kindergarten and first grade.

Mrs. Johnson, Sally's teacher, began to suspect that Sally might be marginally maltreated by receiving harsh punishment at home because of an incident that occurred soon after school opened. While working on an art project, Sally knocked over her paint can, began to cry, and pleaded hysterically that it had been an accident. She begged Mrs. Johnson not to hit her, although the teacher had made neither verbal nor nonverbal threats in that direction. Later, in a private conversation, Sally revealed that her mother became very angry over any incident that created a mess, such as spilling a glass of milk or breaking a dish. Sally confided that although she knew she deserved to be severely punished for her clumsiness, she wished her mother would not hit her so hard. In such cases Sally's mother had kept her home from school until the marks disappeared. When asked how her mother treated her when she was pleased with the youngster, Sally responded, "She doesn't hit me."

When all the facts of the case were presented to the child study group, in-school recommendations included giving Sally opportunities for praise, tolerance of accidents involving spilling, and a sizeable demonstration of affection to the child by the teacher. Mrs. Johnson made plans to encourage Sally to have contact with her peers through nonthreatening situations designed to bring her success.

Even before the case was aired at the child study group meeting, Mrs. Johnson communicated by phone with Mrs. Smith, Sally's mother. She seemed guarded and suspicious of the teacher's contact, although it was obvious that she was concerned about her child's academic progress. The mother asked to be notified if Sally caused any trouble in class, and Mrs. Johnson assured her that she would stay in contact both in regard to problems and successes Sally encountered in school.

It was decided that a parent-teacher conference should be held to make the mother aware of the child's problems and to deal with the dual issues of harsh punishment and lack of positive reinforcement within the home. Although the mother was somewhat reluctant to meet with the teacher, Mrs. Johnson conveyed to her that the conference was not tied to any specific problem, but was intended as a meeting to assess how the school and home could work together to facilitate Sally's development. In that spirit the mother and teacher set a conference time for after school several days later. The dialogue of the conference went as follows:

*Mrs. Johnson:* Thank you for coming to school today, Mrs. Smith. I like to get to know the parents of as many of my students as possible.

*Mrs. Smith:* Well, I hope Sally's not giving you any trouble. She can be a stubborn, willful child when she makes up her mind.

*Mrs. Johnson:* No, Sally's not presenting problems in class. She is coming along in her reading and has even moved up to the next reading group. She likes to play with the younger children and sometimes protects them from the teasing and bullying of the older youngsters.

*Mrs. Smith:* Well, I'm glad to hear all that. I guess she isn't really a bad girl, but sometimes she can be so clumsy.

*Mrs. Johnson:* I think all children have that tendency, Mrs. Smith. But I've noticed that Sally gets extremely agitated when she drops something or when she is afraid she will displease me in some way. I know we are both concerned about her academic progress, and it seems that if she were not so afraid of mistakes and had more self-confidence, she might do better in her schoolwork.

*Mrs. Smith:* I try to keep her in line as best I can. My husband is too busy to devote much time to the kids, and so I have to do everything for them.

*Mrs. Johnson:* That must be a difficult burden for you. (Pause) I'm sure you know that the way a child performs in school is often related to his home life. I wonder if we might discuss how you deal with Sally at home.

*Mrs. Smith:* I treat her just like the two older boys. I try to tell her how important it is to be good. But I think you've got to be firm with children today. You can't let them get away with murder. You've got to punish them when they're bad, like when they disobey you.

*Mrs. Johnson:* I agree that children must have rules to live by, and it is important that they know what is expected of them. Just as parents have responsibilities, so children must know what their responsibilities include. Children also need to be shown love and given rewards when they are good. All of us need praise and appreciation, don't we? How do you treat Sally when you are proud of her or pleased with something she has done?

*Mrs. Smith:* Well, I sometimes tell her that she did a good job. Other times, I buy her a treat.

*Mrs. Johnson:* You know, gifts are signs of a parent's love, but the most direct praise a child can receive is some physical affection — a hug, a pat, or a kiss. Children who aren't shown love daily often feel negative about themselves, and this opinion can interfere with their learning in school.

*Mrs. Smith:* Well, it's hard to come up to a kid and just kiss or hug her. I don't feel very comfortable doing that. I mean, I hug the baby, but with Sally and the boys, it's much harder.

*Mrs. Johnson:* A lot of parents have the same feelings that you do about showing their children love. What kinds of discipline do you use when Sally displeases you?

*Mrs. Smith:* Well, when she makes a mess, I have her clean it up. I'm so busy with the household chores and the baby that she's got to learn to take care of herself. When I tell her to do something and she doesn't, I get really mad. Sometimes I spank her. She's a big girl now, and I want her to know that I mean what I say.

*Mrs. Johnson:* It is good to use reasonable punishments. If Sally knocks something over accidentally, she should take some responsibility for repairing the damage, but if you know it was an accident, the two of you might clean it up together. Have you thought about explaining to her why you have rules around the house?

*Mrs. Smith:* She knows I'm busy.

*Mrs. Johnson:* Of course you are, but a little explanation can sometimes solve a number of problems. At other times, you might take away a privilege she enjoys for a brief period. For instance, if she misbehaves, you could restrict her television viewing for an hour or two as a punishment. Usually short, nonharsh punishments are effective with children. You mentioned that you spank Sally from time to time. How frequently do you do that?

*Mrs. Smith:* Well, sometimes she needs a good swat to show her that I mean what I say. When she talks back, I slap her face. Other times when she disobeys, I give her a good spanking. Maybe I hit her twice a week, but that's a lot less than my parents beat me. I used to get it all the time when I was a kid.

*Mrs. Johnson:* From the way you say that, I get the feeling that you did not like to be physically punished when you were a child. You know, it has been shown that physical punishment does not really stamp out undesirable behavior. Sometimes it makes children strike out at others; sometimes children respond by becoming timid and fearful. Also, it has been demonstrated that children who receive regular physical punishment have lower IQ scores and lower achievement rates than youngsters who receive other kinds of punishment.

*Mrs. Smith:* Yes, but sometimes I get so frustrated with that girl that I don't know what else to do.

*Mrs. Johnson:* You might try rewarding her when she is good and taking away her privileges when she displeases you. Also, the more you can convince her by actions and words that you love her, the harder she will try to please you.

*Mrs. Smith:* I try to praise her from time to time, but it seems she's usually making me mad.

*Mrs. Johnson:* But the more positive things you say to her, the more she will want to hear. We all need to hear good things about ourselves, and children need it more than adults. We have a program here at school that allows the school and home to work together on helping children feel good about themselves. It's called the happygram project.

*Mrs. Smith:* I've never heard of that.

*Mrs. Johnson:* Well, a happygram is a round yellow sticker with a smiling face on it that means your child's performance in school was good or showed improvement that day. It is given to children when they have earned extra praise for their efforts in school, and they can take it home to share with their family.

*Mrs. Smith:* What does it mean if Sally doesn't get a happygram?

*Mrs. Johnson:* It is a sign that her work for the day was average or below average. It can also indicate that she showed no noticeable improvement. But happygrams are given even for small improvements or small increases in effort so that children understand that they can earn them if they try.

*Mrs. Smith:* How am I involved in the idea of the happygram?

*Mrs. Johnson:* When you first see Sally after her school day, give her some physical affection, like a hug or a kiss. If she received a happygram that day, compliment her on it. If she did not earn a happygram, encourage her to try harder the next day.

*Mrs. Smith:* So you mean I only hug her if she gets a happygram?

*Mrs. Johnson:* No. You want to show Sally that you care about her with or without the happygram. If she earns one, congratulate her. If she doesn't, remind her to try harder. But in either case, show her you love her with some physical affection as soon as you see her after school.

*Mrs. Smith:* I guess it would be good if I hugged her more.

*Mrs. Johnson:* Well, there are some times of the day that naturally might include a hug or kiss. When you first see Sally in the morning, when she leaves for school, when she returns, and at bedtime, show her that you love her. Of course, feel free to show her physical affection any other time that you wish.

*Mrs. Smith:* That all seems like a good idea, I'll try. Is there anything else I can do to reward her?

*Mrs. Johnson:* Well, many parents hang the happygram in a prominent place in the home so that the whole family can share in the child's success. Aside from the happygram, notice the activities Sally enjoys and use them as rewards. If she likes you to read to her and she has helped you set the table for dinner, try to find a few minutes in the evening to read a story to her. Or set aside some time to play a game with your daughter. Sally can probably tell you other rewards she would like to earn.

    *Mrs. Smith:* But Sally isn't always good by any means. I've got to punish her when she's disobedient or when she misbehaves in some other way.

*Mrs. Johnson:* Of course you do, but as we discussed before, there are some better methods you can use to punish Sally than spanking her. Explain to her why she makes you angry when she disobeys. Then back up those words with a nonphysical punishment like withdrawal of the privilege to watch a special television show or to go outside to play after school. These kinds of punishment do not cause the resentment or fear that hitting does, and they teach the lesson that Sally must accept responsibility for her actions.

    *Mrs. Smith:* I don't know if I can make all the changes you want.

*Mrs. Johnson:* Are you willing to try for Sally's sake?

    *Mrs. Smith:* Yes, I'll try to give her more affection and to punish her in ways other than hitting her.

*Mrs. Johnson:* Good. Let's bring Sally in and tell her what we have discussed.

    *Mrs. Smith:* All right.

*Mrs. Johnson:* Sally, your mother and I have been talking about ways we can work together to help you do better in your schoolwork. We also want to help you be less afraid of making mistakes. So each day you show some improvement in your work or put forth extra effort, you'll get a happygram to take home. On days when your work does not show something special, you won't get a happygram. Your mother is going to encourage you to bring home happygrams, but remember that she loves you whether you earn happygrams in school or not. And she's going to reward you when you are good and take away privileges you have when you misbehave. But for us to help you, you must decide if you will try hard in your schoolwork and make an effort to be friends with the other children. Will you try?

    *Sally:* Yes.

*Mrs. Johnson:* Well, I think we have made some good plans today. Let's keep in close touch for the next few weeks to see how things are progressing. I'll call you in a couple of days, Mrs. Smith.

    *Mrs. Smith:* Good. I want Sally to make progress in school.

*Mrs. Johnson:* We all do. Thank you for coming in this afternoon. Good-bye.

A great deal was accomplished in the conference recorded above. In many cases, however, a single meeting is not sufficient to cover all the areas in which a child needs help from a parent. If it is not, additional meetings must be scheduled, each covering some part of the problem until all have been discussed. Although parents are frequently defensive at the beginning of meetings with teachers, the skillful educator senses this discomfort and attempts to dispel it. Listening with a "third ear" to both the words and feelings of parents is the most useful tool the teacher possesses.

### Follow-up of a conference

At this point a word of caution and clarification is essential. Although numerous follow-up sessions to provide continued reinforcement and guidance for parents may be necessary, teachers should not define such treatment as psychotherapy. As a professional classroom teacher, even after considerable in-service training, a teacher can make no such claim. Certainly, teacher awareness of the basis for parent or family dysfunction is important in helping to modify parent behavior. Furthermore, teacher relationships with parents can be therapeutic, but the primary functions of the teacher-counseling role are to provide encouragement, support, and direction for parents in their relationships with children. If, in the process of achieving this goal, in-depth treatment is necessary in the opinion of the teacher to promote continued growth for child or parent, teachers may feel comfortable recommending it, after having established a trusting relationship with the parent.

The child's behavior in school is the primary method for a teacher to use in evaluating the success of a parent conference. If the youngster makes even small gains in the areas in which he or she has been experiencing difficulty, the conference can be viewed as a positive meeting. The increased attention the child receives from both parent and teacher often changes his or her self concept significantly, for it shows the youngster that people care. When this factor is coupled with even minor alterations in the classroom and home environments, many children make substantial progress when measured against reasonable expectations. The more cooperative the parents and the less severe their parenting problems, the greater the potential for improvement. Further, the younger the child at the time of teacher intervention, the more responsive he or she is to change, for the youngster's habits and attitudes are not well formed and lend themselves to relatively easy modification.

It is important that the teacher take time to evaluate the course of the conference itself. It may be that the initial hostility of a parent did not diminish during the meeting. In such a case the teacher must investigate alternatives to bring about parental cooperation and change for the good of the youngster. It may be wise to enlist the support of the principal whose position as school leader carries more authority than that of a teacher. Community and governmental social agencies can be contacted to offer specific kinds of assistance to the family. As a last resort a meeting of the parent, agency personnel, and teacher can be held at the school to demonstrate to the parent the depth of concern about the child. However, if possible, it is well if the case remains within the control of the school, with outside agencies involved only to provide leverage to the teacher.

In all follow-up evaluations it is important to remember that not every child is going to be helped and that change cannot be expected to occur overnight. Sensitivity to the uniqueness of each situation is essential. With cooperative families, reassurance that they are helping their child is an important element that encourages progress. Although the temptation to apply hefty pressure to uncooperative parents is great, it may be counter productive, for it often alienates those the teacher wishes to help. In short, the teacher must be prepared to face both success and failure in dealing with parents; yet, if he or she enters into a conference with a plan of action and remains sensitive to the feelings of the parent, the potential is tremendous for improving the lives of both the child and the parent.

In monitoring the progress of a child as a result of a parent-teacher conference and of changes in the classroom environment, it is essential that patience, consistency, and concern be demonstrated. If a system such as the happygram program is instituted, a built-in basis for communication exists between school and home. It is well to ask the child periodically how the parent responds to the happygram or to the child's arrival home without it. Because children understand that they and their parents are part of a team working in the youngster's best interests, they generally accept such questions willingly and answer them openly. If it appears that the parent is not adhering to the plans formulated during the parent conference, it is imperative that attempts be made to correct the situation at the first signs of its breakdown.

A planned program of follow-up by the teacher reinforces the school's concern for the welfare of the child. By making weekly telephone calls to the home, the teacher can stress positive changes observed in the child. By so doing, the parent is rewarded for his or her effort. Phone contacts also give parents the opportunity to air questions or problems they continue to have with regard to their children. This two-way communication is the key to the team approach involving school and home.

Follow-up conferences scheduled as appropriate offer the parent the chance to refine his or her interactional skills with the child. In such meetings parental concerns can be aired and plans for future action formulated. Because the goal of a successful follow-up program is to encourage positive parenting patterns that benefit the whole family, reinforcement is an important element that must be provided on a continuing basis throughout the school year. If the school or community offers parenting classes or courses designed to show parents how to help their children with their schoolwork, parents can be made aware of these opportunities and encouraged to develop their skills through them. Further, the teacher can invite the parent to observe and assist in the classroom to learn more about dealing with children while making a positive contribution to their learning. Thus, any technique the teacher employs to involve parents in positive activities about or with children serves as an important part of a follow-up program.

Yet, even when the school year has ended, the teacher's responsibility to the family has not ended. He or she must encourage placement of the child for the next year with a teacher who understands the dynamics of the youngster's situation and is willing to continue to monitor his or her progress. In some cases the teacher who initiates parental involvement may find it advisable to maintain contact with the parent, even though the child has moved on to a new grade and teacher. In this matter the teacher must evaluate each situation to decide if he or she should relinquish all or only some contact with the child and parent.

## Conclusion

One teacher, working alone or with the assistance of a few colleagues, can implement a successful program to help maltreated children and their families. The chief attributes required are concern for children, empathy with parents, and a sense of responsibility that extends beyond the regular school day. The key to success lies in employing a systematic approach that leaves little to chance but remains flexible enough to meet the unique circumstances of each situation.

From the first day of school, evaluation of children's needs and progress is an ongoing process. Gathering data on a child, evaluating its significance, hypothesizing causal factors, checking teacher suspicions against child and parent statements, conferencing with parents, and monitoring parent and child change are integral steps in the teacher's plan to maximize the growth of each youngster.

Most people become teachers because their school experiences were positive and because they want to play a part in shaping the lives of successive generations. In this light there could be no greater reward for a teacher than to know that he or she has helped a family develop constructive patterns that facilitate the growth of a child. Yet, if one teacher can have such tremendous impact on the lives of children and parents, it staggers the mind to imagine the accomplishments possible if an entire school were to put forth a concerted effort to help its families. The next chapter investigates the potential for change when a school or district is committed to the task of assisting maltreating families.

# CHAPTER 8

# Beyond the classroom: what is the role of school and community in the maltreatment program?

In Chapter 7 the effect a single teacher or small group can have on mal-treated children and their families was discussed. For a program within the school to be broadly effective, the principal must back it and must employ the collective talents and resources of the school and community. This chapter investigates the impact of a coordinated school and community thrust in identifying and assisting maltreating famlies.

## The principal as effective school leader

An effective school is more than a group of teachers working in the best interests of their students. It is a body of people and organizations that rec-ognize that education extends beyond the classroom's four walls and that it must be encouraged by all citizens. Research and experience strongly sug-gest that the key to the success of a school is its principal, whose decisions, priorities, and skills affect hundreds or thousands of lives each year. It is to the principal that teachers and other school staff look for leadership. It is the principal who shapes both community concerns and action. The princi-pal is called upon by social agencies to identify families needing assistance and to monitor the sufficiency of the aid they receive. Further, he or she is given front-line management responsibilities by the central staff of the school district and is expected both to conform to existing policies and ini-tiate innovative practices as appropriate. Thus, the principal's job is one of tremendous responsibility to many sectors; it becomes his or her task to balance the demands of these sometimes competing forces while working for the betterment of both the school and the community.

Successful principals understand all aspects of a school's operation, for their position as school leader provides them with a perspective that is unique. They understand the ways in which programs and practices com-plement or contradict each other, for they view the school both as a multitude of individual facets and as a functioning entity. They possess the ability to perceive how one change in the school's policy affects other seemingly unrelated aspects of the school's operation, either for good or ill. Further, they are sensitive to the amount and kinds of change that can be accepted by the educational institution and its members. They understand that too much innovation can overload a previously sound system, while too little leads to complacency and inefficiency.

When dealing with people, effective principals know how to work with others to maximize their growth and productivity. They are able to communicate both with staff and the broader community to foster understanding and improve cooperation. They appreciate that there are situations in which they must remain uninvolved to allow events to take their course and other times when their intervention is mandated. Their goal is to enhance the effectiveness of all aspects of the school's operation and to allow and encourage the development of all the people involved in the educational process.

Dynamic school principals lead by example rather than by lecture, although they recognize the importance of a well-timed pep talk. They understand that to spur staff and community to activity, they must expect no less and often more of themselves than they ask of anyone else. Their job involves the establishment of educational priorities, the design of innovative programs, and the implementation of activities that attempt to meet the broad needs of children and the community as dictated by analysis of both present and future concerns. In short, the principal possesses both a philosophy of life and a set of goals for education that must be translated into programs that benefit youngsters and their community.

Perhaps more than any other personal quality, successful school principals must possess empathy for others. Such sensitivity to the feelings of others is a product of their ability to understand and accept their own emotions. When dealing with teachers, students, and parents, school principals must listen constantly to ensure that they are keyed in to the emotional lives of those with whom they work. Good human relations skills are an important prerequisite for the successful school leader.

There is no attempt made here to include an exhaustive analysis of the skills and characteristics the principal must possess if he or she is to provide effective leadership to the school. Yet, familiarity with all aspects of the school's program, coordination of the efforts of the school and community through communication, establishment of priorities based on current and anticipated needs, and sensitivity to the people with whom he or she deals are minimal skills a successful principal must demonstrate if the challenges of the post are to be met effectively. The principal's concerns must include the needs both of the general population he or she serves and of the individuals within it who require special consideration.

## The principal's role in initiating a program to help maltreating families

Ideally, the principal should lead the school's efforts against maltreatment. As head of the school, he or she is in a unique position both to utilize the talents and resources of the staff and community and to integrate this aspect of the school's concern into the total school program.

As school leader, the principal possesses power that must be utilized responsibly. It would be foolish to believe that the principal does not have leverage over his or her faculty that can be employed in either a positive or a negative manner. Certainly, the effective principal understands that the weight of the position must be brought to bear judiciously or not at all, for his or her goal is to achieve cooperation and not to foster intimidation. In regard to the establishment of a school program to alleviate maltreatment, the principal's enthusiasm for the project and obvious concern for the welfare of children and parents alike acts as a stimulus to the faculty. Further, the principal who takes the lead in such an effort usually gains the staff's heightened respect for his or her humanistic sentiments and willingness to translate them into action.

Yet, it is not enough for the principal to state concern for maltreated children and then expect the staff to proceed without further guidance. Even before initiating the idea of a cooperative school and community effort to combat maltreatment, the principal must assess the status of the school as a nonabusive environment for children. He or she must apply concerted effort to the elimination of practices such as corporal punishment and harsh verbal abuse that contradict the stated goal of the school to foster the development of each child through positive means. In place of such procedures the principal must see to it that alternative policies are substituted that are consistent with the humane treatment each youngster deserves.

In addition, the principal must evaluate his or her skills and knowledge in the field of maltreatment. He or she must understand the dynamics of the maltreating family and recognize that abusive and neglecting parents need help rather than blame. The principal must learn of programs and practices being employed elsewhere that hold promise of success. The principal must analyze his or her skills in dealing with others on as emotionally charged an issue as maltreatment. He or she must evaluate the willingness of staff and community to become involved in a coordinated effort to deal with maltreatment. As a complement, the principal must identify the skills already possessed and those that must be developed by the staff if such a program is to be successful. The principal must understand that an extensive in-service program will be required to outfit the staff with the necessary equipment to help maltreating families. In short, the principal must realize that unless commitment, cooperation, and competence can be cultivated in the staff, the project is doomed to failure; with those three qualities, the accomplishments can be tremendous.

What should a principal do prior to establishing a comprehensive maltreatment prevention program in the school? The list below can be a useful tool in evaluating the principal's and school's readiness for program development. The principal should—

1. Be familiar with state law and local policy and guidelines, including the role of social service workers
2. Examine his or her concept of the role of public education
3. Examine his or her attitudes and beliefs regarding child-rearing practices as well as those of staff and community members
4. Examine internal practices in the school or school system relative to professed beliefs to determine the discrepancy between belief and practice
5. Analyze reasons for inadequate student performance
6. Develop a working knowledge of the dynamics involved in child maltreatment
7. Assess the development of a support system within the school or school system for the initiation of a maltreatment program
8. Be aware of resources: organizations, materials, and texts that could help in the establishment of a maltreatment prevention program
9. Become knowledgeable of what other persons in the field have accomplished
10. Be concerned about the risks involved in establishing a program in this sensitive area, but have the courage and skills to develop a support system in order to succeed

Once the principal has determined that a program to combat child maltreatment is both desirable and feasible, it becomes his or her task to recognize the unique contributions that can be made to such an effort by members of the staff. The knowledge and skills possessed by school personnel can be pooled into a comprehensive program that runs efficiently with the continued support of the principal but without his or her involvement at every stage. Let us examine the roles that can be played by school workers in a functioning school-based maltreatment program.

## The guidance counselor, school nurse, and school social worker

Although they are not full-time employees in most schools, the guidance counselor, school nurse, and school social worker bring their services to most schools on at least a part-time basis. Because of their specialized training and the nature of the abilities they possess, these school workers can be useful in all phases of a maltreatment program, including the identification, diagnosis, and treatment of abused and neglected children and their families. They act as valuable resources to individual teachers, while they perform important roles in the school-wide program to combat child maltreatment.

Guidance counselors are standard parts of most secondary school staffs, and their number is rapidly increasing on the elementary level. The job description of counselors includes many tasks, some of which are only tangentially related to children. Their training involves a series of graduate courses leading to a master's degree that certifies their preparation. Although their professional education prepares them to counsel students in a wide variety of problem areas, many are so deluged with administrative tasks that they have little time to devote to working with students individually. Because of the range of their responsibilities, counselors are unable to maintain close daily contact with children. In this regard, teachers must accept that their relationships with youngsers are more deeply established in most cases than are counselors'. Further, teachers have far greater opportunities to develop rapport with parents than do counselors. Thus, in a school-based maltreatment program the counselor cannot be expected to shoulder the responsibilities that must rightly fall to teachers, although he or she can play an important role in the overall effort to eliminate maltreatment.

The guidance counselor can act as the reporting official in the school's maltreatment program. When it is believed that abuse or neglect conform to legal definitions, he or she can be called upon to assemble known information and report the case to the appropriate child protective services section for investigation. There is an advantage in vesting this responsibility in one person who can become expert both in the legal aspects of maltreatment and in structuring reports so that all pertinent information is conveyed. Such standardization eliminates much of the uncertainty that surrounds the "to report or not to report" issue and allows for more objective analysis and follow-through as indicated.

On the counseling level, guidance personnel can provide supportive individual and small group sessions for children experiencing difficulty at home. Because their schedules are flexible, they can visit children's homes to acquire information about the family and its functioning. In other cases the counselor can observe children in and out of the classroom to gather information and provide feedback to teachers.

If the school has a child study team, it may be well to select the guidance counselor as its leader because he or she possesses greater familiarity with the case presentation method than do most teachers. Further, his or her expertise can be employed in the preliminary testing and preparation of students who are identified as requiring special services. The guidance counselor's job may include working with teachers on effective parent counseling techniques they can employ when dealing with adults. In addition, the counselor may train teachers in alternatives to harsh punishment in an effort to eliminate marginal maltreatment from the school.

Perhaps the most important role of the counselor in a school-wide program to fight maltreatment is as coordinator of school and community resources. Because guidance counselors have knowledge of the services available within the community on both the governmental and private levels, they can insure that children and their parents are afforded every assistance that exists either within or beyond the province of the school. The ability to draw on the total community as a source of aid is vital to an effective maltreatment program, and the counselor's training and experience prepare him or her to guarantee that all available resources are utilized.

The specialized medical training of the school nurse ensures that he or she brings to the staff knowledge not possessed by any other school personnel. Although many schools throughout America lack the services of a full-time nurse, one is normally available on either a part-time or a rotating basis. In other communities, public health nurses can be consulted as deemed appropriate by the school principal.

The school nurse's skills can be made an important segment of a comprehensive maltreatment program. One part of his or her function centers on diagnosis of medical conditions needing treatment. This staff member can assess the likelihood of malnutrition in cases in which severe physical neglect is suspected. In cases of medical neglect the nurse performs the vital roles of diagnosing the child's needs and counseling parents on the importance of seeking medical care to remedy them. Further, the school nurse can evaluate evidence that suggests physical or sexual abuse when a child sustains injuries of a suspicious nature.

Another vital role that the nurse can undertake involves the coordination of a comprehensive school health program, including testing of vision, hearing, and teeth. He or she can call upon community organizations to provide such specialized services as sickle cell screenings. The public health service can be enlisted to provide immunization against the common diseases of childhood either before or after children are enrolled in school.

A third role that can be assumed by the school nurse focuses on direct services for teachers. The nurse can educate other school personnel to the signs of physical abuse, physical neglect, and medical neglect through in-service programs. In this way teachers are alerted to the symptoms of maltreatment and can perform the preliminary screening of children. Further, because of their own experiences in dealing with parents, school nurses can often suggest to teachers nonthreatening ways to counsel parents. In other cases the school nurse can be included in parent conferences to discuss the medical aspects of a child's case and suggest remedies for his or her physical problems. Often, the expertise of this staff member increases the parent's awareness of the depth of concern the school feels for the youngster.

The school social worker is rarely available to individual schools except on an emergency basis. For this reason the social worker cannot perform as integral a function in a comprehensive school-based maltreatment program as either the guidance counselor or the nurse. However, the knowledge and skills of the trained social worker can be invaluable to a school as it tackles the problems of maltreating families.

More than any regular school staff member, the social worker is likely to have experience with abused children and their maltreating parents. This practical knowledge can be shared with the rest of the school staff through in-service workshops and in more informal contacts with teachers. Because the social worker is charged with the investigation and disposition of severe maltreatment cases, he or she often can provide needed guidance to school personnel as they spot seriously abused or neglected children and observe the early signs of marginal maltreatment in other youngsters. In serious cases reported to the social worker by either the school or an outside source the coordination of both the school's and social agency's efforts affords the opportunity both for continual monitoring of the case and for delivery of complementary services, thus enhancing the chances for a successful resolution of the family's problems.

Thus, trained guidance counselors, nurses, and social workers play important parts as auxiliary members of a school-wide maltreatment program. Certainly, they cannot replace teachers as the front-line professionals in identifying and assisting abused and neglected children, for their contact with youngsters is intermittent. Nor are they in the teacher's unique position to monitor day-to-day changes in the status of children. However, as resource people with specialized areas of expertise, these workers can perform vital roles that augment the efforts of teachers and principals in the battle against maltreatment.

## The role of nonprofessional staff

People knowledgeable about the operation of a school are well aware of the importance of supportive staff in its overall efficiency. Often called nonprofessional or noncertificated personnel, their jobs involve secretarial, custodial, and cafeteria duties vital to a school's total functioning.

If principals were asked whether it is more disruptive to the efficient operation of a school when a secretary or five teachers must be replaced, most would say that the loss of a good school secretary is greater. Because supportive staff interact in important ways with children, it is critical that their talents be utilized and their assistance be enlisted in the school's effort to deal humanely with all children.

It is easy for people who see bus driving, food preparing, or letter typing as their jobs to overlook the fact that children are the primary business of all school personnel. Often a school's problems are significantly increased by the hostility expressed by nonprofessional staff members when they deal with youngsters. Supportive personnel must be trained and encouraged to interact with children in positive ways and, thus, to view themselves as part of the total effort to make the school a constructive force in the lives of youngsters.

Although supportive staff need not be trained specifically in the area of child maltreatment, these employees do need guidance in developing human relations skills that foster communication. Their attitudes should be positive toward their jobs, should reflect a caring both for tasks and people, and should demonstrate ability to cope with the pressures of their duties. When interacting with children, supportive staff members must abide by the rules of the school. If corporal punishment is prohibited, nonprofessional workers must understand that they are not to strike children, but are to follow clearly defined rules regarding the reporting of misbehavior to the appropriate professional in the school. In short, it is important that the supportive staff be committed to the goals of the school and recognize both its opportunity and responsibility to help the school achieve its desired ends.

Because nonprofessional staff members often reside within the community, they can have tremendous impact on the neighborhood's view of the school. If they are convinced that their contributions to the school's efforts are significant, both their perceptions of their own worth and of the school's as a potent force for good will be enhanced.

Anyone familiar with schools can remember countless incidents in which a teacher's aide, secretary, cafeteria worker, bus driver, or custodian has befriended a child with special problems. The impact such contacts have had on children's lives cannot be minimized. Indeed, school personnel must recognize supportive staff members as powerful allies in the school's effort to establish meaningful and beneficial relationships with youngsters and families.

## The school and community child advocacy team

Even when the principal, teaching staff, auxiliary personnel, and nonprofessional workers combine to implement a coordinated plan for helping maltreating families, their efforts are insufficient to meet the total needs of abused and neglected children and their parents. For the school alone this job is overwhelming; it demands enlisting the aid of others in the campaign. The entire resources and cooperation of the community must be sought to ensure that the fight against present and potential maltreatment will be successful.

As both school leader and a respected member of the community, the principal is the natural choice for coordinator of a broad-based maltreatment program. Because of his or her role as spokesperson for the school, the community listens to the principal's statements with interest. It has come to trust his or her judgments as sound and his or her concern as genuine. Because the principal recognizes the value of generalized parent and community support, he or she has cultivated contacts and developed mechanisms to maximize adult involvement in both school and community projects. These same channels of communication can be employed and increased in the construction of a joint school and community child advocacy team.

The major goal of any school is to foster the growth of its students. By utilizing the concerted effort of the school staff and the active participation of community resource people, the aim of education seems nearer realization. Together, educators and lay people can form a team devoted to the development of specific programs to assist currently maltreating families and to forestall the likelihood of future parents falling into patterns of abuse and neglect.

### Who should be involved on the child advocacy team?

It is important that those who participate in the activities of the child advocacy team be sincerely interested in its success and willing to devote the time and energy necessary to ensure it. Because the team stands as a link between both school and community, it is vital that its membership represent these two groups. Although there is no ideal number of members for the team, experience with groups suggests that a body with more than twelve to fifteen participants has difficulty reaching consensus on issues, while a team with fewer than seven or eight members lacks the broad influence necessary to involve the variety of resources available within the community.

Quite naturally, the membership of the child advocacy team should include the principal, who may enlist the assistance of others in screening prospective participants. If there is a community school coordinator at the school, he or she should be a member of the team. It also seems advisable to enlist one professional educator and one nonprofessional school worker, both of whom live in or near the community served by the school. Representatives from existing organizations, such as the PTA or school advisory committee, bring both familiarity with school programs and concern for the welfare of children to the child advocacy team. In addition, a local businessperson provides valuable knowledge of community needs and resources. Representatives from civic service organizations, clubs for children like the Boy and Girl Scouts, or religious groups might also be encouraged to participate on the team. Health care personnel could perform useful services on the team in terms of their specific medical knowledge, contacts with colleagues, and familiarity with community needs and sources of assistance. It is possible that a local politician could be a member of the team, utilizing his or her knowledge and influence to advance the goals of the group. However, caution must be expressed in regard to this last member, since some politicians might see the team as a way to gain publicity and increase their personal prominence rather than as a community-oriented effort to provide needed services to families that require them.

In short, the child advocacy team's members should be representative of all the major segments of the school and community. The broader its membership, the greater its likelihood of learning of and employing the full resources of the community. Whoever its members, it is essential that they understand the depth of commitment required of them and the amount of energy they will have to expend in the course of the team's work. They must realize that their efforts may not advance along a smooth path to success, but may encounter many bumpy spots that can be traversed only with ingenuity and cooperation.

### What can the child advocacy team accomplish?

Since the child advocacy team concept must be based on local needs and actions, the team's first task should be to assess the status of the family as a basic institution within the community. It must evaluate existing services and organizations attempting to meet family needs and note areas in which assistance is lacking but desirable. Team members should understand the close relationship that exists between the home and a child's present and future development. Further, they should receive orientation regarding research and practical findings in the field of child maltreatment, including its causes, effects, and possible remedies. Armed with this knowledge, the child advocacy team can then begin to develop specific programs consistent with both local needs and knowledge in the field of maltreatment.

To gain a foothold in this area it is wise for the school and community child advocacy team to formulate programs at its inception that have a high probability of success. Further, their projects should be nonthreatening in their thrust; otherwise, there is a significant risk of alienating not only the community members targeted for help, but also possible future participants on the team. The aim of initial projects is both to aid the community and win support for the endeavors of the team. As broad-based support and acceptance grow for the efforts of the team, it can begin to expand its efforts, incorporate other resources, and launch more innovative programs.

As the school and community child advocacy team begins to examine existing school and neighborhood programs, it may notice gaps in services that it can fill. For example, if the school has no program to meet the health needs of its students, the team can develop plans for medical and dental examinations by voluntary community practitioners or by public health personnel. Vision and hearing screenings form a good jumping-off point for this effort, with the later addition of complete medical examinations, if possible. An immunization campaign for students and preschoolers is another sound first effort, as is a dental screening procedure to uncover children whose teeth need attention.

As important as these initial diagnostic services are, however, they are meaningless without the development and implementation of programs to correct diagnosed problems. In this regard, doctors, nurses, and dentists, again from the community, can be enlisted to volunteer their services to perform the necessary corrective work. Only if both the diagnostic and treatment phases of a coordinated community effort are developed does the program provide a truly beneficial service to the neighborhood.

Another good starting point for a school and community child advocacy team centers on meeting the basic needs of children for adequate food and clothing. With the advent of federal assistance programs for the poor, many schools and communities have deemphasized help for needy families, expecting government to provide all the essentials of life. However experience continues to demonstrate that, to paraphrase the Bible, the poor are still with us, and they deserve the concern of their neighbors. Although this is an area that must be handled with sensitivity to protect the feelings of the recipient families, most parents appreciate such assistance for their children, particularly if it is provided in response to an emergency or crisis in the family.

Another problem area for many families today makes a good starting point for the efforts and energies of the school and community child advocacy team. Both personal experience and national statistics attest to a significant rise in the number of "latchkey children." Because their single parent or both parents are employed outside the home, these children lack adequate adult supervision, particularly in the late afternoon. Under the auspices of the child advocacy team, necessary care can be provided in many communities using the school building as its site. Some projects of this sort operate from 6:00 AM to 6:00 PM and ensure that the children will be supervised by volunteer adults or paid staff during after-school hours.

If there is a cooperative university in the vicinity, the child advocacy team can utilize the school or some other available building as a location in which to offer courses to community members. Existent plans suggest that either day or evening scheduling of classes is possible, depending on the needs and preferences of participants. Course offerings might include a study of prenatal care for expectant mothers, a course on human sexuality, a class in communication skills, or a program on child development and growth. Such classes provide essential knowledge to present and future parents, while they encourage nurturing relationships between parents and their children.

Another effort of the child advocacy team might involve the school even more directly. The team could schedule a series of parent visits to classrooms so that adults would feel part of the educational process of their children. Some communities have implemented volunteer parent aide programs in which parents not only view the happenings in the schoolroom, but also actively participate in learning activities with children. Both these plans are designed to improve parent-child interaction as they expose parents to positive ways of dealing with their youngsters.

Even as seemingly simple a project as a bumper sticker drive may gain support for the efforts of the child advocacy team while it performs a useful educational function for the community. Many neighborhoods have initiated campaigns around the slogan "Have You Hugged Your Child Today?" in an attempt to spur the community to think seriously and positively about its responsibilities to its young people. Although the stickers may seem little more than an advertising gimmick, their effectiveness in consciousness raising on the need for a demonstration of love between parent and child has been clearly shown in countless neighborhoods throughout America. Such a campaign may seem a small, somewhat symbolic start; yet, it can pave the way for more significant later efforts.

In earlier chapters of this book a number of additional suggestions were included that might be adopted as projects by the child advocacy team. The key to their success depends on a careful assessment of local needs and the matching of those needs to activities that fulfill them.

## Regional and district-wide coordination

For a community to establish a comprehensive program to assist maltreating families, it must reach beyond its neighborhood to encourage broad-based cooperation. In a small community the school district may take the lead in ensuring that the policies are consistent both in theory and practice. It can function as a clearinghouse for information on services available within its bounds and halt the inefficiency of unnecessary duplication. In large school districts the need for coordination and articulation is even more pressing as the area attempts to maximize its resources. For a program to be effective within a large district, it must be administered with an eye both to consistency of programs and communication of their existence to the total community.

Many large school districts are routinely administered on an area basis. Because there is both geographic and social homogeneity within sections of a large district, regional planning and administration units often function as efficient coordinating subsystems. A regional approach to maltreatment allows communities to learn from the successes of other groups in the same geographic area. Further, careful articulation can lead to the adoption of innovative approaches by a number of neighborhoods within a region, while it can minimize the chances of several areas' implementing similar unsuccessful plans.

How can regional or district-wide coordination be accomplished? Representatives from each neighborhood child advocacy team can meet on a regularly scheduled basis to share their ideas concerning plans and programs. Often they draw upon resource people to inject new ideas into their discussions. In small communities the coordinated team approach facilitates the identification and servicing of local needs. In larger districts the regional team acts as an important link to city and area-wide resources available at the local level. Because it represents the thought and action of a number of local organizations rather than only one, the regional team addresses with greater solidarity the concerns of its members and commands with increased authority the attention of policymakers in the area.

In large school districts it is necessary to establish not only regional child advocacy teams, but also a district-wide coordinating group. Its membership is drawn from the regional teams that function on the local level. Its task is to advise both the school board and administrative staff of the priorities that must be met. Whether established by school board, central staff, regional group, or local team initiative, the district child advocacy team recommends priorities and direction necessary to ensure that the needs of all citizens are met.

In addition to the district-wide group drawn from local levels, it is advisable to establish a steering committee of trained professionals to provide expert knowledge to both the district team and school board. Its members may already be part of the district's central administrative staff; more preferable, however, is a group composed both of district administrators and governmental agency heads. Such a combined membership allows for more thorough articulation among many facets of the community that attempt to serve the same clients. When a school district has access to the input not only of its own employees but also of representatives from the health and rehabilitative services division, family services, and other social service agencies, its potential for concerted effort to meet the comprehensive needs of children and families is greatly enhanced.

## Role of the school board and central staff

It is the function of the school board to establish priorities for a school district based on the philosophy it espouses and goals it lays down. The central staff is charged to carry out the dictates of the school board. Further, it assumes responsibility for recommending for review to the board a variety of program alternatives designed to serve the best interests of both the school and community.

Either the school board or central staff may provide the impetus for the development and coordination of a district plan to help maltreated children and their families. Certainly, a district-wide statement on child maltreatment and programs to deal with abuse and neglect when they occur form the backbone of a comprehensive remediation and prevention effort. A policy that stipulates guidelines and procedures for the reporting of severe cases of child maltreatment is an important first step as a school district assumes responsibility for what in most states is the legal obligation of educators. From that basis the school board may next encourage pilot programs developed on the local level. Later, it may call for implementation throughout the district of the most successful of these plans.

In developing a policy statement, whether at the school board, administrative staff, or local school level, it would be helpful to review the guidelines developed by the Child Abuse and Neglect Division of the Education Commission of the States. That division of the commission continues to provide valuable direction, particularly in policymaking issues as they relate to child maltreatment.

### CONSIDERATIONS FOR POLICY DEVELOPMENT*

A policy regarding child abuse and neglect is a commitment by the school (or other education group or institution) to cooperate with other agencies and professions in identification, treatment and prevention programs. The ultimate purpose of a child abuse and neglect policy is to protect children whose health or welfare is threatened through nonaccidental injury or neglect by parents, guardians or caretakers.

The guidelines that follow are practical suggestions to help education policy makers develop and implement effective child abuse and neglect policies. These are not intended to be cookbook instructions that spell out what to do and how to do it. Rather, the guidelines are offered as points to consider when developing policy. They are designed to assist in the development of policies suitable to the needs of institutions and groups. Because of variations among state laws and among school district policies and regulations, it is impossible to develop uniform "model" policies and procedures applicable to all the American school systems.

The first and strongest suggestion is that every school system adopt and issue a child abuse and neglect policy, particularly a policy on reporting. Almost every state reporting requires or encourages school personnel to report suspected child abuse and neglect. An effective child abuse policy should inform school personnel of their legal obligations and immunities in regard to reporting, as well as inform the local community that school personnel are legally obligated or encouraged to report suspected child abuse and neglect.

Any policy regarding child abuse and neglect must be in compliance with state law. To ensure that a proposed policy complies with current statutes, consult an attorney or the state's attorney general. At a minimum, a reporting policy should cite the elements listed below. Sample wording for such citations is listed to the right.

---

*From Education Policies and Practices Regarding Child Abuse and Neglect and Recommendations for Policy Development. (Denver: Education Commission of the States, 1976).

| *Elements to be cited* | *Sample wording* |
|---|---|

*Elements to be cited*

1. A brief rationale for involving school personnel in reporting.

2. The name and appropriate section numbers of the state reporting statute.

3. Who specifically is mandated to report and (if applicable) who may report.

4. Reportable conditions as defined by state law.

5. The person or agency to receive reports.

6. The information required of the reporter.

7. Expected professional conduct by school employees.

8. The exact language of the law to define "abuse" and "neglect"; if necessary, explain, clarify or expand.

9. The method by which school personnel are to report (if appropriate, list telephone number for reporting) and the time in which to report.

10. Whether or not there is immunity from civil liability and criminal penalty for those who report or partici-

*Sample wording*

Because of their sustained contact with school-age children, school employees are in an excellent position to identify abused or neglected children and to refer them for treatment and protection.

To comply with the Mandatory Reporting of Child Abuse Act (Section 350-1 through 350-5), Hawaii Revised Statutes (1968), as amended (Supp. 1975). . . .

. . . it is the policy of the _____ School District that any teacher or other school employee . . .

. . . who suspects that a child's physical or mental health or welfare may be adversely affected by abuse or neglect . . .

. . . shall report to the department of social services . . .

or

. . . shall report to the principal, who shall then call the department of social services . . .

. . . and give the following information: name, address and age of student; name and address of parent or caretaker; nature and extent of injuries or description of neglect; any other information that might help establish the cause of the injuries or condition.

School employees shall not contact the child's family or any other persons to determine the cause of the suspected abuse or neglect.

It is not the responsibility of the school employee to prove that the child has been abused or neglected, or to determine whether the child is in need of protection.

Any personal interview or physical inspection of the child should be conducted in a professional manner. . . .

"'Abuse' means the infliction, by other than accidental means, of physical harm upon the body of a child." "'Neglect' means the failure to provide necessary food, care, clothing, shelter or medical attention for a child."

An oral report must be made as soon as possible by telephone or otherwise and may be followed by a written report.

In Illinois, anyone making a report in accordance with state law or participating in a resulting judicial proceeding is presumed to be acting in good faith and, in doing so, is immune from

| | |
|---|---|
| pate in an investigation or judicial proceeding; and whether immunity is for "good faith" reporting.* | any civil or criminal liability that might otherwise be imposed. |
| | or |
| | In Maryland, there is no immunity from civil suits for untrue statements made by one citizen against another. |
| 11. Penalty for failure to report, if established by state law. | Failure to report may result in a misdemeanor charge: punishment by a fine of up to $500, imprisonment up to one year or both. |
| 12. Action taken by school board for failure to report. | Failure to report may result in disciplinary action against the employee. |
| 13. Any provisions of the law regarding the confidentiality of records pertaining to reports of suspected abuse or neglect. | All records concerning reports of suspected abuse or neglect are confidential. Anyone who permits, assists or encourages the release of information from records to a person or agency not legally permitted to have access may be guilty of a misdemeanor. |

In its child abuse and neglect policy, a school system can specify its role in multidisciplinary cooperation, professional training, public awareness and programs of primary prevention. Although such statements are not necessary, they can help clarify previously ambiguous or ill-conceived positions. The simple process of articulating a clear position can help refocus current programs and even allow new program development.

Policy makers may also find it helpful to articulate a clear policy on evaluation of the school system's child abuse and neglect programs. What are the school system's goals regarding its child abuse and neglect programs? What are the expectations? Are they realistic, measurable? By spelling out realistic expectations and some means to evaluate goals regularly, policy makers can help ensure more effective programs.

A final suggestion: to be useful, the adopted policy must be widely disseminated. Distribute copies to all school employees and parents and throughout the community every year. Well-conceived, clearly written and fully circulated policy is an essential first step toward meeting education's potential role in child abuse and neglect programs.

The statement by the Education Commission of the States provides important direction for school policymakers. There is, however, one point that requires clarification as it relates to the thesis of this text. While the Education Commission of the States specifically states that "it is not the responsibility of the school employee to prove that the child has been abused or neglected, or to determine whether the child is in need of protection," certainly teacher judgment may be a factor in determining that. Ob-

---

*While every state provides immunity for those reporting child abuse, many do not provide immunity for reporters of child neglect. School systems in these states may be able to extend immunity to school personnel via the state public school laws. Many of these laws grant immunity to educators who act under a requirement of school law, rule or regulation. By enacting a regulation requiring school personnel to report suspected abuse and neglect, school systems can ensure full immunity to their employees who report.

viously, a court of law is responsible for "proving" the existence of abuse or neglect even though agency social workers, who may be less capable of determining the need for protection than teachers, are given day-to-day operating power to make such decisions.

## Reporting form

The development of a reporting form is a critical step in the establishment of operating procedures. Although the reporting form is not in itself a policy statement, it does implement aspects of one. For this reason, the development of the form should result from the process of policymaking.

The sample reporting form included is to some extent a compilation of the ones I have reviewed. Some modifications have been made, particularly as they relate to the enlarged role of school personnel.

In addition to its direct action in the field of policymaking in regard to child maltreatment, a school system can make some philosophic decisions that advance the cause of humane treatment of children. The school district that evaluates its policies on corporal punishment and finds them inconsistent with its desire to further the best interests of youngsters may decide to change them. Perhaps the school board accepts a plan to ban the use of corporal punishment on all first graders this year. Each successive year another grade is included in the proscription. Such a procedure provides an opportunity to train teachers in alternative classroom management techniques while it allows time for the community to rethink its attitudes toward corporal punishment. Other school boards may choose to institute immediate bans on corporal punishment because the community and district staff agree that it is counterproductive to the stated goals of education.

Another way a school district can further the cause of both maltreated and well cared for children is through the establishment of hiring practices that place a premium on broad professional training and competence in the classroom. Written tests certifying minimum knowledge in the teacher's area of employment have been required in many school districts for years; other school districts are investigating such tests as a useful screening device for teacher applicants. Further, school districts should establish procedures to judge a teacher's competence in the classroom before he or she is appointed to a position. It seems ironic that school districts rarely require proof that a teacher can manage a classroom and teach children before they hire the candidate. Few prudent people would buy a car without seeing that it performs its functions well; yet, most school boards hire teachers without knowing their teaching abilities. School boards should establish a policy requiring all prospective teachers to demonstrate their skill in dealing with children through in-the-classroom activities evaluated by objective standards. Such prehiring evaluative procedures do not guarantee

## SAMPLE REPORTING FORM

Child's Name _____ Age _____ Birthdate _____

Address _____

Parents' Name: Mother _____ Father _____

Address of parents if different from above _____

Brother(s) (name and age) _____

Sister(s) (name and age) _____

Siblings in this school: If so, list: _____

What have you observed that suggests maltreatment? Be specific.

_____

If you have questioned the child, what does he or she say about the situation?

_____

If you have questioned siblings, what do they say about this situation or others that may add to the understanding of the situation?

_____

What additional information about family or child will be useful in investigating this report?

_____

Optional question: In your opinion, is this an emergency (life-threatening situation)?

_____

Other school employees who could provide information about the child or family or both:

_____

Do you wish to participate in the next phase of investigation? _____

When was the oral report made? Date _____ Time _____

    To whom: _____
                (Name and position)

Signature of person completing report _____ Date _____

If child was questioned in the presence of other adults, signatures of such persons should be included:

_____

Directions: This report should be made in quadruplicate: original to social service agency; copies to school district agent designated by policy; principal or designee for placement in a confidential file; teacher preparing report.

perfection in hiring, but they represent an improvement of present screening devices used in regard to teaching candidates. Furthermore, present teacher placement practices all too often result in less capable and experienced educators being assigned to the most impoverished predominantly minority schools. To say that some children, particularly poor or minority students, are miseducated as a direct result of their placement in teachers' classes is not startling news. What is frightening is administrative and school board inability and unwillingness to provide our most needy youngsters with the best qualified teachers. Until that is achieved, such schools cannot be expected to focus on the special initiatives required to help maltreated children.

With specific reference to maltreated children, school districts can encourage changes in state certification requirements to ensure that prospective teachers are both knowledgeable and skilled in effective methods to identify and deal with maltreated children and their families.

In addition, to supplement its direct-action plans to eliminate child maltreatment, the school board can take the initiative in related areas of child health. A sampling of the policy decisions a school board can enact includes the following:

1. The requirement that all students be immunized against diseases prior to enrollment in school.
2. The requirement that a mandatory physical examination be conducted annually prior to the beginning of the school year. Students whose families cannot afford such checkups and who are not eligible for government-supported physicals should be examined by volunteer doctors from the community or at school board expense.
3. The requirement that a mandatory dental examination be conducted annually sometime during the school year, with alternative arrangements for needy children similar to those suggested in regard to physical examinations.
4. The expansion of the school breakfast program to provide free and reduced-price breakfasts for children who qualify for this federal program. It seems somewhat ironic that although the importance of a well-balanced breakfast is universally recognized as a necessary prerequisite to normal development, many school boards deny youngsters the benefits of this federally subsidized program.
5. The inclusion of medical and dental clinics in school buildings to provide comprehensive community health services to families of the neighborhood. In existing schools unused rooms may be transformed into functioning clinics, while such facilities may be planned into proposed new schools. The cooperation and resources of governmental care-providing agencies can be enlisted in these endeavors.
6. The adoption of a philosophy that acknowledges the need for more school nurses and school social workers as a high priority. Further,

the school board must allocate the necessary funds to implement an expanded program of aid and assistance to children.

Such policies as those outlined above can be important in allowing school personnel to identify and assist abused and neglected children in regard to untreated medical problems, inadequate diet, and continual monitoring of the health of youngsters. Many school boards have already enacted these and similar policies; still others need to follow this course to offer children the comprehensive services they require.

From a leadership standpoint, a school board chairperson or district superintendent committed to aiding maltreated children can use his or her influence to focus public attention on their plight. This official's familiarity with community leaders, local governmental officials, university personnel, business people, and religious leaders allows him or her to enlist their assistance in coordinating a full-service system within the area. Further, this position affords the official the opportunity to monitor the development of a comprehensive community program, expand successful phases, and alter poorly functioning elements.

Thus, tremendous advantages are to be gained by a district-wide commitment to the cause of maltreated children. Although one teacher can make a significant difference in the lives of a few children, educators' power to ameliorate maltreatment is multiplied many times when their efforts are part of a comprehensive district and community thrust.

## The legislature and state department of education

Either by statute or recommendation, each state can promote the expansion of services to children with special needs. For example, although a majority of states do require educators to report suspected cases of child maltreatment, relatively few have developed training programs to help teachers comply with the laws. Fewer still have provided funding to pay for the in-service education of teachers in this field.

It seems essential that states not yet mandating that teachers report serious cases of maltreatment pass such legislation. This is not to say that a legal obligation to report is a panacea, for certainly it is not. It has even been suggested that invoking civil penalties for failure to report is one way to impress teachers with the magnitude of their responsibility to maltreated children.

Certainly, there is a real need for training in the detection and treatment of abusive and neglectful families. States could fund such education for those groups, including educators, who are required by law to report. Another tactic that could be taken in this regard involves the state department of education. Each state department could prescribe training in the area of maltreatment as a condition for initial certification or as a prerequisite for recertification. The state departments of education can mandate that in-service training in this field be supplied for all school personnel and could allocate funds on a continuing basis for this purpose.

As we have seen, there is no shortage of plans that could be implemented to encourage educators to assume their professional and human responsibilities to maltreated children and their families. The plans and provisions of two communities may differ drastically; yet, each may be providing an adequate program to meet the special needs of maltreating families. However, experience in the field demonstrates that the most effective way to deal with the problems of abuse and neglect is through a comprehensive process that utilizes the resources and expertise of as many individuals and organizations within the community as possible. The school district that coordinates its efforts with the services provided by public and private agencies reaps tremendous rewards in the field of maltreatment.

Teachers, school districts, and even states have some natural allies in the fight against child maltreatment. In addition to governmental and private agencies that supply vital services to the community, there are a number of other groups whose aid can be enlisted to help maltreating families. Either on the school or system level, the invaluable assistance of these established groups and organizations should not be wasted, but actively cultivated.

## Major support groups at the local and district levels

Education has long had support from individuals and groups within the community. They have given time, money, and resources to schools almost since the inception of formalized educational institutions. It is these same organizations that can become powerful allies in the efforts of schools and school systems to eliminate child maltreatment. Let us briefly examine the roles that can be played by a few of these groups.

### Parent-teacher association

The Parent-Teacher Association is committed to helping children and aiding school personnel in their efforts to assist youngsters. The PTA is responsible in large part for the broad community support many schools receive. One of the most important functions of the PTA is to foster communication between the school and the community it serves. In addition, the PTA focuses the attention of the community on the efforts of the school and provides for a vital interchange of ideas between professional educators and lay people.

The PTA has shown its effectiveness as a lobbying group on the local, district, state, and national levels. Its voice is respected as it commands attention from the general public and from policymakers in education and government. The PTA's most recent national efforts have focused on the issues of violence on television and in the family. Its concern with reducing violence reflects sentiments akin to those that spur people to fight child maltreatment.

On the local and district levels the PTA can provide more initial support to the efforts of the school to eliminate maltreatment than any other single group. It is incumbent upon those who realize the schools' responsibility in this regard to enlist the assistance of the PTA as they attempt to gain widespread public support for their programs.

### The business community

Business people have a stake in their communities, the importance of which can hardly be minimized. The healthier and more productive the area, the greater their chances for success. Further, organizations like the chamber of commerce continually receive questions concerning the quality of education and of human services provided in an area from representatives of companies contemplating expansion of their operations. Since there is a link between maltreatment, deviant behavior, and crime, it is in the best interests of businesses to become involved in the prevention of abuse and neglect. For all these reasons, the business community has an important role to play in educators' efforts to eliminate child maltreatment.

An actively supportive business group can encourage good family relations through a number of techniques. Many large companies have established preschool care centers at the sites of their businesses, thus fostering the healthy development of youngsters, decreasing absenteeism among their employees, and boosting worker morale. Others provide release time for parents to attend school functions. Still others have flexible work schedules that allow parents to visit their children's schools. Many businesses have established counseling services for troubled employees, while others offer courses in good parenting and communication skills at the job site. All these programs have the potential to decrease maltreatment; for this reason, they should be encouraged, and their expansion urged.

### The religious community

Because religious institutions are vitally concerned with the quality of family life and because they have considerable influence in the community, the school should recognize the potential for support and assistance from neighborhood clergy members. Many schools presently have ongoing relationships with local clergy who are willing to aid troubled families. In other cases, religious leaders have been named to local and district child advocacy teams.

The clergy can be encouraged to cosponsor with schools such events as family days, which emphasize the positive nurturing roles of family life. Space in religious facilities can be utilized for day care or to house programs that supplement the school's efforts in regard to the elimination of child maltreatment. Because of the respect they receive from the community, every effort should be made to encourage members of the clergy to stress the positive aspects of parent-child relationships as expressed in the Old and New Testaments.

### Colleges and universities

The expertise to develop many of the programs needed in the field of child maltreatment can be found within the academic settings of colleges and universities. Further, both the professional preparation of future teachers and the advanced training of current educators are the responsibility of the university. Each school and system must tap the resources of university personnel to meet its unique needs.

Because the university has as its main task the advancement of knowledge, it is only natural that it should be an ally to the school concerned with child maltreatment. Research in the field must continue, as must pilot and demonstration projects that suggest alternative ways to diagnose and deal with abused and neglected children and their parents. Worthwhile courses on the dynamics of child maltreatment must be devised for students who plan to enter the field of education. In this regard the university can lobby its state's department of education to make such courses mandatory for professional certification. Further, specialized courses in normal child development can be formulated and offered both to parents and teachers who need such knowledge. Thus, it is apparent that the university has a vital role to play in support of a comprehensive maltreatment program.

### Teacher organizations

Although teacher organizations have as their primary goal the promotion of their membership's needs in regard to salary and security, such priorities are not incompatible with the needs of children and the community. As advocates of education, teachers' unions have stimulated important innovations in the schools of many neighborhoods. These changes have made positive contributions to the educational process.

At the local level it is imperative that school principals apprise the union leadership through school representatives of efforts in the field of maltreatment since these plans affect teachers. It is well to get union representatives involved in the process of assessing school needs as well as in planning strategies to deal with the information uncovered by analysis. By enlisting their concern, the broad support of the union leadership is encouraged and, by extension, of the union membership as a whole.

At the district level the leadership of the teachers' organization should be encouraged to participate in the system policymaking deliberations and to actively promote this important effort. The teachers' union may take a leadership role in planning in-service education, petitioning for state and federal funding of special projects, and explaining to its members the legal requirement to report suspected maltreatment and the complementary immunity from prosecution such reporting ensures.

So it is clear that at the school level a variety of interest groups should be enlisted to support a program to fight child maltreatment. Each organization has a unique contribution to make to the total task of developing a comprehensive plan of action. On the system level the district is wise that utilizes all the resources of its community; indeed, it is only by drawing from all bases of support and assistance that a truly coordinated comprehensive plan can be devised and implemented.

## The secondary school program

The major emphasis of this book centers on the role of educators in dealing with both maltreated children and their maltreating parents. Although it is true that the basic models that are included for the prevention, diagnosis, and treatment of abusive and neglecting families were developed within an elementary school setting, their applicability with some modifications extends to the secondary school as well. It seems appropriate to examine some basic similarities and differences between maltreatment programs to be employed with young children and those developed for implementation with teenagers.

From the onset it must be remembered that the background data on maltreatment is not age specific, but generalized to help explain the phenomena of abuse and neglect, shed light on characteristics common to maltreating parents regardless of the ages of their youngsters, and to suggest behavioral clues that abused and neglected children as a group display more frequently than nonmaltreated youngsters. Further, processes like case presentation before the child study team are not limited to use with young children; rather, they have equal utility with secondary school students. The model for counseling maltreating parents may need some modification when applied to parents of older students; yet, the extent of change should not be great.

It is essential to recognize that this book is intended as a starting point for all educators regardless of the ages of the young people they serve daily. Its thrust is not prescriptive but suggestive. Since each community represents a unique set of factors that differentiate it from all other neighborhoods, it is impossible to walk into any school with a ready-made model and expect it to meet all the needs of students. Therefore, adaptability and creativity stand as important qualities any educator must have, either on the elementary or secondary level, if he or she is to have any chance of structuring and implementing a successful program to combat child maltreatment. In short, there are no general blueprints for dealing with either young or older maltreated children; instead, local needs and realities determine the shape of any maltreatment plan.

When dealing with secondary school students who are maltreated, it is well to remember that the pattern of abuse or neglect is likely to have existed for some time. From a realistic standpoint, longevity makes its negative effects more severe for the youngster and lessens the chances of significantly changing the parents. There is nothing startling to educators to suggest that the earlier remediation is begun, the greater the possibilities of success. Significant change in a kindergarten student is more likely than in a fifth grader, although the fifth grader has a better chance of being helped than an eighth grader. All stand a higher probability of being successfully assisted than an eleventh grader.

On the other hand, it is not rare for maltreatment to begin within a family as or after a youngster reaches adolescence. For instance, the highest rates of sexual maltreatment are found among preadolescent and adolescent girls. Neglect frequently replaces physical abuse as teenage boys become too large for their parents to hit. In other cases, drastic changes in life circumstances, such as death of a spouse, divorce, or remarriage, can correspond with the onset of maltreatment among teenagers. The likelihood of breaking such recently acquired patterns of abuse and neglect in older children represents a hopeful area for educators.

It cannot and should not be accepted as a reality that a maltreated child of secondary school age is irredeemable, nor is it sensible to assume that all can be helped. Aid on a one-to-one basis may be successful in ameliorating the effects of maltreatment and in changing parental attitudes and behavior in a number of cases. Yet, it must be acknowledged that the pathology that causes long-term cases of maltreatment may be beyond the expertise of school personnel because of its resistance to change. Such cases may require professional psychiatric treatment for both parents and offspring.

One important element in any comprehensive program to eliminate maltreatment involves the education of secondary school students for satisfactory family relationships as adults. Such efforts attempt to stem the probability of maltreatment through educational experiences that analyze the responsibilities and rewards of healthy family living. Although such instruction ideally should begin in the elementary schools to adequately prepare youngsters for the tasks of adulthood, it is imperative that secondary school students receive such knowledge.

Certainly the structure of the traditional secondary school mitigates against successful implementation of a child maltreatment program. Because a student spends less than an hour a day in any teacher's classroom and is one of at least one hundred fifty students with whom that educator deals, close student-teacher relationships are inhibited. Further, because the orientation of upper schools is toward acquisition of academic skills and knowledge, there is less social and emotional involvement between teacher and student than in the elementary classroom. While teachers in elementary schools usually handle nearly all their students' special needs and problems within the self-contained classroom, secondary teachers are more likely to refer youngsters from class to deans and counselors. Because most secondary schools have insufficient staffing in these areas, the youngsters are often dealt with only in terms of immediate discipline for wrongdoing rather than with regard to the underlying causes of their maladjustment.

It is not the purpose of this book to change the structure of the secondary school program, although many drastic alterations are needed. When we recognize the breadth of student needs, it becomes apparent that diversified alternatives based on demonstrated student concerns must be incorporated into secondary school programs. The possibilities in this regard are endless. For instance, young people who have never established intimate, trusting relationships with any adults should have the opportunity to do so. Since the traditional secondary school structure cannot accommodate this need, an alternative school pattern may be developed. Perhaps sixty young people who need close adult relationships are enrolled in a yearlong program in which two teachers handle all basic subjects for four hours a day; during the rest of the day, the students are free to participate in other school projects that interest them. In such an environment, secondary students have a better chance to interact on an intimate level both with adults and with each other than they do within a traditional school structure.

Yet another factor that makes secondary school youngsters more difficult to deal with concerns the peculiar problems of their age group. Often, their behavior is erratic and bizarre. The pressures they experience from their peers are frequently intolerable. Their insecurity tied to a desire to rebel against parental control is responsible in large part for teenagers' experimentation with alcohol, drugs, and sex. It is an understatement to say that it is difficult to be a teenager; likewise, trying to reach and deal with secondary students is equally hard. Yet, most teenagers have needs that interested teachers can meet. In spite of the factors that complicate efforts to deal with maltreated youngsters, the task is not impossible; further, its importance mandates that secondary educators formulate methods to diagnose and treat abused and neglected young people. By employing a system of individual analysis, educators learn a great deal about youngsters and their families that becomes the basis for action.

### Recommendations for the secondary school

Even with the uniqueness of the age group, the structure of the secondary school program, and the other obstacles encountered, there is much that secondary school personnel can accomplish in the field of maltreatment. Individual teachers with both interest and energy can investigate their suspicions of maltreatment. Once confirmed, they can perform intervention counseling with parents following the same basic model that has been presented in Chapter 7. It is often a good idea on the secondary level to inform the guidance department of the case and enlist the assistance of trained counselors in helping both the student and the family.

In cases in which a counselor learns of marginal maltreatment and no teacher can or wishes to investigate, the guidance person must take the initiative in confirming the case and planning a course of treatment. Group counseling at the secondary level holds much promise for youngsters identified as maltreated. Indeed, this treatment technique is more appropriate for teenagers, who are more verbal and more perceptive, than for elementary school students.

Ideally, each secondary school should establish a child study team as described in Chapter 7. Utilizing the interests and training of teachers, administrators, school psychologist, and guidance personnel, this group is an important link in the establishment of an in-house mechanism for dealing with maltreatment cases in a systematic way. When serious cases of abuse or neglect that fit legal definitions are discovered, they must be reported immediately to the appropriate social service agency for investigation. Therefore, it is necessary that each school formulate a procedure for reporting. As suggested earlier, it is well to charge one person with the reporting of severe maltreatment cases and to have that person act as the liaison with the social worker assigned to the case.

The basic requirement of any successful maltreatment program involving the schools is the formulation of a comprehensive training program for teachers, parents, and students. Let us turn our attention to the unique elements included in such a plan on the secondary level.

Students should be involved in the planning of a comprehensive maltreatment program on the junior and senior high school levels. Currently, at least one national high school service club has adopted child maltreatment as a recommended project. The interest and concern of students can be utilized as an important element in the development of a program, general acceptance by the community, and enthusiasm for it within the school's faculty and student body. It may be that students will be trained to spot maltreatment in younger children within their neighborhoods and familiarized with citizens' responsibilities to report suspected serious maltreatment to the proper authorities. Assemblies and meetings can be organized by students to provide either the entire student body or an interested segment of it with the knowledge and skills required to forward the battle against maltreatment. It may be that students will be trained to help their peers overcome the effects of maltreatment that interfere with healthy development. Self-reporting of maltreatment can be encouraged by establishing a total school environment willing to offer assistance to abused and neglected young people. Secondary students provide a useful resource that should be maximized to increase the effectiveness of a comprehensive school and community effort against maltreatment.

A second major component of the secondary school program involves expansion of curriculum offerings in the related areas of maltreatment and family living. To avoid abuse and neglect when they become parents, secondary school students should acquire awareness of the nature of maltreatment and its causes and effects. In addition, courses in positive child-rearing practices should be offered to expose future parents to constructive techniques to employ with children. Classes in child development, homemaking, consumer education, psychology, human sexuality, communications, and parent-child relationships should be available to secondary school students. Further, self-awareness classes emphasizing understanding of peer and parental pressures can also be incorporated into the curriculum.

The recommendation that additional courses be included in the already overburdened secondary school no doubt stirs some controversy. Many people believe that learning that centers on family living should occur in the home and is not the legitimate province of the school. In addition, the current cry for basic education may be viewed as in conflict with the suggestions made above. Further, individual communities present added considerations and contraints, as in the still controversial area of sex education. However, it seems clear that if the home is not willing or able to perform its educational function in regard to adult living, then the school must assume this responsibility. Although there are many worthwhile areas of learning incorporating basic skills, it cannot be seriously denied that adjustments to adult living and parenthood involve important fundamental knowledge that is essential to a satisfying life.

Thus, it is clear that educators' involvement to end maltreatment should not end at the elementary school level. Indeed, secondary schools have a vital role to play in the elimination of abuse and neglect both as experienced by students and as inflicted by prospective parents. Just as educators in each elementary school must shape a program fitted to its unique circumstances, so secondary school personnel must consider their special role in the educational process. They must evaluate the needs of their students as well as the strengths and weaknesses of existing programs. In light of such assessments. secondary school educators must establish a philosophy and set of goals that include the prevention, detection, and treatment of maltreatment as priorities.

## Conclusion

For a maltreatment program to meet all the needs of the children and parents who require its services, it is imperative that people concerned with education from the classroom level upward be committed to the elimination of abuse and neglect. Teachers need the support of their principals, who, in turn, must enlist the backing of their superiors at the central administrative level. The school board must establish maltreatment procedures that clearly reflect its sense of responsibility to deal effectively with this problem. The state department of education and legislature must likewise formulate and approve plans with an eye to the reduction of maltreatment. Furthermore, all educators need the support and involvement of an active lay community. Thus, every level of the educational hierarchy in concert with citizen groups must reflect commitment to the goal of ending abuse and neglect. In addition, each must be aware of the efforts of others in an attempt to provide a comprehensive set of programs and services to accomplish their mutual goal.

As important as involvement of all levels of the educational structure is, however, it must be remembered that the classroom teacher and school principal are the critical agents in the fight against maltreatment. They face a number of technical problems for which they must devise effective strategies if their program is to have a chance for success. Let us turn our attention to some pragmatic considerations that face the front-line workers in the effort against child maltreatment.

# CHAPTER 9

# What strategies and practical considerations are involved in the development of a comprehensive maltreatment prevention program?

Initiating innovative programs in any sphere of activity is a difficult task. When the environment is an educational institution and the change involves patterns of human interaction, the task is monumental. First, the development of a comprehensive maltreatment prevention program demands alterations in in-house operations, for teachers must learn to identify, plan for, and try to meet the needs of abused and neglected youngsters. Second, for such a plan to be more than minimally effective, educators must develop techniques and strategies to work with maltreating parents. Because of the sensitivity and understanding required in both these categories of interpersonal encounters, the individual skills of teachers and the mechanisms for interaction and assistance they employ must be finely tuned.

It must be acknowledged that when the subject of installing a maltreatment prevention program is first broached with school and community personnel, some resistance to the plan can be anticipated. Some educators question the wisdom of tapping so sensitive an area as child maltreatment. Others view such a program as an added set of duties piled atop an already overburdened number of responsibilities. Some community members believe that it is inconceivable that maltreatment could exist in their neighborhood and dismiss the subject rather than investigate it to learn that their beliefs are unsupported by fact. Yet, all these arguments against the establishment of a comprehensive maltreatment prevention program make two basic erroneous assumptions: that schools have not always been faced with and concerned about abused and neglected children and that schools do not initiate change. Schools continually incorporate innovative programs to improve both student performance and behavior. Schools regularly utilize the joint resources of school and community to help families whose needs become known. Schools constantly employ new techniques to improve parent-teacher communication for the purpose of helping children through greater parent involvement. Both school and community members search unendingly for ways to increase the interaction between the neighborhood and the educational institution that serves it. The initiation of a child maltreatment prevention program is compatible with all these areas of action; indeed, it is potentially an innovation that advances the cause of education more than any other single change.

Because the principal and his or her staff of teachers are key elements in the process of developing programs for the prevention and elimination of child maltreatment, it is essential that they plan carefully and thoroughly before beginning their efforts in this field. As with any kind of change, if a maltreatment prevention program is not painstakingly planned and structured before implementation, it is doomed to failure almost from the start. This fact is especially important in the development of a comprehensive prevention program because such a project consists of many complementary components and involves a large number of people. Therefore, it seems advisable to devote some attention to strategies and considerations that should be explored both prior to launching a maltreatment prevention program and in its early stages of implementation. These concerns relate to central school staff and local school personnel and will vary from locale to locale depending on the unique needs and circumstances of the community.

## Role of the district's central staff

Although it has been stated repeatedly and remains true that the involvement of school-level educators in maltreatment prevention programs is the critical element in their success, the importance of the school district's central staff should not be underestimated. It is desirable for central staff administrators to provide strong leadership in support of child maltreatment prevention programs conducted on the local school and community level. Further, the central staff must recognize the needs and concerns of individual neighborhoods and facilitate local efforts in response to them. Just as local governmental officials often feel misunderstood by the broader federal bureaucracy, so many school-level people believe that central staff personnel display a callous disregard for local problems. It is the task of central staff administrators to dispel this belief and advance individual school efforts.

In some communities it may be the decision of the central staff of a school district that the entire system should develop plans to prevent child maltreatment. In such circumstances, central staff should exert leadership in this field; yet, it should also rely heavily on the input of local school personnel as it develops a district-wide plan. To ignore an individual school's needs and suggestions does little except build resistance among the very people who must implement such a program. To mandate policies that may be viewed by teachers either as burdensome or beyond the province of the school is certainly counterproductive to the goal of helping maltreated children and their parents. In a parallel way a sudden school district edict concerning the elimination of corporal punishment may lead to school-level resistance if teachers have come to rely on it and know few other classroom control techniques. Thus, it behooves central adminstrators to be sensitive to the rate and amount of change they can reasonably require of local school staffs. Further, they must recognize that involvement of school personnel in policy decisions not only broadens support for the plan, but also improves its quality.

When the central administrators of school districts are committed to the concept of school- and community-based maltreatment prevention programs, they can be of tremendous assistance to local efforts. They can provide funds for hiring and training aides and community personnel, stipends for in-service workshops for teachers, and moneys for program development, initiation, and continuation. Such financial support may not require additional revenue, but rather restructuring of a school district's priorities to make moneys allocated to less critical areas available to maltreatment prevention programs. Further, central district personnel can assist local educators in acquiring funds through state and federal grants and foundations. Thus, the central administrators of a school system can play a positive, vital role in facilitating the local child maltreatment prevention programs of individual schools and neighborhoods.

## Role of the principal

As a principal begins to plan and initiate a comprehensive program of maltreatment prevention for the school and community, he or she is faced with a number of critical decisions. The quality of these early choices in large part determines the later success of the program. Because of the far-reaching effects of these preliminary plans and because of the multitude of factors that must be assessed, it is desirable that the principal involve both key staff and community people in all stages of program development. Yet, ultimate responsibility for the success or failure of a maltreatment prevention program must rest with the school leader. Therefore, the principal must consider such questions as —

1. How can I prepare myself to understand and correctly evaluate student needs in the area of maltreatment and devise strategies to meet them?
2. What should be the process and the timetable in preparing the school staff and community to plan and implement a comprehensive prevention program?

3. What special knowledge and training do teachers and community members need to increase the probability of establishing and maintaining a successful maltreatment prevention program?
4. Once the program is under way, what checks can be employed to defuse possible problem areas before they sabotage the entire effort?

Ideally, the principal should be intimately involved in every aspect of the maltreatment prevention program from the earliest discussions of the feasibility of such an undertaking to its actual implementation. His or her commitment to the project is vital in initiating and maintaining staff and community enthusiasm; the more active the principal's leadership, the greater will be the dedication of others to making the program work.

Before others can be trained in the processes necessary in a maltreatment prevention program, the principal must increase his or her knowledge of the subject. The most desirable way in which this basic educational task can be accomplished is for a group of principals to develop their own training program over several months. Perhaps they can meet for a few hours each week to gain knowledge in the field and familiarity with the interpersonal skills so necessary to such a project. Between meetings, they can study and practice the techniques to which they have been exposed. Much of the training in the sessions can be accomplished by the principals themselves since many already have experience with good human relations skills. In specialized areas such as counseling and process training, it may be necessary and desirable for the principals to recruit outside assistance. The important element is that the preparation of principals to begin a maltreatment prevention program should be comprehensive. It must deal with all the areas that have been reviewed in this text and must focus on a number of critical process issues. Let us turn our attention to several of these concerns.

### Analyzing student needs

The process of needs assessment as it relates to the student body of a school is an ongoing dynamic carried forward by an effective principal. As school leader the principal is concerned constantly with evaluating new programs in regard to the special needs of students. Perhaps the most recent national movement in this area is the thrust toward the acquisition of basic math and reading skills. Based on standardized test scores, the needs of students become apparent; in response to this information, extensive curriculum changes have been implemented in many schools with an eye toward improvement of these basic skills.

Just as a school leader analyzes the academic requirements of students, so he or she assesses the social and emotional needs of the children in the school. In this regard it is important to evaluate both the individual needs of youngsters and the general attitudes and expectations of our society. For example, a program such as Big Brothers or Sisters has long recognized that a child needs an adult of the same sex to talk and interact with, not only because it is personally satisfying to the younster, but also because such contact helps the child grow into a productive and well-adjusted adult member of society. In the same way, it is the principal's task to evaluate his or her school's students to learn of the hindrances that exist both to their personal happiness and healthy development as responsible citizens.

In analyzing the needs of children, the principal should consider answers to the following questions:

1. How does my school compare to other schools within the community in regard to such factors as academic achievement, student behavior, and socioeconomic level? What does this information reveal about the special needs of my students?

2. What are other schools doing that my school is not to help children who have similar needs? Are their techniques adaptable to this unique school setting?

3. How are children performing at each grade level? Does there appear to be a significant difference in either achievement or behavior at one level when compared to another? If the answer is yes, what factors may account for the variation?

4. How are children performing in each classroom in the school? Are there differences in student achievement in varying classes? If the answer is yes, what successful techniques are being used to advance learning in some classrooms and what factors appear to hinder progress in others?

5. What changes should be made in the in-house program to provide children with more humane and successful school experiences? Are there procedures or attitudes that should be altered to more adequately meet the needs of children?

6. What goals should the school staff adopt to improve the efficiency of our educational task? Is there general agreement among school personnel as to the direction we should go to better meet the individual needs of our students?

7. What factors beyond the school walls have impact on students, either for better or worse? Are there elements within the community that positively or negatively affect the children? How can the school lend its support to advance desirable community action and use its influence to diminish the effect of negative neighborhood forces?

8. Who are the children in the school experiencing the greatest difficulties? What are their families like, and do they conform to any discernible pattern or patterns? As the population is analyzed, are any generalizations apparent? How many of these students' problems can be successfully remedied by the school alone? How many of their difficulties require the involvement of parents or community resources? In short, what needs of children are not being met and what action can be taken to correct this situation?

There are many benefits to be derived from a careful analysis of student needs. Such information provides insight to school planners concerning both strengths and weaknesses in their programs. Even if the decision is made not to launch an all-out maltreatment prevention program, the process of needs assessment aids the principal in making informed choices in regard to the school and its policies. Further, it focuses attention on children's requirements and suggests those that the school can reasonably be expected to meet and those that are beyond the school's province. This long-range goal-setting process is an important part of a school's self-evaluation and is critical to a successful ongoing educational program.

### What sequence should be followed in preparing staff and community for the planning and implementation of a maltreatment prevention program?

Schools have long involved themselves in assessing student needs and initiating special efforts for children and families with unique requirements. Therefore, the orientation toward and framework of a maltreatment prevention program is not alien to school staffs. Further, many schools have established in-service programs in such areas as discipline, general classroom management, and improved student-teacher communications. Therefore, teachers are accustomed to receiving training directly related to school and student needs and view workshops on child maltreatment as fitting within that category. However, few schools have developed a comprehensive overview of and systematic process for improving both in-house student-teacher interaction and school-family-community involvement. To do so requires more than mere lip service to the formulation of a philosophy and goals; it calls for more than just the willing participation of many school and lay people. Such a comprehensive approach to the role of the school in the lives of children requires that a process be designed that takes into account the needs of students, as well as the potential of the staff and community to assist children both in and out of school.

When the principal believes he or she understands the dimensions of student needs as related to the maltreatment problem in the school and has grasped the specific in-house policies and attitudes that must be modified to facilitate the assistance of maltreated children and their families, the principal is ready to involve other educators in the school in planning programs to improve the lot of abused and neglected youngsters. At this point the principal is knowledgeable in the field of child maltreatment in general and as it affects individual youngsters in his or her school population in particular. Therefore, the principal is prepared to provide leadership to staff and community members as they work together to structure a program to combat maltreatment.

If one does not exist in the school, a steering committee including the principal and a few especially concerned teachers should be established to perform a twofold task. First, this group should investigate methods to improve in-house procedures for dealing positively with children within the confines of the school. Second, the steering committee should investigate strategies to reach out to maltreating families in the community. After a number of sessions during which the principal shares his or her learning and teachers provide input, some basic decisions can be made. Some initial steps to be taken are discussed below.

A decision may be made for the school to embark on a pilot program for the improvement of in-school disciplinary procedures and student-teacher interaction. The school may decide to eliminate corporal punishment in the lowest grade or grades (i.e., primary elementary, seventh grade in junior high school, tenth grade in high school) as a first step in modifying disciplinary practices. Such a ban can be extended as both teachers and students begin to feel comfortable with discipline alternatives. Further, it may be decided that harsh verbal comments should be scrupulously avoided.

To make these modifications, teacher training should be provided in disciplinary strategies, general classroom management, and student-teacher communication. It is hardly productive to call for change and ban some established practices unless a range of alternatives is provided to help teachers adapt to the new in-school policies.

A third preliminary step may be the identification of a group of teachers committed to helping maltreated children by reaching out to deal with their parents. This group will be trained in the field of maltreatment and schooled in the interpersonal skills necessary to deal successfully with maltreating parents.

A note at this point seems appropriate concerning in-school changes as they relate to the initial stages of program development. Although it is not absolutely necessary to install policy changes to improve in-house conditions prior to the outreach effort to help maltreating parents, it seems a wise first step. For one thing the school must get itself in order before it can go to parents and request the same of them. The school staff must improve its interaction with children before it can reasonably expect parents to establish positive interpersonal relationships with their children.

Some schools may decide that their initial pilot projects represent the full extent of their maltreatment prevention programs and that no other components should be added. In such cases the only training that is necessary is a brief staff orientation that provides for the acquisition of a knowledge base in the general field of child maltreatment, an understanding of laws pertaining to abuse and neglect, and the development of an in-house reporting procedure in suspected severe cases of maltreatment. While this approach is a step in the right direction, it reflects only limited commitment to the plight of maltreated children and their families.

If it is the school's decision to accept responsibility to assist maltreated youngsters through a comprehensive process of aid, the next step is the establishment of a school child advocacy team to identify abused and neglected children and prescribe a course of action to eliminate their maltreatment. Team members should be familiar with all aspects of child maltreatment and knowledgeable concerning school and community resources that can be pressed into service to assist maltreated children and their parents.

In later stages of the development of a comprehensive school-based maltreatment plan, it seems wise and natural to train more school and community personnel to significantly broaden the scope of the program. Such expansion should occur after the discovery and remedying of initial program problems.

The general format, including the vital elements of preparation of the principal, committee planning, limited teacher training, pilot projects, establishment of a child advocacy team, and later expansion to facilitate greater staff involvement, is not a mandate, but rather the suggestion of one process that can be employed. Several advantages this process possesses include affording ample opportunity for advance planning, offering the chance for involvement to those especially concerned about maltreated children, and providing a structure that is compatible with usual school procedures. The strongest recommendation for this process is that it has been tested and found to be sound. Variations on this plan may involve the principal to a greater or lesser extent; yet, to be successful, it is imperative that a school-based maltreatment prevention program have the strong and vocal support of the school leader.

## Special concerns in implementing a teacher training program

Teacher training is an important element in a successful maltreatment prevention program. It is well to be aware of potential hazards and pitfalls before training begins so that efforts can be made to eliminate crises before they arise.

Teachers are a cynical group, especially those who have been in the profession for any length of time. Their skepticism is understandable, because too often education has followed any innovation like a will-o'-the-wisp and without sufficient data concerning the effectiveness of new programs. Many new approaches have been heralded as panaceas; too often, they have created more and larger problems than they have solved. Teachers who are not committed to the goals of a child maltreatment prevention program are not good candidates for participation in such a plan. Their beliefs that the process will not work become self-fulfilling prophecies that destroy any hope for its success.

In the initial pilot training program it is advisable to elicit the participation of volunteers who are predisposed toward the success of the plan and committed to working hard to ensure it. Ideally, volunteers to be trained should reflect experience spanning a variety of grades or subject areas to increase their impact on the total school population. Those trained initially provide a source of strength and continuity to the prevention program and may train other teachers when the program is expanded.

Prior to the first phase of training on improvements in in-house procedures, a number of very practical considerations must be dealt with by the steering committee. These questions include the following:

1. How many teachers will be trained?
2. Where will training sessions be held?
3. How many training sessions are necessary?
4. How long should each training session last?
5. When should training sessions be held?

Both practical experience and research suggest some answers to these questions. Sessions should include no more than fifteen participants, with between eight and twelve the optimum size. Session length should be approximately an hour and under no circumstances more than an hour and a half. Teachers should be provided release time during the school day to attend the training sessions if such a plan can be devised. Their classes can be covered by any of a number of strategies commonly employed in schools, including placing students in a large group or requesting a teacher to cover a participant's class during a planning period. Training sessions should be held once a week in a comfortable area of the school for as many weeks as necessary.

One advantage gained by scheduling training sessions during the school day involves immediate reinforcement. Teachers can return to their classrooms from a session and begin to practice the skills in which they have just been instructed. While many teachers do not like to lose valuable teaching time by being out of the classroom for training, they greatly appreciate a principal's concern and effort not to extend the school day for training. As with so many issues, however, local policies and circumstances will determine the actual strategies employed in structuring a training program in a school. These recommendations are included for consideration only and are not designed to be prescriptive.

During the second phase of training, which is directed at child maltreatment, its prevention, detection, and amelioration, a number of specific problems can be anticipated. Teachers experience little difficulty helping children and counseling parents regarding medical, dental, and other physical needs of children. Similarly, situations involving inadequate supervision, the need for parents to spend more time with their children, and the requirement of parents to attend to the material needs of their youngsters create little conflict in teachers. However, disagreement and emotional resistance often arise among teachers in regard to children who are diagnosed as emotionally neglected or "unloved" or as harshly punished.

It should come as no surprise to learn that some teachers have been harshly physically punished, while others have been deprived of needed affection by their parents. While some realize that these circumstances represent child-rearing deficiencies and have consciously changed parenting patterns with their own children, others believe that the rearing they received was correct. They argue that because they survived under such circumstances, other children should be able to do so as well.

For an educator to recognize the need for parents to change their behavior, the teacher must perceive his or her own childhood circumstances to have been different from those of the child in question or must understand that both he or she and the youngster have experienced the same poor parenting. For example, although many teachers received physical punishment, most were probably loved and knew it. This situation makes them very different from many of the children with whom they deal who do not believe their parents have positive feelings toward them. A teacher who recognizes the qualitative difference between his or her early life and that of a maltreated child understands the importance of helping the youngster by counseling the child's family to end maltreatment.

The emotionalism that surrounds as personal and highly charged an issue as child maltreatment is potentially destructive to those who would establish a systematic program to assist abusing and neglecting families. For this reason it is important that training sessions for teachers provide an opportunity for trainees to express their feelings. The person who conducts the training must proceed slowly as he or she listens to the responses of participants and assesses their abilities to accept the roles of parent-counselor and child-advocate for maltreating families.

Another area of concern in regard to trainees centers upon their reaction to the amount of additional work a comprehensive maltreatment prevention program demands from its participants. The data-gathering preliminary stages and the later case conference approach to the evaluation of possibly maltreated children are time-consuming processes. Add to these time expenditures the parent conferences and the follow-up necessary to reinforce parental behavioral changes, and the enormity of the effort becomes apparent. One way to minimize the amount of time required of teachers is to provide them with release time both for preparing and presenting cases. If case conferences before the child advocacy team can be scheduled during regular school hours, the extra time demanded of teachers will be curtailed. Certainly, concern about the amount of time required is a valid one; yet, when the potential positive results are compared to the waste in human lives when maltreatment is allowed to continue, the investment of time can be seen as a small price to pay for tremendous returns.

From a motivational point of view, some consideration should be given by the principal to reinforcing teachers for their efforts in the field of maltreatment prevention. Too often teachers do not become involved in projects because their work goes unrewarded and seemingly unnoticed. This circumstance is even more likely to arise in an area like prevention of child maltreatment since it has not historically been perceived as a legitimate role of the school. Many teachers claim they need no outside reinforcement to pursue a prevention program, for helping children and their families is sufficient reward in itself. Certainly, this altruistic spirit is laudable, but people being what they are, it is likely that not everyone is so easily gratified. One kind of reward for teachers' efforts might include the use of school budget money to purchase teaching materials requested by those involved in the prevention program. Teachers who invest extensive out-of-school time in the program might be permitted to leave school a couple of days a week at or near the dismissal bell, rather than have to remain the stipulated amount of time after the departure of the children. A letter of commendation placed in the file of a participating teacher is another reinforcing technique a principal can use to show recognition of a teacher's effort. Certainly, frequent notes of appreciation and on-the-spot congratulations for a job well done are easily accomplished rewards that mean a great deal to recipients and spur them to continue their endeavors.

Perhaps the greatest reinforcer is a sense of group spirit that exists among those who work on the maltreatment prevention project. Time should be set aside for participants to share both their successes and frustrations and receive feedback from others. Teachers really want and expect so little appreciation from others for their work that when they receive it, they respond with renewed vigor to continue and increase their efforts.

To maximize the productivity of training sessions, it is suggested that they be carefully structured and follow a written agenda or format. In addition, weekly assignments should be required as follow-ups from the actual workshops. For example, if a session on improved classroom management is concerned with supplying children with positive reinforcement for activities they complete successfully, teachers may be asked to chart or count the relative numbers of positive and negative comments they make to children in the course of each day. In the area of maltreatment, teachers can be assigned behavior checklists to complete on each child. They may be asked to practice and evaluate their questioning skills with children or to participate in role-playing exercises involving counseling and later assess their own strengths and weaknesses. Such activities are a natural follow-up to training sessions in that they call for the participants to put into practice the information and skills in which they have been instructed.

## Debugging the program

Regardless of how well planned a training project or how carefully structured a school plan, there are bound to be technical difficulties that tax the ingenuity of the planners and those directing the program. It goes without saying that the more attention paid to the particular circumstances of the local center, the fewer the problems that are likely to arise. Yet, the director of the training sessions must be prepared to make changes when they are necessary; if he or she fails to respond swiftly to such difficulties, the effectiveness of the program can be severely diminished. Practical experience suggests that the following technical problems are similar to those any school might face.

One school decided to hold its training sessions during the school day and to provide coverage for the classes of the participants. A well-coordinated program was established for this purpose, utilizing teacher aides and resource teachers. However, absenteeism was not considered, and when three of the covering teachers called in sick on the day of a training period, the session had to be canceled. After that experience a backup system was devised that included provisions to take into account the possibility of absenteeism.

Interruptions during training sessions can destroy their effectiveness; therefore, it is essential that both trainees and trainer plan ways to minimize them. For example, a particular student may behave acceptably when the regular teacher is present in the classroom, but may become a problem to a substitute. A plan can be formulated that provides for the student's removal from the class and his or her supervision in a more desirable location until the regular teacher finishes a training session. If such a procedure is outlined ahead of time, there will be no interruption to the teacher during training.

No matter how carefully planned, changes in the training program will be necessary based on the needs and desires of trainees. Each session should be evaluated by the participants using anonymous written forms that provide feedback to the workshop director. This information should then be shared with the committee involved in development of the training curriculum, and modifications made as appropriate.

Once training has been completed and teachers begin to confer with parents, a whole different set of potential problems arises. If an appointment between parent and teacher is scheduled during the school day, arrangements for coverage of the teacher's class must be made. A desirable place affording privacy must be found in which parent and teacher can talk. A schedule for the use of that room must be established and cleared through one person so that it is not in demand for two conferences at the same time. If small children accompany the parent to the conference, procedures should be developed to remove preschoolers from the conference area and keep them under adult supervision until the conclusion of the counseling session. Solutions to these logistic problems are local ones. In some school situations an aide can take charge of watching small children during conferences and of scheduling the use of the conference room.

A more basic problem concerns the transporting of parents to and from the school for conferences. Because the counseling element is basic to the school's outreach program to assist maltreating parents, it is essential that parents be provided with transportation if they are unable to supply it themselves. Further, parents may need transportation to such places as clinics for themselves and their children so that the youngsters can receive the care they need. In this regard, teacher aides or volunteer parents can be utilized to pick up the parent at home, bring him or her to the the school for the conference or the clinic for an examination, and take the adult home. An alternative involves transporting parents from their work sites during their lunch hours and returning them to their places of employment after the conference with little work time lost. Similarly, parents who find before-school conferences convenient can be given rides to their work sites so that they will not miss any of their scheduled work shift. It is important that advance consideration be given to these issues so that the process of conferencing is facilitated, and, of course, each school staff must devise solutions adapted to its resources and circumstances.

After the completion of their training, participants are generally eager to begin work with maltreating parents. Their expectations are high in regard to the amount of positive change they can bring about. Armed with their newly acquired skills, teachers begin conferencing with parents and expect immediate results. Yet, just as the parents took a long time to develop unsatisfactory parenting patterns, so it requires some time to change them. Often teachers become discouraged by their lack of instant success, and their morale flags. They may decide their efforts are in vain; thus, the entire school-based outreach program is threatened.

One way to combat this potentially damaging situation is to prepare teachers for some frustration even before they begin to work with parents. They should understand that a tremendous amount of exertion over a long period may be necessary to effect even the smallest changes in parental behavior. Further, educators must accept from the start that they will not be successful in every case they undertake.

An important component of a maltreatment prevention program and one way to evaluate progress over time is through accurate records on the progress of both the child and his or her parents. These reports may point up subtle alterations in learning or attitudes of which the teacher is unaware. In cases in which no growth is observed over a reasonable length of time, additional case conference presentations before the child advocacy team may be advisable to decide upon new directions with more possibility of success than the techniques used to that point. In such cases it may be that new information has come to light that suggests the need to redefine a youngster's problems and concentrate efforts in a different area. The important issue here is that the evaluation of a family's progress must be an ongoing dynamic process that allows for reexamination, particularly when initial endeavors are unsuccessful.

Not only can progressive records pinpoint cases in which little growth has occurred, but they can also graphically demonstrate when tremendous strides have been made. Surprisingly rapid student growth academically and socially is often recorded in cases in which maltreating parents learn to deal positively with their youngsters. Initial behavioral checklists should be periodically updated to note patterns of growth, as should in-class performance and standardized test scores over a period of time. Such evidence of growth can do much to boost the morale of those who work within the maltreatment prevention program, for after all, healthy student growth and adjustment are the ultimate goals of the educators' efforts.

## The dilemma of when to report a case

As has been emphasized time and time again, one of the most difficult aspects of any maltreatment program centers on the individual judgments of educators. When is it appropriate for them to report a suspected incident of child maltreatment to the social service agency charged with handling such cases? Some questions each educator must answer in reaching a decision in this area are as follows.

### What is child maltreatment?

In a broad sense, every educator can define child abuse and neglect, but such definitions differ from teacher to teacher. Further, it is difficult to apply the comprehensive scope of maltreatment to individual child and family circumstances. Thus, the first step an educator must take is to define child maltreatment in a manner that is useful and practical for him or her.

### How does the state define child maltreatment?

Each educator must learn the legal definition of child abuse and neglect in his or her state to understand what cases fit statutory guidelines and are reportable to the appropriate social service agency. Yet, because state laws are often nonspecific in defining child maltreatment, it is frequently difficult to discern if, in fact, an individual case meets the statutory criteria for reporting.

### Will the case be investigated?

Even though a case fits the legal definition of child maltreatment, will the social service worker investigate it? Because much of the work of child protective agencies is crisis oriented, cases in which permanent harm to a child does not appear to be imminent are often put aside in favor of more dangerous circumstances. Furthermore, while the number of reported cases of child maltreatment increases, the number of social workers who investigate and work with families remains totally inadequate. Therefore, a practical consideration involves assessing if, in fact, a case that fits legal standards for maltreatment will be investigated promptly. If not, what can you do to expedite the process? The literature in the field is replete with tragic cases of reported maltreatment that go uninvestigated for months and that grow more severe in the interim between the initial report and social service action.

### When does a marginal case become reportable?

When does a marginal case of maltreatment become serious enough to be reportable in accordance with state statutes? No doubt the vast majority of maltreatment cases educators see fall into the marginal category of abuse and neglect. Relatively few correspond to statutes that define maltreatment as endangering the life, health, or safety of a youngster. Yet, family circumstances can change radically within the course of only a few weeks. The concerned educator must continually reevaluate cases of marginal maltreatment to discern if and when they conform to legal definitions of reportable maltreatment.

### Summary

Is it enough to follow the old axiom "When in doubt, report"? Such an attitude may not serve the best long-range interests of either the child or the family. Certainly, educators must report cases of maltreatment that they suspect fit legal definitions; failure to do so is itself a violation of the law in most states as well as an obvious denial of an educator's professional responsibility to children. Yet, the teacher's obligation does not end with reporting. Those trained to deal with maltreating families can become part of the investigating team to ascertain the kinds and amount of maltreatment occurring. In cases in which the teacher knows the family suspected of maltreatment, the teacher can conduct the initial investigative interview in the presence of the social worker. Often, the school is a nonthreatening environment in which to stage this preliminary meeting to gather data on the circumstances of the family's life. Such a cooperative venture requires coordination and planning between social service agencies and educators; yet, pilot projects of this sort have demonstrated several advantages to this approach. Often, better rapport is established between parents and the teacher–social worker team than would be possible if only the social worker were investigating the case. Further, the teacher can monitor the family's progress through daily contact with the child; no social worker alone could manage such close, ongoing observation. This cooperative procedure between social service agencies and educators can be implemented within the requirements of existing child maltreatment laws if both social workers and teachers recognize that the welfare of children may well be better safeguarded through such joint efforts. Nor should the teacher–social worker team approach be discarded after the initial case investigation. The teacher can continue to participate in the case as treatment for the family is begun and as follow-up evaluations of family progress are conducted. Thus, close contact between parents, teachers, and social workers can facilitate the positive development of maltreating families more than the efforts of either teachers or social workers alone.

## Criticism of maltreatment prevention programs

Schools and communities that develop programs to aid maltreated children and their families should be prepared for criticism. The form it takes and the source of criticism will no doubt vary. Because the nature of the programs developed, particularly in the early stages of implementation, can affect long-range success, it is prudent to begin with a noncontroversial program. For example, programs in the area of medical and physical neglect are less likely to arouse criticism than those involving psychological or sexual maltreatment.

Although criticism is likely, it should not deter the well-organized, thoughtful team from program implementation. On the contrary, the school and community that anticipate negative responses to specific programs can effectively plan counter strategies useful in neutralizing opposition. The best strategy in the long run is to design meaningful, thoughtful, and well-organized programs. Successful programs geared to the best interest of children are the strongest argument to detractors.

Successfully established maltreatment programs are likely to address the question, "Should maltreated children be encouraged to report their parent abusers?" Certainly, this significant issue is likely to stimulate lively debate among policymakers. If the school environment is positive and loving, one in which children feel free to discuss personal experiences with understanding adults, the question may be moot. In such environments, knowledgeable and caring adults will develop understandings and relationships enabling them to help all children. Children will feel free to relate sensitive and highly charged experiences to their trusted teachers. By words and actions teachers will have imparted confidence and caring to children, which are often prerequisites to the sharing of unpleasant experiences.

In school environments that do not meet the conditions so described, the establishment of a policy that encourages reporting of the parent abuser will probably not be very successful. Still, the establishment of such a policy to encourage self-reporting is far better than not to endorse such action. The potential for both misunderstanding and malicious reporting by children is a calculated hazard outweighed by probable benefits. In either case, student-initiated reports of maltreatment should be carefully reviewed by school personnel who may need to call upon other appropriate social service agencies prior to involving parents.

Another area in which criticism is likely but action necessary concerns sexually abused children. Because of the sensitive nature of sexual abuse, it is frequently difficult or impossible for a teacher or concerned lay person to take action except to report. Statistics demonstrate that there are thousands of reported cases of sexual abuse of children every year. However, it can only be estimated that the vast majority of sexual abuse goes unreported, hidden behind the four walls of individual households.

One of the chief reasons why people are reluctant to report suspected cases of sexual maltreatment involves legal considerations. Sexual abuse is usually treated as a criminal offense rather than as a personal and family problem that requires solving. Generally, the police and courts become involved in sexual abuse cases as soon as they are discovered, and the offender is indicted and tried. Rarely is any attempt made to provide the kinds of psychological help and counseling necessary to allow family members to begin to function as a unit.

As part of a city-wide program on child maltreatment the issue of sexual abuse must be addressed and action taken. In preparation for action a first step in this effort is a call for the decriminalization of some types of sexual abuse and the evaluation of each case on an individual basis. Because the ultimate goal of any program to eliminate child maltreatment is the strengthening of positive family units, it is often counterproductive to place a family member in jail when individual or group therapy might eliminate the abuse and keep the family intact. Such community-based alternatives are viable options, as evidenced by the success of the Santa Clara, California, effort to treat sexual abusers and their young victims.

## Conclusion

The process of preparing the principal to begin a maltreatment prevention program, developing a functional steering committee, building a pilot program to improve in-house procedures, training teachers to be sensitive to the needs of children and parents, and constructing and implementing an effective program to combat maltreatment is a long, hard road that requires the pooling of the dedication and skills of all who are involved. To complete the first wave of such plans within one year, including the establishment of a child advocacy team, may be a realistic timetable for some schools but beyond reach for others. In either case it is advisable to view efforts in the field of maltreatment prevention from a long-term perspective in which quality and success outweigh too speedy and impermanent false impressions of change. It is possible that between two and three years may be required to implement a comprehensive maltreatment program employing not only the teacher-counselor component, but also the full range of community resource agencies and personnel in the battle against abuse and neglect. In the planning stages and as the program evolves, great care is necessary to eliminate technical problems and to deal with criticism that can sabotage it; however, thoughtful, skillful, and creative planners can do much to ensure the success of their projects. As always, the degree of resourcefulness and ingenuity of local educators will determine, in large part, the level of accomplishment of the school's effort to prevent and ameliorate child maltreatment.

# CHAPTER 10

# What key resources are available in the planning and implementation of your local program?

Child abuse is a centuries-old problem that has gone virtually unheeded until the past decade and a half. Yet, each time a child is mistreated represents a new and unique tragedy both for the youngster and the abusive parent. In a larger context, every case of maltreatment holds the potential to destroy a human being and entire families, whose abilities to be productive members of society are jeopardized. Who must share the responsibility for allowing such waste to occur? Obviously, all adult Americans must accept some responsibility for the recent past; even more for the present and future. In a more specific context, educators must now accept the responsibility to actively participate in the initiation of planned programs to help maltreated children and their families. It is more than a legal obligation; it is a fulfillment of our human responsibility.

It is incumbent upon educators to gain knowledge of the general field of child maltreatment, of procedures for reporting life-threatening circumstances in which children live, and of alternative processes for helping marginally maltreated youngsters and their parents. This book has attempted to review the major components of child abuse and neglect and to encourage educators to begin thinking about strategies they can employ to help both children and families. The effective educator must evaluate his or her level of commitment to both children and the community while deciding on the action he or she will take. The educator must assess the magnitude of the maltreatment problem in his or her neighborhood, the abilities he or she has to effect positive change, and the amount of support that can be expected from both professional co-workers and community sources. The educator must understand that he or she cannot save every child from maltreatment; yet, such a realization does not mean that the task is futile. If he or she genuinely cares about children, the educator knows that even one salvaged youngster stands as a triumph.

To formulate an effective comprehensive program to deal with child maltreatment, individual educators need to be part of a coordinated thrust involving community agencies and residents, school principals, central administrative staffs, school boards, state departments of education, and schools of education. All groups concerned with the welfare of children must accept the challenge of eliminating child maltreatment both through publicizing the plight of abused youngsters and developing programs designed to help maltreated children and their parents.

Child abuse is a problem that will not go away if we ignore it. It can no longer be swept under the community rug; its prevalence denies that it represents the actions of a few psychotic adults. If we can call our society humanistically oriented, we can wait no longer to take steps to prevent and eliminate maltreatment. Will educators and community members accept the challenge of maltreatment? They must. Is it now time for plans to be formulated and implemented to help maltreated children? The time is long overdue.

The resources available to those interested in the field of maltreatment are legion. Since serious research in the field was begun in the early 1960s, dozens of books, hundreds of pamphlets, and thousands of articles have been published on the subject. These publications include detailed descriptions of demonstration projects in the field as well as documented research studies of the structure of maltreating families. Various public and private funding sources have supported the development of curricula for teachers, pupils, and community members to increase awareness of the dilemma of maltreated children and their families. Many of these projects have produced tapes, films, and filmstrips that are available to interested persons at little or no charge. In short, the resources in the field of maltreatment are plentiful if you know where and how to look for them.

There are several agencies that can be contacted to aid educators concerned about maltreated children. Some of the most useful include the following:

Education Commission of the States
Child Abuse and Neglect Project
300 Lincoln Tower
1860 Lincoln Street
Denver, Colorado 80203

National Center for the Prevention and Treatment of Child Abuse and Neglect
University of Colorado Medical Center
1205 Oneida
Denver, Colorado 80220

National Center on Child Abuse and Neglect
Children's Bureau
Office of Child Development
Department of Health, Education, and Welfare
P.O. Box 1182
Washington, D.C. 20013

National Committee for Prevention of Child Abuse
Suite 510
111 East Wacker Drive
Chicago, Illinois 60601

Parents Anonymous, Inc.
2810 Artesia Blvd., Suite F
Redondo Beach, California 90278
Toll-free number: 1-800-421-0353

American Humane Association
Children's Division
5351 South Roslyn Street
Englewood, Colorado 80110

Child Welfare League of America, Inc.
67 Irving Place
New York, New York 10003

These agencies can supply interested citizens with comprehensive listings of all media available. In addition, they offer many free and low-cost resources that can be useful as a community begins its own program to fight child maltreatment. Being on the mailing lists of such organizations often results in receiving periodic newsletters telling of innovative programs and upcoming conferences. Such groups are eager to publicize child abuse programs and accept materials submitted to them for dissemination.

## Conclusion

Thousands of children die every year at the hands of their parents. Hundreds of thousands more suffer from maltreatment that takes many forms. Yet, the future is hopeful. We as a nation have begun to develop a sensitivity to the plight of maltreating families and via legislation and policy have established positive, far-reaching procedures and programs. In leading the way, the federal government has enacted laws and established policies for the protection of children in general and as it relates to maltreatment specifically. For example, the federal government requires that persons working with children in Head Start programs report their suspicions of child maltreatment (see Appendix D).

State governments have also been active in protecting children, particularly in the past decade. The enactment of child abuse and neglect laws, state registries, and hot lines have been implemented in almost all states. Of course, much remains to be done at both the federal and state levels. Still, we have witnessed significant progress in one decade.

In our nation the nurturance of our children cannot be left to government leaders distant from local communities. It is in every village, town, and city that persons who care about children and families must be awakened to the needs of our young people In that effort, school persons participate in what may be their most vital educational role.

If at this point the message to "get involved" is still unacceptable, perhaps the figures presented below will stimulate your participation in a campaign to assist maltreated children and their families.

The cost of child abuse to society in terms of dollars is staggering. Injuries to the head and central nervous system are among the most common forms of physical injury suffered by abused children. The cost of caring for one permanently brain-injured child in a public facility for one year is $15,162. If that child lives for an additional 47 years, the cost to the taxpayer is $712,614. The cost of caring for one permanently brain-injured child in a private facility for one year is $28,800. If that child lives for an additional 47 years, the cost is $1,353,600.

The most common form of treatment for child abuse ordered by a court is temporary foster care. The cost of foster care for one child for one year is $4,500, and the average length of foster care is four years. There is a demonstrable correlation between child abuse and juvenile delinquency. The cost of incarcerating one juvenile for one year is $8,900. There is also a demonstrable correlation between child abuse and the commission of felonies by adults. The cost of incarcerating one adult for one year is $6,500. [Fraser, 1977]

# Annotated bibliography of books, pamphlets, and films

The following annotated listing of books, pamphlets, and films about child maltreatment may be helpful to professionals, students, and lay persons. A variety of selections have been included with special emphasis on the significant roles of school personnel, social service workers, and lay persons.

## BOOKS AND PAMPHLETS

Armstrong, Louise. *Kiss Daddy Goodnight*. New York: Hawthorn Books, Inc., 1978.

In this book the author reports her personal experiences and those of other victims of sexual abuse. This is a compelling, honest, and often emotional account of the trauma associated with incest. *Kiss Daddy Goodnight* explodes the myth of incest as a taboo. For as Armstrong states, a taboo is a deterrent, and incest is too widespread for it to fit that definition.

Bakan, David. *Slaughter of the Innocents: A Study of the Battered Child Phenomenon*. San Francisco: Jossey-Bass, Inc., Publishers, 1971.

Child abuse has existed throughout the history of humankind. Today we flatter ourselves about our society's humanistic love of children; yet, maltreatment continues largely unchecked. By exploring the historical, legal, and medical aspects of child abuse and neglect, the author delves into the dynamics of parent-child relationships and reveals the universality of adults' potential to maltreat their youngsters. This book's style makes it both readable and useful for professionals in the field of maltreatment as well as for the general public concerned about the problem.

Berkeley Planning Associates. *Evaluation of Child Abuse and Neglect Demonstration Projects, 1974-1977*. Springfield, Va.: National Center for Health Services Research, 1978.

This major study was an evaluation of eleven federally sponsored child abuse and neglect projects operative between 1974 and 1977. The findings are significant for professionals and lay persons involved with or planning counseling programs for abusive parents. Results indicate the need for long-term treatment for abusing parents. The complete evaluation study is available in twelve volumes.

Borgman, Robert D.; DeSaix, Christine; and Polansky, Norman A. *Roots of Futility*. San Francisco: Jossey-Bass, Inc., Publishers, 1972.

This book is based on research findings obtained through seven years' work in a section of Southern Appalachia. Its thrust is to determine those factors responsible for both marginal neglect and severe deprivation. It concludes that although poverty does not appear to have a direct causal relationship to neglect, it underlies the apathy-futility syndrome common to many neglecting mothers. Because it suggests both preventive and treatment techniques, this book is useful reading for social workers, hospital and mental health personnel, educators, law enforcement employees, and lawyers.

Chase, Naomi Feigelson. *A Child is Being Beaten: Violence Against Children, An American Tragedy*. New York: Holt, Rinehart and Winston, 1975.

This book highlights the need for awareness and action at the community and national levels if maltreated children and their parent abusers are to be helped. Child abuse is viewed as one result of the breakdown of family life and the failure of institutions that serve the family. This book can serve as a good general introduction for those not knowledgeable in this area.

Child Abuse and Neglect Project. *National Advisory Committee on Child Abuse and Neglect*. Denver: Education Commission of the States, 1978.

This report of the National Advisory Committee highlights specific recommendations for legislative action and policy implementation. A total of sixteen recommendations are directed to the federal government, state governments, and education agencies. The committee also voices opposition to the use of corporal punishment in schools. This pamphlet is valuable to persons interested in influencing legislation and policy for the prevention of child abuse and neglect.

Child Abuse and Neglect Project. *Trends in Child Protection Laws, 1977*. Denver: Education Commission of the States, 1978.

This pamphlet is an updated edition of the 1976 report, *Trends in Child Abuse and Neglect Statutes*. The primary focus is on state laws to protect abused and neglected children. New sections added include a discussion of the adjudication and disposition procedures that follow the report of a suspected case of child abuse or neglect. The data reported includes legislation enacted through 1977.

Child Abuse and Neglect Project. *Trends in Child Abuse and Neglect Reporting Statutes, 1976*. Denver: Education Commission of the States, 1977.

This useful pamphlet is designed for the reader concerned about the legal status of reporting laws in the fifty states. It may be of special value to policymakers, legislators, and state and national advocates of maltreatment prevention policies. Topics surveyed include state definitions of maltreatment, people required to report, and penalties for failure to report. Readers should note that some state laws have been changed since the publication of this pamphlet.

Child Abuse and Neglect Project. *Teacher Education: An Active Participant in Solving the Problem of Child Abuse and Neglect*. Denver: Education Commission of the States, 1977.

The survey investigates teacher education programs in Region VIII to determine the existence and extent of instruction on child abuse and neglect provided to prospective and current teachers. The writers advocate the development and implementation of such courses in schools of education. This publication provides direction to people involved in planning preservice and in-service programs for educators.

Child Abuse and Neglect Project. *Child Abuse and Neglect: Model Legislation for the States.* Denver: Education Commission of the States, 1976.

Child abuse laws are often too vague to be either enforceable or constitutional; this publication suggests legislation to overcome both these problems. Included is a model child abuse law suitable for adoption by all state legislatures. Its language includes defined legal terminology, and its content is both detailed and comprehensive. An explanation of each section of the law is contained in a "Comments" section. This model law is designed to serve as a guide for persons evaluating their states' child abuse and neglect laws.

Child Abuse and Neglect Project. *Education for Parenthood: A Primary Prevention Strategy for Child Abuse and Neglect.* Denver: Education Commission of the States, 1976.

This publication presents a concise and thoughtful rationale for the initiation of comprehensive parent education programs. The authors summarize the current status of parent education projects and encourage their expansion and proliferation. Specific shortcomings within existing programs are discussed, and strategies for their elimination are offered.

Child Abuse and Neglect Project. *Education Policies and Practices Regarding Child Abuse and Neglect and Recommendations for Policy Development.* Denver: Education Commission of the States, 1976.

In 1975 the Child Abuse and Neglect Project of the Education Commission of the States surveyed professional educational groups in all fifty states to assess existing policies and instructional programs related to child abuse. The methodology and findings of their research are presented along with sample responses from school districts. Also included is a rationale for educator involvement in the field of child maltreatment.

DeCourey, Peter, and DeCourey, Judith. *A Silent Tragedy: Child Abuse in the Community.* Port Washington, N.Y.: Alfred Publishing Company, 1973.

This book poignantly calls for modifications in social attitudes and legal procedures in the field of child maltreatment by recounting the case histories of twelve children whose stories were known to authorities but who suffered continuing abuse. Either because the professionals failed to take any or the proper remedial action, the maltreated children incurred additional harm or death. This book is applicable to both professionals and laymen concerned with improving services available to maltreated children.

DeFrancis, Vincent. *Protecting the Child Victim of Sex Crimes Committed by Adults.* Denver: American Humane Association, Children's Division, 1969.

Although completed in 1969, this study continues to stand as a significant analysis of sexual abuse in America. It represents both a substantial research document and, by extension, a powerful plea to professionals and communities to act on the behalf of both the sexually abused victim and the abuser. Although its sample was small and predominantly urban, the findings of this study have broad applicability to the general population.

Fontana, Vincent J. *Somewhere a Child is Crying.* New York: MacMillan, Inc., 1973.

The book provides an overview of the subject of child maltreatment with particular reference to both the positive and negative efforts of New York City in this regard. The author's perspective is as a doctor in an urban setting, and his thrust is designed primarily to stir public interest in the plight of abused children and encourage programs to aid maltreated youngsters. The book serves as a case-study introduction to the problem of child abuse and is applicable to the general public.

Fraser, Brian G. *The Educator and Child Abuse.* Chicago: National Committee for Prevention of Child Abuse, 1977.

This booklet attempts to make educators aware of their legal and moral obligations to recognize and report suspected cases of child maltreatment. It defines the problem, explanations for its occurrence, symptoms that suggest abuse, steps taken in response to a report, and the legal status of educators in regard to reporting. Further, it proposes a model school reporting policy to be used when maltreatment is suspected. This booklet serves as a useful introduction to educators as they begin to learn of their responsibilities to maltreated children.

Gil, David G. *Violence Against Children: Physical Child Abuse in the United States.* Cambridge, Mass.: Harvard University Press, 1970.

Based on the analysis of the nearly thirteen thousand reported incidents of child maltreatment in 1967 and 1968, this study draws some interesting conclusions about the nature and incidence of child maltreatment in the United States. Further, data on surveys of public knowledge, attitudes, and opinions on the problem of child abuse are included to demonstrate the social climate in which the problem exists. This book is of general interest to both professionals and laymen concerned with the extent of child maltreatment and the social attitudes that surround it.

Helfer, Ray E., and Kempe, C. Henry, eds. *Child Abuse and Neglect: The Family and the Community.* Cambridge, Mass: Ballinger Publishing Company, 1976.

The editors have compiled articles from prominent researchers and practitioners. The book is divided into six sections: Dysfunction in Family Interaction; Assessing Family Pathology; Family Oriented Therapy; The Community; The Family and the Law; Early Recognition and Prevention of Potential Problems With Family Interaction. This is a valuable collection of papers for social workers, therapists, and educators working with abused children and their families.

Helfer, Ray E., and Kempe, C. Henry. *The Battered Child.* 2d ed. Chicago: The University of Chicago Press, 1974.

This book is a revised edition of one of the foundation texts on child maltreatment by two of the foremost pioneers in the field. Because there is no single type of parent who maltreats his or her child, the authors advocate a multidisciplinary team approach to deal with the multifaceted phenomenon of child abuse. After delineating the historical, social, and legal aspects of the problem, attention is turned to the role of health care personnel, including radiologists and emergency room workers, to recognize and report suspected cases of maltreatment. Further, law enforcement and social service workers are challenged to investigate and supervise the cases until they are resolved. This book is especially useful for hospital personnel, social service workers, mental health professionals, and law enforcement officers.

Herner and Company. *Multidisciplinary Teams in Child Abuse and Neglect Programs.* Washington, D.C.: National Center on Child Abuse and Neglect, Office of DHEW, 1978.

When community resources are combined to form a multidisciplinary team, abused and neglected children and their families can be served efficiently and effectively. This pamphlet includes a rationale for developing a multidisciplinary team and describes ways in which teams function. The appendices list names and addresses of functioning teams and guidelines developed by child abuse and neglect multidisciplinary teams in Virginia and Pennsylvania.

Herner and Company. *Volunteers in Child Abuse and Neglect Programs.* Washington, D.C.: National Center on Child Abuse and Neglect, Office of DHEW, 1978.

Volunteers are making significant contributions in a wide range of programs designed to help maltreated children and their families. This pamphlet includes a brief summary describing ways in which volunteers can be utilized effectively. A comprehensive listing of child abuse and neglect programs in which volunteers are involved is presented, as is a bibliography particularly relevant to the subject.

James, Howard. *The Little Victims: How America Treats its Children.* New York: David McKay Co., Inc., 1975.

This book is a strong indictment of adult behavior toward children. According to the author, parents, teachers, institutions, and society as a whole are responsible for the maltreatment of children. This book is powerful reading and a call to arms to help children realize their potential.

Justice, Blair, and Justice, Rita. *The Abusing Family.* New York: Human Sciences Press, 1976.

The authors, practicing psychologists, make a strong case for understanding child abuse in terms of family structure. The book reviews theories on why parents maltreat their youngsters as well as complementary treatment plans that have been devised and implemented. The authors recount the success they have encountered with group treatment involving both parents, even though only one may be abusive. This book is of special interest to social service workers and mental health personnel because of its discussion of alternative prevention and treatment programs.

Kempe, C. Henry, and Helfer, Ray, E. *Helping the Battered Child and His Family.* Philadelphia: J.B. Lippincott Company, 1972.

This collection of seventeen articles presents a contemporary overview of abusive parents' needs and desires for assistance, maltreated children's right to help, treatment delivery systems that have been and can be developed, and the legal and judicial roles in combating maltreatment. Written by experts involved in various phases of child abuse and neglect, the essays contain practical advice on programs and practices that have proved successful in dealing with abusive families. Essays have particular applicability to professionals in the areas of social work, law, hospital care, mental health, and education.

Kline, Donald F. *Child Abuse and Neglect: A Primer for School Personnel.* Reston, Va.: The Council for Exceptional Children, 1977.

A summary of major issues and concerns relating to school personnel working with maltreated children, this publication serves as an excellent introduction. Its application extends both to educators and lay people who are interested in exploring the school's role in diminishing the incidence and severity of maltreatment.

Martin, Harold P., ed. *The Abused Child: A Multidisciplinary Approach to Developmental Issues and Treatment.* Cambridge, Mass.: Ballinger Publishing Company, 1976.

In this book Martin has compiled articles about the abused child. Recently a considerable amount of writing has focused on child abuse, but few writings have highlighted the impact of child abuse on the child. The multidisciplinary team approach presented in this volume has value to all professionals working with children and families.

National Center of Child Abuse and Neglect. *Interdisciplinary Glossary on Child Abuse and Neglect: Legal, Medical, Social Work Terms.* Washington, D.C.: U.S. Department of Health, Education, and Welfare, 1978.

This publication contains a complete listing of terms used by professionals who work with maltreated children. Educators and lay persons can benefit from knowing and using the vocabulary of other personnel concerned with the field. The pamphlet includes references and acronyms of agency titles in addition to vocabulary used by professionals involved in child maltreatment.

National Center on Child Abuse and Neglect. *Child Abuse and Neglect Audiovisual Materials.* Washington, D.C.: U.S. Department of Health, Education, and Welfare, 1977.

This excellent catalogue includes listings of films, audio tapes, audiovisual tapes, slide tapes, and training packages as well as annotations of items and addresses from which they can be obtained. For those planning an extensive training program this catalogue can be useful.

National Center on Child Abuse and Neglect. *Child Abuse and Neglect: The Problem and its Management.* Washington, D.C.: U.S. Department of Health, Education, and Welfare, 1975.

Together, these three volumes provide a comprehensive overview of problems and issues, recommended roles for professionals and lay persons, and specific suggestions for building a child abuse prevention team. The publications are especially useful for lay people active in their school and community and for others being introduced to the field of maltreatment.

Pupil Services Section, Division of Instructional Services, Wisconsin Department of Public Instruction. *Child Abuse and Neglect: A School-Community Resource Book.* Madison, Wis.: Wisconsin Department of Public Instruction, 1977.

Although prepared for the state of Wisconsin, much of the information included in this publication can be useful to school and community persons elsewhere. A wide variety of resources and detailed in-service programs are included for the reader. In addition, strategies suggested for building school and community teams to combat maltreatment are insightful.

Young, Leontine L. *Wednesday's Children.* New York: McGraw-Hill Book Company, 1964.

This documentary study attempts to delineate the life-styles and personality types of parents who abuse and neglect their children. Further, it seeks out information on the severity of maltreatment and investigates differences between parents who actively abuse their children and those who are neglectful. Young's findings suggest the diversity of problems experienced by maltreating parents and the wide range of forms their treatment of their youngsters takes. This book is especially useful to professionals within the field of maltreatment as a barometer of the personal and familial problems that are typical of maltreating parents.

## FILMS

*Broken Bones — Broken Homes*

This two-part film focuses on the roles of professionals in diagnosing and dealing with child maltreatment from the time of its discovery through legal proceedings. The first part of the film depicts discussions among psychiatrists, mental health personnel, hospital workers, lawyers, and protective services case workers. The second portion focuses on the resulting juvenile court case and its resolution. The complexity of the issues that surround maltreatment are clearly outlined in this film, which is designed to provide educational background for members of the medical, mental health, social service, and legal professions who deal with abuse cases.

Produced by: National Center for Juvenile Justice
Medium: 16 mm film, color
Year produced: 1974
Length: Part I is 30 minutes; Part II is 60 minutes
Approximate rental fee: $50.00
Purchase: $500.00
Order from: National Center for Juvenile Justice, 3900 Forbes Ave., Pittsburgh, PA 15260

*Child Abuse: Cradle of Violence*

The frustrations of parenthood can be overwhelming, as this film demonstrates with the help of formerly and currently abusive parents. Parents who mistreat their youngsters are not monsters, this production emphasizes, but rather adults unable to cope with the pressures of their jobs, isolation, and child rearing. The importance of community resources such as crisis hot lines and self-help groups is noted, as is the necessity for high school parenting courses to prepare future parents to deal nonviolently and lovingly with their children. Foster parents, day-care workers, and the general public make up the principal audience for this film.

Produced by: Mitchell-Gebhardt Film Company
Medium: 16 mm film, color
Year produced: 1976

Length: 22 minutes
Approximate rental fee: $50.00
Purchase: $375.00
Order from: The J. Gary Mitchell Film Company, Inc., 2000 Bridgeway, Sausalito, CA 94965

### Children: A Case of Neglect

This documentary film focuses on the damaging effects of inadequate health care on urban and rural children whose families cannot meet basic medical costs. Areas covered include easily correctable factors that impede learning, retard normal growth, and in extreme cases, cause permanent damage to youngsters. This film is appropriate for a general audience.

Produced by: ABC News, Pamela Hill
Medium: 16 mm film, color
Year produced: 1974
Length: 56 minutes
Approximate rental fee: $55.00
Purchase: $600.00
Order from: MacMillan Films, Inc., 34 S. MacQueston Parkway, Mt. Vernon, NY 10550

### Children in Peril

The offices and meeting rooms of some of the organizations and agencies that help maltreating families serve as the backdrop for this film. Interviews with experts in the field of child abuse evaluate the possible causes, cures, and legal implications of child maltreatment. Emphasis is placed on treatment methods designed to help children and parents, including lay therapy, group therapy, and Parents Anonymous.

Produced by: ABC
Medium: 16 mm film, color
Year produced: 1972
Length: 22 minutes
Approximate rental fee: $30.00
Purchase: $350.00
Order from: Xerox Films, Xerox Educational Publications, 245 Long Hill Road, Middletown, CO 06457

### Cipher in the Snow

Physical abuse is not the only kind of maltreatment that kills, as this dramatization of a true story graphically demonstrates. When a young boy dies without apparent reason, one of his teachers uncovers the emotional deprivation and abuse he had suffered both at the hands of his parents and school personnel. This film is appropriate for incorporation in either a community or school-based training program to help participants recognize and alleviate maltreatment before it reaches disastrous proportions.

Produced by: Brigham Young University
Medium: 16 mm film, color
Year produced: 1973
Length: 23 minutes
Approximate rental fee: $15.00
Purchase: $265.00

Order from: Brigham Young University, Media Marketing, W-STAD, Provo, UT 84602

## Don't Give Up on Me

The efforts of a multidisciplinary team to aid a maltreating mother are chronicled in this production, which was originally produced for use in sensitivity training of social workers. The film takes the viewer from the initial report of abuse, to the court hearing, to protective services' follow-up, and finally to treatment sessions for the parent. An instructor's manual that accompanies the film suggests topics for group discussion and follow up. This production is applicable both to case workers and the general public.

Produced by: Cavalcade Productions
Medium: 16 mm film, color
Year produced: 1975
Length: 28 minutes
Approximate rental fee: $50.00
Purchase: $375.00
Order from: Motorola Teleprograms, Inc., 4825 North Scott Street, Schiller Park, IL 60176

## Fragile: Handle with Care

This film focuses on the case histories of three abusive families in an attempt to explore realistically why parents maltreat their children and the consequences for youngsters. Nonpunitive treatment methods are advocated to assist parents to improve their self-images and thus alter their attitudes toward their offspring. This film is applicable to educators and other professionals whose jobs involve counseling maltreating adults to become better parents.

Produced by: KTAR-TV Productions in Cooperation with the Independent Order of Foresters
Medium: 16 mm film, color
Year produced: 1974
Length: 26 minutes
Rental Fee: No charge
Purchase: $125.00
Order from: High Court of Southern California, 100 Border Avenue, Solana Beach, CA 92075

## Incest: The Victim Nobody Believes

Silence continues to surround the taboo of incest; yet, its reality for three women is dramatically revealed in this film. Fear, frustration, and guilt arise as the lifelong legacies with which these women must live because of the sexual abuse they received as youngsters from members of their families. This production brings to light the existence and effects of incest both for the professional who deals with maltreated children and for the general public.

Produced by: Mitchell-Gebhardt Film Company
Medium: 16 mm film, color
Year produced: 1976
Length: 21 minutes
Approximate rental fee: $50.00
Purchase: $350.00

Order from: The J. Gary Mitchell Film Company, Inc., 2000 Bridgeway, Sausalito, CA 94965

## Mother-Infant Interaction

A mother's reaction to her baby in the first few hours and days after birth can indicate the potential for maltreatment at a later stage in the child's development. This film depicts the reactions of six mothers to their babies immediately and shortly after delivery. The narrator suggests clues that medical personnel should note as they watch mothers and infants interact. In addition to its usefulness to hospital workers, the production is also applicable to paraprofessionals who work with new mothers. Further, its inclusion in parenting class curricula can alert prospective parents to the importance of early bonding between parent and child.

    Produced by: National Center for the Prevention and Treatment of Child Abuse and Neglect
    Medium: 16 mm film, black and white
    Year produced: not known
    Length: 35 minutes
    Approximate rental fee: $10.00
    Purchase: $80.00
    Order from: Mike Williams Associates, Box 564, Manhattan Beach, CA 90266

## The Neglected

This film stresses the job of social workers in dealing with families whose children are placed under the authority of protective services agencies as a result of maltreatment. Emphasis is placed on the role of the supervisor, case worker, and the interaction necessary between the two in helping unstable parents learn good parenting skills. This production can be useful both to professional social service workers by demonstrating positive approaches to maltreating clients and to the general public by delineating the services provided by case workers.

    Produced by: Mental Health Film Board
    Medium: 16 mm film, black and white
    Year produced: 1965
    Length: 30 minutes
    Approximate rental fee: $25.00
    Purchase: $225.00
    Order from: International Film Bureau, Inc., 332 S. Michigan Ave., Chicago, IL 60604

## War of the Eggs

Marital strife as a contributing factor in child maltreatment is explored in this dramatization of the life of an abusing family. A two-year-old becomes the focus of his mother's anger and frustration until the truth of the family's plight is uncovered by a hospital staff psychiatrist. As the film reveals, only after the family acknowledges its problems and examines them can solutions be found.

    Produced by: Paulist Productions
    Medium: 16 mm film, available in color and black and white
    Year produced: 1971
    Length: 27 minutes
    Approximate rental fee: $15.00 for black and white, $20.00 per day for color
    Purchase: $160.00 for black and white, $325.00 for color
    Order from: Paulist Productions, P.O. Box 1057, Pacific Palisades, CA 90272

*We Can Help*

As part of the curriculum "We Can Help," The National Center on Child Abuse and Neglect has produced eleven film strips and seven films. The annotated listing can be requested from The National Center on Child Abuse and Neglect; the audiovisuals can be purchased or rented from National Audio Visual Center (NAC), Order Section, Washington, D.C. 20409.

| Order no. | Title | | Price |
|---|---|---|---|
| 000705 | *We Can Help* audiovisuals—(entire series) | | $1,100.00 |
| | *Filmstrips* | | *Rental fee* |
| 008795 | Set of 11 filmstrips | | $110.00 |
| 000544 | *Physical Indicators: Signs of Alert* | | 12.50 |
| 000549 | *Physical Abuse: What Behavior Can Tell Us* | | 12.50 |
| 000561 | *Identifying Neglect: Before It's Too Late* | | 12.50 |
| 000615 | *Issues in Reporting Child Abuse and Neglect* | | 12.50 |
| 000625 | *Case Planning and Referral of Child Abuse* | | 12.50 |
| | *Medical Indicators of Child Abuse and Neglect* (series) | | |
| 000629 | Parts 1 and 2: *Skin Trauma and Internal Injuries* | | 12.50 |
| 000636 | Part 3: *Skeletal Injuries* | | 12.50 |
| 000643 | Part 4: *Neglect* | | 12.50 |
| 000684 | Part 5: *Sexual Abuse* | | 12.50 |
| 000664 | *Observing Behaviors of Parents and Children* | | 12.50 |
| 000702 | *Child Abuse and Neglect: What the Educator Sees* | | 12.50 |
| | *Films* | *Sales price* | *Rental fee* |
| 000541 | *Working Together* | $150.00 | $12.50 |
| 000612 | *Sexual Abuse: The Family* | $150.00 | $12.50 |
| 000623 | *Investigating Cases* | $150.00 | $12.50 |
| 000562 | *Abusive Parents* | $150.00 | $12.50 |
| 000627 | *Presenting the Case* | $150.00 | $12.50 |
| 000695 | *The Interview* | $150.00 | $12.50 |
| 000696 | *The Medical Witness* | $150.00 | $12.50 |

# Names and addresses of newsletters about child abuse and neglect

For up-to-date information about issues in child maltreatment, new resources, conferences, and innovative programs and projects, newsletters represent a good source. Among the most useful to school personnel are the following.

*Check Points for Children*
Regional Institute of Social Welfare, Inc.
468 N. Milledge Avenue
Athens, GA 30603

*Midwest Parent-Child Review*
School of Social Welfare
The University of Wisconsin
P.O. Box 413
Milwaukee, WI 53201

*Caring*
National Committee for Prevention of Child Abuse
Suite 510
111 East Wacker Dr.
Chicago, IL 60601

*National Child Protection Newsletter*
University of Colorado Medical Center
Department of Pediatrics
The National Center
1205 Oneida Street
Denver, CO 80220

*Child Abuse and Neglect Newsletter*
Children's Hospital National Medical Center
2012 11th Street, N.W.
Washington, D.C. 20009

# Child abuse and neglect grantees funded by the National Center on Child Abuse and Neglect, as of October, 1978

Project Officers in Washington, D.C., can provide specific information of grantees listed below and place you in direct contact with key persons at each grantee site.

*Regional Resource Centers* (James Harrell, Project Officer [202] 755-0593)

1. Region I: Judge Baker Guidance Center, Boston, Mass
2. Region II: College of Human Ecology, Cornell University, Ithaca, NY
3. Region III: Howard University, Institute for Urban Affairs and Research, Washington, D.C.
4. Region IV: Regional Institute for Social Welfare Research, Athens, Ga
5. Region V: Graduate School of Social Work, University of Wisconsin-Milwaukee, Milwaukee, Wis
6. Region VI: Graduate School of Social Work, University of Texas at Austin, Austin, Tex
7. Region VII: Institute of Child Behavior and Development, University of Iowa-Oakdale Campus, Oakdale, Iowa
8. Region VIII: National Center for the Prevention and Treatment of Child Abuse and Neglect, Denver, Colo
9. Region IX: Department of Special Education, California State University, Los Angeles, Calif
10. Region X: Western Federation for Human Services, Seattle, Wash

*National Professional Resource Centers* (James Harrell, Project Officer)

1. Education Commission of the States, Denver, Colo
2. American Bar Association, Chicago, Ill
3. National Association of Social Workers, American Public Welfare Association, Washington, D.C.

*National Minority Resource Centers* (James Harrell, Project Officer)

1. Native American Coalition of Tulsa, Tulsa, Okla
2. Alliance of Black Social Workers, Philadelphia, Pa
3. Puerto Rican Congress of New Jersey, Trenton, NJ

4. National Urban League, New York, NY
5. Texas Migrant Council, Laredo, Tex

*Field Initiated Child Abuse and Neglect Research Projects* (Dave Sears, Project Officer [202] 755-8208)
1. Department of Psychology, Stanford University, Stanford, Calif
2. Department of Sociology, University of Rhode Island, Kingston, RI

*Child Sexual Abuse Demonstration Projects* (Kathleen MacFarlane, Project Officer [202] 755-0593)
1. Parents United, Inc., San Jose, Calif
2. Fairview Southdale Hospital, Family Renewal Center, Edina, Minn
3. New Mexico Department of Human Resources, Family Resource Center Albuquerque, NM
4. Child and Family Services of Knox County, Knoxville, Tenn
5. CAUSES, Illinois Masonic Medical Center, Chicago, Ill

*Adolescent Maltreatment Demonstration Projects* (Kathleen MacFarlane, Project Officer)
1. National Network of Runaway and Youth Services, Washington, D.C.
2. Community Justice Programs, Inc., Augusta, Me
3. New Jersey Division of Youth and Family Services, Trenton, NJ
4. Odyssey House, Inc., New York, NY

*Substance Abuse-Related Child Maltreatment Demonstration Projects* (Kathleen MacFarlane, Project Officer)
1. Graduate School of Social Work, University of Arkansas at Little Rock, Little Rock, Ark
2. Department of Psychiatry, University of Michigan, Ann Arbor, Mich
3. New York Medical College, Center for Comprehensive Health Practice, New York, NY

*Child Neglect Demonstration Projects* (Alice Low, Project Officer [202] 755-8208)
1. University of Colorado Medical Center, National Center for the Prevention and Treatment of Child Abuse and Neglect, Denver, Colo
2. Family Resource Center, St. Louis, Mo
3. University of Texas Health Science Center at Dallas, Dallas, Tex
4. Muckleshoot Tribal Council, Auburn, Wash

*Remedial Services for Abused and Neglected Children Demonstration Projects* (Kathleen MacFarlane, Project Officer)
1. Children's Hospital Medical Center, Children's Trauma Center, Oakland, Calif
2. Urban League of the Pikes Peak Region, Inc., Child Care Department, Colorado Springs, Colo
3. Hill Health Corporation, Hill Health Center, New Haven, Conn
4. Children's Hospital of Pittsburgh, Parental Stress Center, Pittsburgh, Pa

*Improved Juvenile Court Handling of Child Protective Cases* (Jay Olson, Project Officer [202] 755-0590)
1. Office of Navajo Economic Opportunity, Fort Defiance, Ariz
2. Los Angeles Superior Court, Los Angeles, Calif
3. Jefferson Parish Juvenile Court, Gretna, La
4. Monroe County Family Court, Rochester, NY

*Investigation and Correction of Child Abuse and Neglect in Residential Institutions* (Jack Corrigan, Project Officer [202] 755-8208)
1. Commonwealth of Massachusetts, Office for Children, Boston, Mass
2. New Jersey Division of Youth and Family Services, Trenton, NJ
3. Department of Social Services, Division of Family Services Salt Lake City, Salt Lake City, Utah
4. Social Rehabilitation Administration, Department of Human Resources, Washington, D.C.

*Child Protection Agency Program Improvements Projects* (Roland Sneed, Project Officer [202] 755-0593)
1. Clayton County Department of Family and Children Services, Jonesboro, Ga
2. Illinois Department of Children and Family Services, Springfield, Ill
3. Caroline County Department of Social Services, Denton, Md
4. Lewis and Clark County Welfare Department, Helena, Mont
5. Ohio Department of Public Welfare, Columbus, Ohio
6. Iowa Department of Social Services, Davenport, Iowa
7. Department of Social Services, Virginia Beach, Va
8. West Virginia Department of Welfare, Charleston, WVa

*Community Based Prevention and Treatment Projects* (Karen Mitchell, Project Officer [202] 755-0593)
1. Children's Hospital, Birmingham, Ala
2. Cook Inlet Native Association, Anchorage, Alaska*
3. Phoenix South Community Mental Health Center, Phoenix, Ariz*
4. Urban Indian Child Resource Center, Indian Nurses of California, Inc., Oakland, Calif
5. Child, Inc., Wilmington, Del
6. South County Mental Health Center, Delray Beach, Fla
7. Kapiolani-Children's Medical Center, Honolulu, Hawaii
8. Family Advocate Program, Boise, Idaho*
9. Inter-Church Council Pastoral Care and Counseling Services, Inc., New Bedford, Mass
10. Minnesota Chippewa Tribe, Social Services Division, Cass Lake, Minn
11. Clark County, Las Vegas, Nev*
12. Sponsored Activities, Dartmouth College, Hanover, NH
13. United Day Care Services, Inc., Greensboro, NC
14. Children's Medical Center, Dayton, Ohio*
15. Hillcrest Medical Center, Tulsa, Okla*
16. Family Counseling Service of Lane County, Eugene, Ore*
17. Eagleville Hospital and Rehabilitation Center, Eagleville, Pa
18. Woonsocket Family and Child Service, Woonsocket, RI
19. Chicano Training Center, Houston, Tex
20. Visiting Nurses Association, Inc., Burlington, Vt
21. Red Caboose Day Care, Inc., Madison, Wis*

*Evaluation Contracts* (Jack Corrigan, Project Officer [202] 755-8208)
1. The Clinical Demonstration grants will be evaluated by Berkeley Planning Associates of Berkeley, Calif (Susan Shea [415] 549-3492)
2. The Child Protection Agency Program Improvement Projects and the Community Based Projects will be evaluated by E. H. White of San Francisco, Calif (Earl Doty [415] 668-0076)

---

*Roland Sneed, Project Officer (202) 755-0593.

# Head Start policy governing the prevention, identification, treatment, and reporting of child abuse and neglect

The Chapter N-30-356-1 in the Head Start Policy Manual reads as follows:

N-30-356-1-00 Purpose.
10 Scope.
20 Applicable law and policy
30 Policy.

AUTHORITY: 80 Stat. 2304 (42 U.S.C. 2928h).

**N-30-356-1-00 Purpose.** This chapter sets forth the policy governing the prevention, identification, treatment, and reporting of child abuse and neglect in Head Start.

**N-30-356-1-10 Scope.** This policy applies to all Head Start and delegate agencies that operate or propose to operate a Full-Year or Summer Head Start program, or experimental or demonstration programs funded by Head Start. This issuance constitutes Head Start policy and noncompliance with this policy will result in appropriate action by the responsible HEW official.

**N-30-356-1-20 Applicable law and policy.** Section 511 of the Headstart-Follow Through Act, P.L. 93-644, requires Head Start agencies to provide comprehensive health, nutritional educational, social and other services to the children to attain their full potential. The prevention, identification, treatment, and reporting of child abuse and neglect is a part of social services in Head Start. In order for a State to be eligible for grants under the Child Abuse Prevention and Treatment Act (hereinafter called "the Act"), P.L. 93-247, the State must have a child abuse and neglect reporting law which defines "child abuse and neglect" substantially as that term is defined in

189

the regulations implementing the Act, 45 CFR 1340.1-2(b). That definition is as follows:

A. "(b) 'Child abuse and neglect' means harm or threatened harm to a child's health or welfare by a person responsible for the child's health or welfare."

"1. 'Harm or threatened harm to a child's health or welfare' can occur through: Nonaccidental physical or mental injury; sexual abuse, as defined by State law; or neglectful treatment or maltreatment, including the failure to provide adequate food, clothing, or shelter. Provided, however, that a parent or guardian legitimately practicing his religious beliefs who thereby does not provide specified medical treatment for a child, for that reason alone shall not be considered a negligent parent or guardian; however, such an exception shall not preclude a court from ordering that medical services be provided to the child, where his health requires it."

"2. 'Child' means a person under the age of eighteen."

"3. 'A person responsible for a child's health or welfare' includes the child's parent, guardian, or other person responsible for the child's health or welfare, whether in the same home as the child, a relative's home, a foster care home, or a residential institution."

In addition, among other things, the State would have to provide for the reporting of known or suspected instances of child abuse and neglect.

It is to be anticipated that States will attempt to comply with these requirements. However, a Head Start program, in dealing with and reporting child abuse and neglect, will be subject to and will act in accordance with the law of the State in which it operates whether or not that law meets the requirements of the Act. Thus, it is the intention of this policy in the interest of the protection of children to insure compliance with and, in some respects, to supplement State or local law, not to supersede it. Thus, the phrase "child abuse and neglect," as used herein, refers to both the definition of abuse and neglect under applicable State or local law, and the evidentiary standard required for reporters under applicable State or local law.

N-30-356-1-30 Policy — A. *General provisions.* 1. Head Start agencies and delegate agencies must report child abuse and neglect in accordance with the provisions of applicable State or local law.

a. In those States and localities with laws which require such reporting by pre-school and day care staff, Head Start agencies and delegate agencies must report to the State or local agencies designated by the State under applicable State or local Child Abuse and Neglect reporting law.

b. In those States and localities in which such reporting by pre-school and day care staff is "permissive" under State or local law, Head Start agencies and delegate agencies must report child abuse and neglect if applicable State or local law provides immunity from civil and criminal liability for goodfaith voluntary reporting.

2. Head Start agencies and delegate agencies will preserve the confi-

dentiality of all records pertaining to child abuse or neglect in accordance with applicable State or local law.

3. Consistent with this policy, Head Start programs will not undertake, on their own, to treat cases of child abuse and neglect. Head Start programs will, on the other hand, cooperate fully with child protective services agencies in their communities and make every effort to retain in their programs children allegedly abused or neglected — recognizing that the child's participation in Head Start may be essential in assisting families with abuse or neglect problems.

4. With the approval of the policy council, Head Start programs may wish to make a special effort to include otherwise eligible children suffering from abuse or neglect, as referred by child protective services.

However, it must be emphasized that Head Start is not nor is it to become a primary instrument for the treatment of child abuse and neglect. Nevertheless, Head Start has an important preventative role to play in respect to child abuse and neglect.

B. *Special provisions* — 1. STAFF RESPONSIBILITY. Directors of Head Start agencies and delegate agencies that have not already done so shall immediately designate a staff member who will have responsibility for:

a. Establishing and maintaining cooperative relationships with the agencies providing child protective services in the community, and with any other agency to which child abuse and neglect must be reported under State law, including regular formal and informal communication with staff at all levels of the agencies;

b. Informing parents and staff of what State and local laws require in cases of child abuse and neglect;

c. Knowing what community medical and social services are available for families with an abuse or neglect problem;

d. Reporting instances of child abuse and neglect among Head Start children reportable under State law on behalf of the Head Start program:

e. Discussing the report with the family if it appears desirable or necessary to do so;

f. Informing other staff regarding the process for identifying and reporting child abuse and neglect. (In a number of States it is a statutory requirement for professional child-care staff to report abuse and neglect. Each program should establish a procedure for identification and reporting.)

2. TRAINING. Head Start agencies and delegate agencies shall provide orientation and training for staff on the identification and reporting of child abuse and neglect. They should provide an orientation for parents on the need to prevent abuse and neglect and provide protection for abused and neglected children. Such orientation ought to foster a helpful rather than a punitive attitude toward abusing or neglecting parents and other caretakers.

[FR Doc.77-2284 Filed 1-25-77;8:45 am]

# Index